HITLER'S DEFEAT IN AUSTRIA, 1933–1934

Death mask of Engelbert Dollfuss.

GOTTFRIED-KARL KINDERMANN

Hitler's Defeat in Austria

1933-1934

Europe's First Containment of Nazi Expansionism

TRANSLATED BY
SONIA BROUGH AND DAVID TAYLOR

WESTVIEW PRESS
Boulder, Colorado

German edition *Hitlers Niederlage in Österreich.*
Bewaffneter NS-Putsch, Kanzlermord und
Österreichs Abwehrsieg 1934
© 1984 by Hoffmann und Campe Verlag, Hamburg

This translation © 1988 in London, England,
by Gottfried-Karl Kindermann

Published in 1988 in London by
C. Hurst & Co. (Publishers) Ltd.,
38 King Street, London WC2E 8JT

Published in 1988 in the United States of America by
WESTVIEW PRESS
Frederick A. Praeger, Publisher
5500 Central Avenue
Boulder, Colorado 80301

Library of Congress Cataloging-in-Publication Data

Kindermann, Gottfried Karl, 1926–
  Hitler's defeat in Austria, 1934.

  Translation of: Hitlers Niederlage in Österreich.
  1. Austria——Politics and government——1918–1938.
  2. Austria——Foreign relations——Germany. 3. Germany——
Foreign relations——Austria. 4. Hitler, Adolf,
1889–1945. I. Title.
DB97.K5513 1988   943.6'051   87–25426
ISBN 0-8133-0594-2

Printed in England on long-life paper

ACKNOWLEDGEMENTS

I should like to express my thanks to all those who have helped me in the preparation of this book. I am particularly indebted to Dr Bruno Kreisky, former Chancellor of Austria; to Dr Fritz Bock, former Vice-Chancellor of Austria; and to Frau Eva Nicoladoni-Dollfuss for devoting their time to extensive discussions with me on the history of the years 1933–4 and Austria's resistance to National Socialism. I am similarly grateful to Hofrat Professor Dr Erwin Steinböck and to Dr Reichmann, former Austrian Ambassador to the Holy See, for profitable conversations on this subject. In my native Austria, I would further like to thank the staff of the Institut für Zeitgeschichte of Vienna University for help and advice, and in particular express my gratitude for their support to the Institute's director, Professor Dr Erika Weinzierl; to Austria's leading authority on Engelbert Dollfuss, Dr Gerhard Jagschitz; and to Dr Isabella Ackerl. For their assistance in speedily providing important documentary matter, my especial thanks go to Dr Ekkehard Früh of the documentary department at the Arbeiterkammer in Vienna and to the staff of the Austrian National Library photo archives, as well as to Dr Weinandy, formerly Director of the German Foreign Ministry Archives in Bonn, and Professor Dr Booms, Director of the Bundesarchiv in Koblenz.

The publishers Hoffmann und Campe (Hamburg), C. Hurst & Co. (London) and Westview Press (Boulder/Colo.) have ventured to undertake unsubsidised commercial publication of this book despite its politically uncomfortable premises and its re-examination of historical events which many find convenient to pass over in silence. Dr Anneliese Schumacher-Heiss at Hoffmann und Campe prepared the German edition with great sensitivity and editorial skill. An article of mine entitled 'Austrians Stood Up to Hitler's Germany' in the *International Herald Tribune* of 3 July 1986, attracted Mr Christopher Hurst's attention to the book. Mr Frederick A. Praeger of Westview Press had personal experience of the early years of Austria's First Republic. All that remained was to find the funds necessary to provide the British publishers with an English translation. These were generously donated by Governor Siegfried Ludwig and the Government of Lower Austria. Dr Sonia Brough and Mr David Taylor translated the main text with great commitment and proficiency. Working with them was a highly rewarding and instructive experience. Dr John Maressa and Elke Teichmann translated a large part of the appended documents.

My colleagues Dr Peter Streitle and Reinhard Meier-Walser in the Centre for International Politics at the Geschwister-Scholl-Institut of Munich University assisted me with alacrity and expertise in compiling documentary and bibliographical material. Dr Streitle has, in addition, been most assiduous and resourceful in helping to prepare the English edition. I am grateful for the assistance of Herr Robert Holzbauer in Vienna for locating and providing copies of important source-material relating to the Austrian government's internal security policy in the period under review. Frau Gisela von Thielen typed the greater part of the German manuscript with unflagging patience, while Heike Czarhetzki and Corinna Voss helped with technicalities and corrections. Thanks are due also to the Deutsche Forschungsgemeinschaft for enabling extensive gathering of source-material in Austria. Last but not least, I should like to thank my little daughter Ada-Jasmin for affectionate encouragement during the more difficult stages of writing this book.

Munich,   G.-K. K.
September 1987

Photo Acknowledgements

Indicated by a capital letter following the relative caption on the photo pages (frontispiece and between pages 92 and 93), as follows:

Austrian National Library, Vienna, *A*; Institute for Contemporary History, University of Vienna, *B*; private archive of Frau Eva Nicoladoni-Dollfuss, *C*; *Der Heimatschützer*, *D*; Lothar Rübelt, Vienna, *E*; John D. Gregory, *Dollfuss and his Times*, *F*; Otto Reich von Rohrwig, *Der Freiheitskampf der Ostmarkdeutschen*, *G*; *Kanzler Dollfuss im Bild*, *H*.

PREFACE I

On 20 December 1933, Chancellor Engelbert Dollfuss delivered a commanding foreign policy review to the Executive Committee of the Christian Socialist Party of Austria. Pointing out the great threat posed to Austria's independence by the policies of Adolf Hitler, he expressed his apprehensions over the possibility that Mussolini and Hitler might reach an understanding, which would result in Austria's internal affairs being controlled from Rome and Berlin. Two years later the threat was to become reality, and the end of Austrian sovereignty merely a question of time.

On 25 July 1934, the outlawed National Socialists launched a revolt designed to install a National Socialist government in Austria, but encountered fierce resistance from the Austrian government, the Austrian army and the great majority of the Austrian people. Hitler sustained his first major defeat, and Europe was thus given the chance, in the ensuing four years, of frustrating the manifest expansionist desires of the Third *Reich*. It failed to exploit this opportunity.

Professor Dr Gottfried-Karl Kindermann, Director of the Centre for International Politics at the Geschwister-Scholl-Institut of Munich University, provides an authoritative account, supported by comprehensive documentation, of Austria's successful resistance to National Socialist aggression in the summer of 1934.

Since the early 1920s, successive Christian Socialist administrations had shelved the idea of *Anschluss* with Germany, viewing this option as a last resort should it prove impracticable to press ahead in some form with the internationally-oriented 'Austrian mission'. With the advance of National Socialism in Germany in the early 1930s, Austrian governments increased their efforts to inculcate a sense of tradition in the population, in the hope that this would provide a buffer against the pan-German propaganda being bruited about by Nazi Germany and the outlawed Austrian NSDAP.

Despite the collapse of Austrian democracy in March 1933 under the weight of the ideological polarisation of the two mass parties — the Christian Socialists and the Social Democrats — and despite the installation of an authoritarian regime following a civil war in February 1934, the great majority of the Austrian people remained opposed to *Anschluss* with a National Socialist Germany.

Following a 'conference' with Hitler at Berchtesgaden in February

1938, Dollfuss' successor, Chancellor Schuschnigg, recognised that a plebiscite on Austrian independence represented the last chance of protecting Austrian autonomy. The plebiscite was set for 13 March 1938, and the few days available for its preparation produced eloquent testimony — as evidenced by a variety of Austrian and German documents — that the overwhelming majority of the Austrian people supported independence.

The emotionally-charged final days of Austrian independence, the experiences of many thousands of Austrians in concentration camps where the protagonists of the civil war were to meet again, and the trials and sacrifices of the Second World War, generated a climate of conviction in which Austrian autonomy was to be resurrected from a Europe laid in rubble and ashes once more.

Today, over ninety per cent of the Austrian people identify themselves with Austrian independence and with this state, the Republic of Austria. Professor Kindermann traces the origins of this deeply-rooted commitment to Austria which first emerged during the country's emphatic defensive victory over Adolf Hitler in July 1934.

DR ALOIS MOCK
President of the European Democratic Union

PREFACE II

Engelbert Dollfuss — towards a balanced assessment

Rarely has a personality been more distorted by the approbation and antipathy of political parties than Engelbert Dollfuss. It is, therefore, especially gratifying that a more realistic evaluation of his life has recently begun to gain wider acceptance, and I welcome the present publication as a contribution to this new approach.

As Governor of Lower Austria, I see Engelbert Dollfuss — a native son of this province — as a pioneer of, and martyr to, the cause of a new Austrian patriotism, a movement which was to come into its own in the Second Republic under Leopold Figl. It is my conviction that a fair judgement of the personality and achievement of Engelbert Dollfuss is only possible if one puts aside all personal prejudices and takes full account of the constraints imposed on him by the situation in Austria and Europe at the time. Grave errors were undeniably committed by the political leaders of the First Republic, but the causes are only too often forgotten. The collapse of the Habsburg monarchy, with its far-reaching repercussions, the unpreparedness of much of the population for the new Austrian state, and the severe economic crisis, had all seriously exacerbated the political climate in Austria in the early 1930s. When Dollfuss came to power as Federal Chancellor in May 1932, Austria had, in addition, to contend with the advent of National Socialism and its unprecedented campaign of terror.

The fact remains that in the face of the National Socialist threat — both internal and external — a new Austrian identity began to emerge under Dollfuss' patronage. It was this which made Dollfuss, who spared no effort in the struggle to preserve Austria's sovereignty, the chief target of the National Socialists. He was to become the first martyr to the cause of this new Austrian patriotism, to be followed by countless others in the prisons and concentration camps of the horrific Nazi era.

The time is surely ripe to give Engelbert Dollfuss his long overdue recognition for what he was: a heroic fighter on Austria's behalf in what was a tragic political arena, both at home and abroad. At another level — and this is a fact generally overlooked — Dollfuss was Director of the Lower Austrian Chamber of Agriculture and a highly successful agrarian reformer. His innovatory contributions continued during his tenure of office as Minister of Agriculture.

In looking back on the First Republic, one should not forget that mistakes were made on all sides, often fraught with serious consequences. It ought not to be a matter today of seeking mutual recrimination for errors and misunderstandings of the past. To my mind, the principle of shared responsibility is indisputable.

From our aspect it is to be noted that, in the fateful year 1934, repeated attempts were made by Lower Austria to reconcile the warring Social Democratic and Christian Socialist camps. As a champion of these efforts, Josef Reither deserves special mention. But it was an undertaking destined to fail. Developments in Austria, conditioned by strong pressures from abroad, had already taken on such a momentum of their own that Lower Austria's endeavours could do nothing to avert the tragic clashes that erupted in February 1934 and the subsequent deepening of animosities between the two major political camps.

The lesson to be drawn for the present and for all future times is surely that, regardless of all ideological considerations, a political opponent must never be looked upon as an enemy, and that partnership and cooperation in the interests of the people and the state ought to be paramount. This, in my view, is an incontestable precept.

SIEGFRIED LUDWIG
Governor of Lower Austria

CONTENTS

ILLUSTRATIONS

Death mask of Engelbert Dollfuss   frontispiece

Between pages 92 and 93

Parading units of the Socialist Defence League
Hitler reviewing SA units on the German-Austrian border
Goering speaking in Vienna, October 1932
Goebbels in Vienna, 1932
The Crusader cross, symbol of the Dollfuss era
Group picture of Schuschnigg, Starhemberg and others
Dollfuss speaking at a patriotic rally
Dollfuss with Fulvio Suvich
Dollfuss with Anton Rintelen
Dollfuss meeting wartime comrades
Portrait of Dollfuss
Dollfuss with his children
Cardinal Innitzer visits Dollfuss, wounded in murder attempt
Mussolini in 1934
Prince Starhemberg
Major Emil Fey
Heimwehr unit fighting in Carinthia, July 1934
Heimwehr machine-gun unit
Nazi rebels in Carinthia (St Andre)
Nazi rebel machine-gun unit, Wolfsberg, July 1934
Armoured police-car in action against Nazi rebels, Vienna
Arrest of SS rebels, Vienna, July 1934
Defeated Nazi rebels escape to Yugoslavia
The body of Dollfuss, as found in his office
Dollfuss' coffin borne out of the Ballhausplatz
Crowd in the Heldenplatz, paying last respects to Dollfuss
Nazis destroying a monument to Dollfuss, 1938

GLOSSARY

Ballhausplatz: Synonym for the Federal Chancellor's Office in Vienna and for the Austrian Foreign Ministry, derived from its location.

Heimwehr (also *Heimatschutz* or *Österreichischer Heimatschutz*): Home Defence Corps (non-governmental, politically motivated rightist military formations with primary local roots in the various provinces, and in a less developed structure at the top from 1928).

Landeshauptmann: Provincial governor.

Österreichertum: Austrian identity (the term denotes historically-conditioned cultural characteristics of the Austrian people).

Österreichische Legion: Austrian Legion (a private military party army composed of Austrian Nazi escapees who were organised, trained, armed and stationed by German NSDAP and Third *Reich* authorities in Southern Germany close to the Austrian border).

Schutzbund (full name, *Republikanischer Schutzbund*): Socialist Defence League (a private military party army of the Austro-Marxist Social Democratic Party of Austria founded in 1923).

INTRODUCTION

This book was written in the years 1982 and 1983, and first published in its original German version in July 1984. Its objectives are limited to the following closely related themes.

First, it examines the position of the Austrian state and government during the first two years of Hitler's rule, and his attempt to make Austria the initial target of his expansionist policies. Both the domestic and foreign policy aspects and the ideological and psychological dimensions of Austria's reaction to the complex Nazi onslaught (or, as Hitler termed it, the 'general offensive') against this neighbouring state are investigated. Secondly, the book seeks to provide an explanation of how Austria, economically impoverished and riven by fratricidal domestic conflicts, was able to inflict on Hitler in 1934 what he admitted to be his first major foreign policy defeat — indeed, his only one before 1943. The historical legacy that Austria has gained from its successful resistance to National Socialism is also outlined.

The book's scope is therefore confined to the grave and many-faceted German-Austrian crisis of the years 1933 and 1934. It does not pretend to offer a comprehensive account of this period, nor to supply a history of the First Austrian Republic. Where appropriate, however, background information on the events in question is sketched in. In its approach, the book follows — implicitly and by no means stringently — the analytical methods adopted by the Munich School of Neo-Realism in International Politics.* As a general didactic principle, the book takes issue with widespread tendencies in Austrian politics to portray the First Austrian Republic (1918–38) in terms of simplistic, black-and-white partisan clichés, or indeed to ignore significant events for lack of a consensus view of them on the part of Austria's political parties.

Two years after publication of this book, the controversy surrounding the election of Kurt Waldheim to the presidency of Austria brought calls for a closer examination of the Austrian record regarding National Socialism. The National Socialists, by exploiting popular pan-German sentiment in Austria that went back to the democratic revolution of 1848–9, had successfully persuaded a sizeable number of Austrians to

*Cf. Gottfried-Karl Kindermann, *Grundelemente der Weltpolitik*, 3rd edn, Munich, 1986.

reject the new idea of an independent post-Habsburg Austria and collaborate with the Third Reich. This is an abject side of Austrian history in the 1930s and '40s. Less known is the remarkable fact that right at the beginning of the Nazi era, Austria, small and both politically and economically fragile, possessed leaders who very clearly discerned the true nature and aims of National Socialism at a very early stage and, undeterred by threats to their lives, mounted a spirited and comprehensive resistance to it.

Austria was the first country to outlaw the NSDAP, the first to take up arms against Nazi expansionism, and the first to lose a government leader in that struggle. The eventful and highly dramatic history of this resistance effort is little known outside Austria and largely minimized or ignored in Austria itself for the reasons noted above.

A brief synopsis follows.

1. On the first page of *Mein Kampf*, Hitler calls for the annexation of Austria by the German *Reich*. He repeatedly emphasises his '*deep hatred for the Austrian state*'. After his seizure of power in 1933, this hatred was to be focused with increasing intensity on the new Austria and its leaders. In 1932, internal policy guidelines of the NSDAP had already stated the notion that '*he who possesses Austria controls Central Europe*'. In the same year, Hitler had taken the decision to launch his 'general offensive against Austria'.

2. Less than four months after taking power, Hitler embarked on his 'cold war' against Vienna. He began by eliminating German tourism to Austria by the imposition of a 1,000-mark visa fee, and subsequently applied increasing economic pressure with a view to bringing about the collapse of Austria's already crisis-ridden socio-political system and teetering economy. At the same time, Nazi control of the German media allowed a massive propaganda campaign to be conducted against Austria with the purpose of undermining its integrity as a state. During a secret meeting of the Cabinet of the Third *Reich* in May 1933 Hitler explained that *a new Austrian ideology* was luring the Austrians away from pan-German sentiments; that Austria was drifting away from the *Reich* towards 'Switzerlandisation'; that the Vatican, Habsburg monarchists and Jews were increasingly influential in the political and social life of Austria; and that therefore a determined fight had to be launched against Austria — it was 'now or never'.

3. Concurrently, and with the support of the *Reich*, the Austrian National Socialists (who were under the direct command of the German NSDAP) initiated propaganda and terror campaigns unprecedented in

Austrian history, with a series of bomb attacks against public institutions and political opponents. Assassination attempts, some of them successful, were made against many of Austria's political leaders including Dollfuss, Schuschnigg, Fey, Starhemberg and Steidle. The task of Hitler's 'fifth column' in the war against Austria was to effect a political *Gleichschaltung* or satellisation of Austria. The *de facto* breakdown of Austria's independence was to be followed at an appropriate moment by *de jure* annexation.

4. Forced on to the defensive by a continuing spate of bomb attacks, killings, economic sanctions, propaganda campaigns and the massing of armed Nazi units along Austria's borders, the Austrian authorities in 1933 started to hit back with vigorous security measures, and launched an ideological and diplomatic campaign to defend Austria's integrity. This was to be the beginning of *Europe's first state-organised resistance to Nazi imperialism.*

5. In the ideological conflict with National Socialism, Austria's leaders developed a new concept of the Austrian state which rejected *Anschluss* and for the first time adopted permanent independence as a basic goal. This was a major turning-point in the history of the Republic and in the history of Austrian political thought, and foreshadowed the political identity Austria was to assume after 1945. In the 1930s, Dollfuss and his supporters outlined an 'Austria ideology' which rested on the view that German-speaking Austrians, having constituted the ethnic core of the multinational Habsburg empire, had developed a distinct way of life and cultural identity by virtue of their five centuries of co-existence with Magyar, West Slav and Latin peoples. The 'Austrian identity', they contended, required the framework of a state to guarantee its survival. By defending itself the new Austrian state was also to be a guarantor of peace in Europe and a champion of the new Pan-European movement. Members of the Austrian government warned publicly that if Austria, in its strategically crucial position, were conquered, this would shatter the peace of Europe. Austria's struggle to check the Third Reich's expansionist drive, they correctly predicted, therefore had important implications for the whole of Europe.

While the Austrian government battled with National Socialism, it was also making an attempt to replace the crisis-ridden parliamentary system and the constitution with the first 'Christian corporate' system in history. It was hoped that Austria would play a model role as the first country in the world to incorporate the social teachings of papal encyclicals into its socio-political system. This hastily improvised experiment, clothed in crusading zeal, was intended to confer ideological

legitimacy on the new state and sanction what were in fact grave violations of the existing constitutional order. The main practical objective of
this experiment was to effect a dictatorial concentration of power in the
face of serious threats from the Third *Reich*.

6. Austria's leaders, irrespective of their firm defence of the country's
sovereignty, felt that the Austrian people were a more Europeanised but
nevertheless integral part of German civilisation in its broadest sense. In
their critique of National Socialism, they pointed to traditional German
and Christian cultural values as constituting the real essence of German
civilisation, and emphatically rejected the equation by the Nazis (and,
paradoxically, by some of their later critics) of *Deutschtum* — or the
essential German identity — with National Socialism. Austria, they
maintained, was the last bastion of Christian-German civilisation, on
behalf of which they claimed the right and acknowledged the duty to
resist National Socialism by every possible means. The Austrian
government's denunciation of National Socialism came earlier and was
more vehement than that from the other governments of Europe at the
time. Many of its arguments were to be echoed a decade later during the
July 1944 anti-Nazi resistance in Germany.

In the course of the ideological war waged between Germany and
Austria, the Austrian Chancellor Engelbert Dollfuss described National
Socialism as a system of political crime rooted in a criminal ideology. He
was the first statesman publicly to challenge the German and Austrian
people, in June 1934, with the question: 'Do you really want to have
anything in common with this gangsterism? I appeal to you . . . to
draw the line at their methods, and at the philosophy that makes these
methods possible. Only one thing can be said about these methods, and
it is this: "I am against them!" Anyone who fails to say that is an
accomplice.' Shocked by the outrages perpetrated in the name of
National Socialism's racial policies, Austria's bishops, in a pastoral letter
read out to all congregations at Christmas 1933, unanimously condemned
the Nazis for their racism, anti-Semitism and nationalistic megalomania.
The key passages of this strongly-worded letter were taken up into the
Fatherland Front's platform in 1935. This was a significant historical
precedent. For the first time, Church and state had both taken an explicit
stand against racism, and in particular against the anti-Semitism which,
in other countries too, enjoyed the support of vocal minorities. Austria's
Fatherland Front was probably the first ruling party in Europe to include
such an explicit passage in its programme.*

*See Appendix, Documents 25 and 26 (pp. 164–5).

7. Fascist Italy, which had a strong interest of its own in preserving the *status quo* on its northern borders, backed up the beleaguered Dollfuss government in its struggle against National Socialism on the home and foreign fronts. France and Britain, anxious to play Mussolini off against Hitler, sanctioned Italy's stance while remaining more passive themselves. Before Italy's conquest of Abyssinia (Ethiopia), Austria thus became the cause of a serious conflict between the two Axis powers, in which Mussolini encouraged Austria's resistance to Berlin. Seeking to exploit this controversy and to enhance its external security, Austria therefore entered into a form of alliance with Italy and Hungary in 1934. Complying with an explicit assurance given to Dollfuss the previous year, Italy was the only European power to back up Austria's armed defence in July 1934 with military gestures against the Third *Reich*.

8. In 1933, Austrian parliamentary democracy broke down — though in circumstances very different from those in Germany. Since 1918, Austria had had to contend with a lack of consensus among its politicians on two vital issues. First, its parties saw Austria's independence as a state not as a common, unifying value but as a provisional and unwelcome condition. Secondly, each of the parties ranked its particular ideologies and interests higher than the fundamental order of pluralist democracy. It was symptomatic of the deep mistrust that existed between the ideologically and socially polarised political camps that they had at their disposal large private armies, to be committed in the event of a civil war, and parliament was unable to force them to disarm. A civil war was thus regarded as bound to break out sooner or later. The Austrian government had thus in effect lost one of the prerogatives of any modern state, namely a monopoly on all means of physical force. When irresponsible procedural machinations on the part of opposition party leaders led to bizarre and apparently symptomatic self-paralysis of Parliament, the Dollfuss government seized the opportunity to suspend parliamentary proceedings and establish illegally a new, authoritarian corporate system. One of the primary tasks it set itself was the concentration of all levels of political control in the hands of the government so that there could be effective resistance to the menacing and far superior power of the Third *Reich*, in a struggle where Austria's very existence as a state was at stake.

9. The establishment of an authoritarian minority regime seriously weakened the domestic basis of Austria's resistance to National Socialism. The government was fighting on two fronts — against the National Socialists and against the Austro-Marxist Social Democrats. Radical

minority groups in both the government and Social Democratic camps engineered a confrontation. A four-day civil war in February 1934 between government troops and units of the Austro-Marxist military defence league in Vienna added to the dimensions of domestic division, and when the government outlawed Social Democratic institutions and activities, little hope was left for the realisation of previously discussed ideas for a broad anti-National Socialist coalition. The situation was compounded by the fact that the Italian government, which alone of all European powers was prepared to support Austria against Hitler, had since 1933 been fiercely opposed to Austro-Marxist Social Democracy.

In seeking dependable allies against the Third *Reich*, Dollfuss thus seems to have believed — for a time, at least — that he had to opt either for Italy or for the Austrian Social Democrats. One important factor in this is often neglected — namely that, contrary to the Dollfuss government and its Austrian ideology, the Austro-Marxists continued to insist upon a policy of *Anschluss* with Germany, though now with the proviso that it should come about 'after Hitler'. In practical terms, this meant that even in the face of Hitler's general offensive against Austria, the country's two major parties held irreconcilable views on the vital question of whether to preserve or abandon Austria's independence as a state. 10. In July 1934 — twenty years, almost to the day, after the historic assassination of Archduke Franz Ferdinand at Sarajevo — an armed National Socialist revolt was launched in Austria, the most serious crisis in German-Austrian relations since the war of 1866. Chancellor Engelbert Dollfuss, Hitler's chief antagonist in Austria, was brutally murdered — the first foreign government leader to be killed in a face-to-face struggle with Third *Reich* expansionism. There were armed clashes in six of the nine Austrian provinces.

The revolt was successfully put down everywhere by the Austrian army with the support of loyal voluntary defence units to both of which the Nazi insurgents had been looking for active support, or at least passive acquiescence. It was the first time in the history of the Austrian Republic that the Army and patriotic militia forces had been called to battle when the very survival of their state was in the balance. Moreover, it was the first time that a European country had taken up arms against the National Socialists.

Nazi hopes that the revolt would spark off a spontaneous pan-German mass uprising against the government were disappointed, and their lack of broad popular support became apparent. On the contrary, in the critical days of battle, over 50,000 volunteers rallied to the support of the authorities in defence of Austria's independence; not a single defection is known to have occurred. With world attention anxiously focussed on the outcome, the Austrian government was quickly able to put down the revolt. Had there in fact been a mass uprising, then not even Italy's military threats would have averted an internal *Gleichschaltung* and *de facto* satellisation of Austria by the Third *Reich*.

11. Shaken by the complete failure of the revolt, Hitler was forced to take drastic and humiliating decisions in this, his first and only serious foreign policy defeat before 1943. He dissolved the regional administration of the Austrian NSDAP, dismissed its leaders, and ordered the cessation of the terror and propaganda campaigns against Austria. The paramilitary units of the Austrian NSDAP were disbanded, and rebels were threatened with arrest and detention in concentration camps if they tried to seek refuge in Germany. Interference by the German NSDAP in Austrian domestic affairs was halted. Hitler had now in effect conceded almost all Dollfuss' demands relating to non-intervention. As for the Third *Reich*'s *Anschluss* policy, Hitler ordered that the unsuccessful short-term 'revolutionary' tactics should be replaced by long-term 'evolutionary' ones. Only four years later, and after much hesitation, did Hitler send the *Wehrmacht* across the Austrian border. Austria's suppression of the revolt had thus thwarted a National Socialist seizure of power from within, leaving Germany with no alternative but to resort to military invasion in 1938.

12. International press comment on the uprising was almost unanimous in stressing that Austria's successful stand against National Socialism had not only safeguarded its own sovereignty, but also contributed significantly to the preservation of peace in Europe. When thirteen states of the U.S.A. celebrated an 'Austrian Day' in July 1942 to commemorate Austria's successful containment of Hitler in 1934, Senator Claude C. Pepper said that it would be recorded in the book of history 'with shining letters' that little Austria had been the first country that, by determined resistance, had halted Hitler's expansionism for a while. It had alarmed the world, and provided a historical breathing-time tragically unused by the Western powers.*

But no effective international measures were introduced to protect Austria's long-term independence following the defeat of the National Socialists, nor were steps taken to strengthen its fragile economy, still reeling from the impact of Hitler's 1,000-mark visa fee on tourist travel.

*See Appendix, Document 100 (pp. 223–4).

Austria's parlous economic position caused an increasing number of Austrians to view some form of *Anschluss* with a Germany whose economy was quickly recovering as an attractive option.

13. The successful prevention by the Dollfuss government of the German-backed attempt by the Austrian NSDAP to seize power, and the bravery of the many citizens who risked their lives to put down this revolt, earned Austria the status of a 'liberated' country after the Second World War. In 1946, the grand coalition of Christian Democrats, Socialists and Communists published its documentary 'Red-White-Red Book', recalling Austria's dramatic role in the first European resistance to Third *Reich* expansionism. From 1945 on, despite the four-power occupation, Austria was ruled by a central federal government. Its first regular Federal Chancellor after the general election of 1946 was the concentration-camp returnee Leopold Figl, a one-time friend and active party colleague of Dollfuss. He and many leaders of his generation symbolised both the *continuity* of pro-Austrian patriotism and the remarkably smooth *transition* towards the life-style of pluralistic democracy that became characteristic of Austria's Second Republic after 1945. In both respects the facts of history have shown the ability of Austria's three major political parties to learn from the lessons of history and act in accordance with them.

14. Compared with the reactions of other states towards the Axis Powers in the 1930s, Austria's record was impressive indeed. While the League of Nations principle of collective security was deserted by the powers, who did nothing decisive to save Manchuria or Abyssinia; while France and Russia sacrificed their ally Czechoslovakia; while the Czechoslovak government offered far less resistance than the Austrians in the Dollfuss era; while Poland gladly profited from Czechoslovakia's dismemberment with territorial gains; while Britain could speak of 'peace in our time' as late as September 1938; while Stalinist Russia covered Germany's rear in 1939–40, dividing Poland, invading Finland and being ousted for that from League of Nations membership; while the world including the Western powers paid tribute to Hitler's 'progress' at the Berlin Olympic Games of 1936 and while the US government did not even dare to respond to China's desperate plea for mediation in the face of Japan's all-out aggression in the summer of 1937 — Austria in 1934 inflicted on Hitler what he himself admitted to be his first foreign policy defeat. Even after 1936, when it was hopelessly penned in by the Berlin-Rome axis, the Austrian government still refused to capitulate and call in the Germans. When, instead, its govern-.

ment dared to challenge Hitler with the proposal of a plebiscite on Austrian independence in 1938, he sent the *Wehrmacht* across the borders. Three Chancellors of the Austrian Republic and one Vice-Chancellor (Schuschnigg, Figl, Gorbach, Bock) and scores of other prominent Austrian leaders were sent to concentration camps. Others escaped to foreign countries or committed suicide. Hitler sought and obtained his revenge: no less than 118 of the 215 members of Austria's first post-war parliament were either direct victims or resistance activists. Commentators alleging 'Austria's complicity with the Third *Reich*' should be reminded that between 1938 and 1945 there was no Austrian Vichy-type government. Hitler hated Austria, the country in which he had repeatedly experienced failure and humiliation; indeed so deep was this hatred that he even forbade the use of its very name. Austria was not even transformed into a '*Land*' of the Third *Reich*; it was dissolved as an administrative unit, and each of its provinces was put *separately* under individual control from Berlin. Betwen 1938 and 1945, there simply existed no 'Austria' in the sense of any administrative or self-representing unit with organs of its own. Consequently, there was in those years no Austria as such capable of forming a collective will or of cooperating with anybody. Those many tens of thousands of Austrians who indeed collaborated voluntarily with Nazi Germany even before the *Anschluss* in 1938 can only be considered as having done so on a purely individual basis, and not as having represented the state and people of Austria after that state had been destroyed. Before its occupation by the German Wehrmacht in 1938, however, Austria's own government and its supporters resisted Nazi imperialism and opposed Nazi ideology. From 1933 to 1938 they denied Hitler the use of their geostrategically most important country for his expansionist designs. This was Austria's historical contribution to the maintenance of peace and the *status quo* in Europe. And in retrospect it reduced the length of Nazi rule in Austria to a period of only seven years, compared to more than twelve in Germany.

15. The annexation in 1938 was indeed a turning-point. Of the hundreds of thousands of Austrians who enthusiastically welcomed *Anschluss* — once it had become a fact of history, only a minority were National Socialists in the strict sense. This was despite the fact that the three major Austrian parliamentary parties had remained *Anschluss*-oriented ever since the fateful dismemberment of the supranational structure of the Austro-Hungarian empire. Moreover the majority of those Austrians who, in a short-lived wave of mass euphoria,

had acclaimed *Anschluss* were motivated by *various* forms of pan-German sentiment, and by the hope that it would lead on to prosperity, full employment and an honoured, if not dominant place for Austria within the newly-formed Greater German empire. The international appeasement of Hitler and a growing international disregard for Austria had deepened the impression there that *Anschluss* had by now become historically unavoidable. Its pan-German supporters in Austria were soon to discover that *Anschluss* led in reality to war and austerity, to contempt for Austrian values by the Nazis, and to total disregard by Berlin of vital Austrian interests such as the South Tyrol.

With regard to Austrian politics in the 1930s, one cannot avoid the fact that the concept of permanent independence for a small, post-imperial Austria — as arbitrarily carved out by the victorious Entente powers in 1918–19 — and the rejection of *Anschluss* were championed only by the Christian Socialist Party (later succeeded by the Fatherland Front) and, after 1932, several small affiliated parties, as well as by the Habsburg monarchists and a grouping of Communists. The autocratic rule of the patriotic centre was understandably resented by the other two major parties.

16. One of the significant historical differences between Germany and Austria in the 1930s lies in the fact that the German Weimar Republic succumbed internally to the Nazi bid for power while Austria's state and government were able to defeat in 1934 the attempted and German-supported Nazi revolt aiming to seize power *from within*. This Austrian success and the fact that in 1938 *Anschluss* had to be imposed *from without* by superior military strength upon a still defiant Austrian government was to have far-reaching and lasting consequences for the post-war Second Austrian Republic.

This configuration of events provided the factual historical basis and moral justification for post-war Austria's treatment as Hitler's first victim and as a liberated country. Austria thus received in 1955 a 'state treaty' and not a 'peace treaty'. Unlike Germany, Italy, Romania, Japan and other countries, it is therefore not subject to the 'enemy-state clauses' of the United Nations Charter. Under certain conditions those clauses confer upon former members of the victorious wartime alliance the right to take unilateral coercive action against states that were formerly their enemies in the Second World War. Psychologically, these consequences of the Austrian state's resistance in the 1930s have had a deep impact upon the state-related political and historical identity of Austria's post-war population. In this book we only deal with the most dramatic and initially successful phase of Austria's struggle against the external and internal challenges of National Socialism. But one of its lasting and most precious legacies — the self-acceptance of the new post-Habsburg Austria as an independent state — was born in this short but decisive period. This legacy has been inherited and expanded by the Second Austrian Republic. It now forms one of the cornerstones of its political life and of its role in the international system of European politics.

THE SUCCESSOR-STATES OF THE DISMEMBERED
AUSTRO-HUNGARIAN HABSBURG EMPIRE

Inset: The European dimension of the Austro-Hungarian Empire.

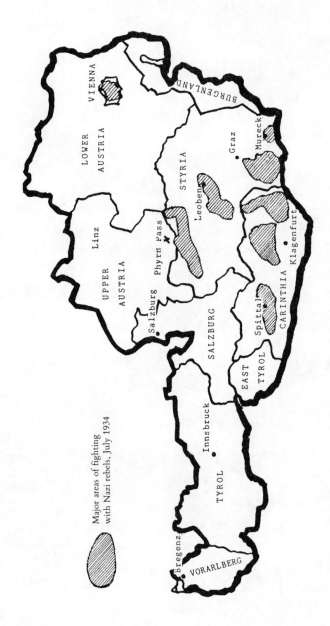

Major areas of fighting
with Nazi rebels, July 1934

THE REPUBLIC OF AUSTRIA

Only 6 million out of 10 million Austrians lived within its borders.

1

THE ST GERMAIN TREATY — AN AUSTRIAN TRAGEDY

The rise and fall of a multinational empire

Historians have frequently characterised the Treaty of Versailles as a 'disaster', but this would be too mild a term to describe the impact of the Treaty of St Germain on German-speaking Austria. The economic and psychological effects of Versailles on Germany were unquestionably severe, but the *Reich* was compelled to cede very little territory populated by German-speaking majorities. It was also able to retain its regional and economic infrastructure virtually intact. By contrast, the Austro-Hungarian Empire — the third largest power in Europe — was comprehensively carved up into no fewer than seven succession states. The Habsburgs, Europe's preeminent German-speaking dynasty from the thirteenth to the twentieth century, were forced to bow from the scene, taking with them the political umbrella they had held over the variegated nationalities of central and southeastern Europe.

The 636-year history of the House of Habsburg had begun at the close of the thirteenth century in the Babenberg hereditary lands which are still part of present-day Austria. In 1306, the Habsburgs acquired Bohemia and Moravia and in 1374, by inheritance, Istria and other Adriatic possessions. In 1490, Maximilian I obtained the crown of Hungary, and during the reign of his grandson Charles V, the Habsburgs acquired the Netherlands and Spain together with its American possessions. In 1556 the Monarchy was divided between the Austrian and Spanish branches of the family; Archduke Ferdinand I, the head of the Austrian branch, was elected King of Hungary, Bohemia and Croatia.

For the Habsburg Empire, built by a skilful dynastic policy of far-sighted marriage settlements and anticipated inheritances rather than by military conquest, the Reformation brought with it a twofold burden: that of acting as a bastion of the Counter-Reformation against the Protestant north, while at the same time shielding Europe from the expansionist pressure of the Ottoman Empire in the south — 1529 had seen the first siege of Vienna by the Turks. The Treaty of Westphalia, which ended the Thirty Years War in 1648, divided Germany into a myriad of sovereign principalities but left the Habsburgs with the greater part of their hereditary lands intact and in possession, though in name only, of the Imperial title.

In the age of Prince Eugene of Savoy (1663–1736), whose life spanned the reigns of three emperors, Austria advanced to the status of a leading European power. It joined forces with England in the north to contain French expansionism under Louis XIV, and in southeastern Europe successfully expelled the encroaching Ottomans from Hungary, Croatia and large areas of Romania, following a second siege of Vienna in 1683. After the reforming reign of Maria Theresia (1740–80) and the repulse of repeated Prussian invasions under Frederick II, Austria did not intervene in European politics on a significant scale again until the early years of the nineteenth century when, in alliance with Great Britain, Russia and Prussia, it played an important role in crushing Napoleon. The Austrian State Chancellor, Count Metternich, played a decisive part in shaping a new European peace settlement at the Congress of Vienna (1814–15), a distinguished chapter in the history of Austrian diplomacy. France, the conquered nation, took part in the Congress on an equal footing and was not subjected to political revanchism. The settlement, despite its short-comings, kept Europe free of coalition wars for a century.

In 1866, a Prussian-Italian alliance forced Austria to engage in a war on two fronts. This war shook the Habsburg Empire to its foundations and prompted structural changes that spelt the beginning of its decline as a major power. In 1867, the Hungarians successfully insisted on consti-tutional reorganisation of the Empire on a dual basis. By this arrange-ment, known as the Austro-Hungarian *Ausgleich* (compromise), the Empire became the 'Austro-Hungarian Monarchy'. The head of the House of Habsburg was thenceforward both emperor of the western half of the Empire and king of the eastern half. The western or Cisleithanian half consisted of present-day Austria, Carniola, Gorizia, Gradiska, Istria, Dalmatia, Bohemia, Moravia, Galicia and Bukovina, while the Hungar-ian or Transleithanian half consisted of present-day Hungary, Transylvania, Croatia and Slovenia. Each half of the Empire had its own government and there was no common imperial cabinet, although defence, economic policy and foreign affairs were controlled by common agencies. Defence was based on the unique supranational Austro-Hungarian army personally commanded by the Emperor/King. The three joint agencies rested on the '*k.u.k.*' ('*kaiserlich und königlich*', i.e. imperial Austrian and royal Hungarian) bureaucracy. What were termed 'delegations', composed of equal numbers of parliamentary representatives from the two halves of the Empire, met alternately in Vienna and Budapest to set the annual budgets for the three agencies.

This bipartite power structure, the product of arduous political infighting, grossly violated the principle inscribed by the Habsburgs over the gate at the main entrance to the imperial residence in Vienna — '*Justitia Regnorum Fundamentum*' (Justice is the Foundation of the Empire) — because it implied a *de facto* predominance of the German-speaking Austrians in one half of the Empire and of the Magyars in the other, to the detriment of the majority of the West Slav nationalities. At the beginning of the twentieth century, Archduke Franz Ferdinand, the designated successor of Emperor Franz Joseph, attempted to shift this dual structure towards a tripartite arrangement to include the West Slavs or, alternatively, towards a federation of nationalities enjoying equal status, somewhat along the lines of a plan for a 'United Nations of Greater Austria' outlined in 1906. Franz Ferdinand was assassinated at Sarajevo in 1914. Two years later Franz Joseph, who had been Emperor since 1848, died. His death marked the end of an era in which he had come to be regarded as the living symbol of the Habsburg multinational Empire.

On 8 January 1918 President Woodrow Wilson delivered his Fourteen-Point Address to the United States Congress, demanding that 'the peoples of Austria-Hungary be accorded the freest opportunity of autonomous development' and that 'readjustment of the frontiers of Italy should be effected along clearly recognisable lines of nationality'. In the wake of the Fourteen Points, the young and idealistic Emperor Karl I, the successor to Franz Joseph, pressed for peace and, on 16 October 1918 proclaimed his 'Peoples' Manifesto'. This included the statement that '. . . Austria should, in accordance with the will of its peoples, become a federal state in which each nationality forms its own political community in the area in which it is settled'. Wilson's reply to an Austrian note of 4 October 1918 seeking an armistice made it clear that the Allies' position had changed. The idea of autonomous nationalities within a continuing Habsburg Empire was no longer acceptable; instead, the constituent peoples of the Empire were to be given the right to establish their own fully sovereign nation-states. This sealed the fate of the multinational Habsburg Empire.

Republican Austria — remnant of a truncated empire

In compliance with the Emperor's 'Manifesto', a constitutive meeting of the German-speaking deputies of the old Austrian Parliament was held on 21 October 1918 and a 'Provisional National Assembly of the State of German-Austria' was formed. The Assembly voted unanimously 'to establish an independent German-Austrian state' claiming sovereignty over the entire German-speaking territories of the Habsburg monarchy. The new state intended to invoke the rights of self-determination that had been extended to the other successor-states, and was determined to resist any annexations of former Imperial territory populated by German-speaking majorities. In addition, international agreement on 'access to the Adriatic Sea' was sought.

The Assembly's declaration of intent to found a German-speaking Austria marks the birth of the new Republic, and it was formally constituted on 12 November. *Anschluss* (union) with the German *Reich* was not among the chief proposals made at the Assembly on the subject of Austria's international future. The Social Democrats proposed that Austria should form a league of nations with the successor-states of the old Empire. If this were unattainable, then, in the words of the party's spokesman Victor Adler, the new Austria would be '. . . compelled to affiliate itself with the German Reich as a federal state'.[1] The Christian Socialists argued for a democratic, but monarchist, form of government and for federation with the successor-states.[2] Only the spokesman of the National Socialist Workers' Party rejected the idea of close links with the successor-states and demanded Austria's integration into a 'unitary German state' of 80 million people.[3]

On 11 November 1918, the Emperor Karl relinquished any part in affairs of state and referred the constitutional question to the German-Austrian people. On the following day, legislative proposals for the 'Constitution and Government of German-Austria', drawn up by Karl Renner, were laid before Parliament in Vienna. Article 1 of the proposals constituted German-Austria as a 'democratic state' while Article 2 began: 'German-Austria is a constituent part of the German Republic.'[4] Details of Austria's incorporation into the German *Reich* were held over for later negotiation. Only one member of the Austrian State Council voted against the *Anschluss* clause. This was Wilhelm Miklas, later President of the Republic in the Dollfuss/Schuschnigg period, who had just carried the point that the ancient Babenberg colours (red, white and red) be adopted for the Austrian flag. His dissenting vote was vindicated fourteen months later when the Treaty of St Germain stipulated in Article 88 that 'The independence of Austria is irrevocable unless the Council of the League of Nations agrees to amendment.' The name

'German-Austria' chosen for the new state by its representatives was changed to 'Austria'.

In late February and early March 1919 the German Foreign Minister, Count Ulrich von Brockdorff-Rantzau, and the Austrian Secretary of State for Foreign Affairs, Otto Bauer, conducted secret negotiations on a treaty of union which, among other things, envisaged Vienna as the 'Second capital of the Reich'. The Treaty of St Germain put a stop to these plans and Austria was reluctantly thrown back on its own resources.[5]

In retrospect, the desire for union with Germany in the early days of the First Republic appears to have been less an expression of unrestrained nationalism — other options had been seriously debated — than the result of a pervading sense of being caught up in a historic disaster and deep scepticism over whether the new, small Austrian state offered a viable long-term solution.

The German-speaking Austrians had, not without reason, seen themselves as the core of the multinational Habsburg Empire which, through the centuries, had evolved into a community of nations with no less than 52 million citizens. At the outbreak of the First World War it extended from Silesia in the north down to the frontiers of Albania and Montenegro in the south, and from Switzerland and Trento in the west across Romania to the frontiers of Tsarist Russia. It is often forgotten that the Habsburg Empire included a 1,300-mile stretch of coastline along the Adriatic. In 1914, the Austro-Hungarian fleet numbered sixteen battleships (some of them modern Dreadnoughts), three battle-cruisers, nineteen destroyers, fifty-one torpedo boats, six submarines and thirty naval aircraft.

For centuries, the Habsburgs had controlled an extensive supranational economic and defence community. This had brought with it multi-faceted interchange among the Empire's ethnic groupings. All this had now disappeared. The break-up of the Empire also meant that the Austrian nucleus had been abruptly severed from its traditional markets and supplies of natural resources. Party leaders and public opinion alike believed that, cut off in this way, the new state's prospects of economic survival were poor. There was no access to the sea and as a minor landlocked state with six other countries as its neighbours, effective military defence posed major problems. While Germany and Hungary had retained their identities as nation-states, the dissolution of the Danube Monarchy radically changed the ways in which the German-speaking Austrians saw themselves and the outside world. As the core element of a multinational empire, they had for centuries upheld concepts of supranationality and ethnic integration that were antithetical to the philosophy of the nation-state. Now they suddenly found themselves members of an exclusively German-speaking country contiguous to the German nation-state and quite unprepared to believe that this rump of a once vast empire had any real future.

The St Germain treaty not only dissolved the Danube Monarchy; more seriously, it sliced up areas of the Empire inhabited by German-speaking majorities. The Austrian Provisional National Assembly laid claim to all former German-Austrian territory, but this was largely ignored by the Allies despite their professed commitment to the principle of self-determination. The 1910 census showed that there were 10 million German-speaking inhabitants in the Austrian (or Cisleithanian) half of the Empire alone. The St Germain map-makers left the new Austrian state with only 6 million out of these 10 million; 3,500,000 were transferred to the newly-created state of Czechoslovakia, against their clearly expressed will. Tirol, regarded for centuries as the 'Heart and Shield' of Austria, was required to cede its entire southern area, with 250,000 German-speaking Tiroleans, to Italy, and the region remains divided to this day.

In 1918 and again in 1919, Yugoslav troops invaded Carinthia with the intention of annexing the southern part of Austria. These incursions were fiercely resisted by the local population. Local militia units were rapidly formed with the support of the Vienna People's Guard. A short-lived occupation of Klagenfurt could not be averted, but the fact that the local population had taken up arms prevented Yugoslavia from creating a *fait accompli*. The fighting prompted the Allies to organise a plebiscite, and this secured the disputed areas for Austria. In southern Styria, however, the local population remained passive in the face of the Yugoslav incursion, and there a *fait accompli* was achieved. No plebiscite was held, and Austria lost the Marburg Basin. Only in the east was Austria successful in laying claim to territory. Allied approval was obtained for the acquisition of the Burgenland. Military action also preceded the Burgenland dispute, but on this occasion Hungary, like Austria, had been on the losing side in the First World War and the award was not influenced by Allied concern for the claims of the victors. Nonetheless, the Allied control authority accepted the result of a rigged plebiscite in the Ödenburg region; this area was awarded to Hungary despite its German-speaking majority.

Thus German-speaking territories in the north, east, southeast and south of the old *k.u.k.* Monarchy were ceded to foreign states. In all, these losses deprived Austria of 40 per cent of its German-speaking population.

The capital city of the rump of the old Empire that now constituted the new Republic — Vienna, with its 2 million inhabitants — was not only disproportionately large, but severed from its hinterland. The much reduced German-Austrian state was obliged to shoulder the debts and reparations of the whole Austrian half of the old Empire. This, combined with the burden of economic concessions demanded by the Allies, induced a general mood of despondency and hopelessness.

Some of the radical implications of the peace settlement were spelt out by Karl Renner, one of the founding fathers of the Republic, in a speech he gave on 11 September 1919:

The world has misinterpreted the notion of Germany's rapprochement with Austria as an effusion of pan-German ambition and excessive nationalism. In reality, our part in it was simply a mark of our desperation and the feeling that we had been abandoned. . . . At the economic level, we shall become dependent on all our neighbours: on the Poles and the Czechoslovakians for coal, on the Poles and the Romanians for petroleum, on the Hungarians for grain, on the Southern Slavs for cattle, and on the Italians for access to the sea.[6]

To the victorious powers at St Germain, Renner addressed the historic warning: '. . . if they force German-Austria to sign the peace treaty, they will be endangering their own victory by laying a corpse on their triumphal carriage . . .'[7]

Two unofficial plebiscites on the *Anschluss* question were conducted in 1921, despite protests by the Austrian government and the Allied powers, and these returned 90 per cent majorities in favour of *Anschluss* with Germany. Another unofficial plebiscite had been held in Vorarlberg in May 1919, and this showed an 80 per cent majority in favour of *Anschluss* with Switzerland.

A deeply negative climate of opinion had been created by the unpropitious circumstances in which the First Republic was created, by the amputation of large and important German-Austrian territories and by the widespread perception that the country was isolated, exposed and encircled by successor-states. Very few Austrians had any confidence in the viability of their new state, which thus lacked popular endorsement. From this attitude stemmed one of the congenital defects of the First Republic, namely the absence of consensus among its political parties as to whether the state could and should survive.

Confronted with serious financial difficulties, the new Republic obtained a League of Nations loan of 650 million gold crowns in October 1922. Backed by Great Britain, France, Italy and Czechoslovakia, the loan was extended on terms that were far from favourable. The conditions attached were expressed in documents known as the 'Geneva Protocols', signed by all five countries on 4 October. Austria undertook 'in accordance with the wording of article 88 of the Treaty of St Germain not to give up its independence', and agreed to 'abstain from every economic or financial obligation which would be calculated to impair this independence directly or indirectly'. Otherwise the Protocols afforded Austria a reasonable degree of latitude in negotiating customs tariffs and commercial and financial agreements with other countries.

Ten years later, the Austrian and German Foreign Ministers, Johann Schober and Julius Curtius, signed an agreement setting up a customs union between their two countries. Carefully formulated to respect Austria's treaty obligations, and open to the participation of other countries, it nevertheless drew a sharp diplomatic protest from the Allied powers, while France abruptly withdrew important credits it had extended to Austrian banks. The Allied powers referred the agreement to the International Court of Justice at The Hague. On 5 September 1931 the Court ruled, by a vote of eight to seven, that it was not compatible with the Geneva Protocols. Two days before the judgement, both Vienna and Berlin had informed the League of Nations Council that they were abandoning the agreement.

In early May the same year, Austria's premier bank, the *Creditanstalt*, revealed that it had debts of 140 million schillings and was close to bankruptcy. National economic collapse was only averted by the introduction of a rigorous stabilisation programme and by British support in the shape of a 150 million-schilling loan. In July 1932, a new administration under Chancellor Engelbert Dollfuss negotiated a second League of Nations loan in London, this time for 300 million schillings.

Dollfuss' administration immediately came under heavy attack from the Social Democrats, the Pan-German Party and the National Socialists, all of whom objected to the acceptance of prohibitions on *Anschluss* and a customs union with Germany as conditions *sine qua non* of the loan. The Bundesrat (Upper House) rejected ratification, and the overriding vote in the Nationalrat (Lower House) on August 23 was carried by only two votes.

The prohibitions on *Anschluss* contained in the Treaty of St Germain, the Geneva Protocols and the Lausanne Agreement paradoxically worked to strengthen perceptions of Austria's statehood and allay doubts about its independence. But at the psychological level, the interference of foreign powers and the restrictions they placed on Austria's freedom of action created a deep fund of resentment which welled over when *Anschluss* became a reality in 1938. Meanwhile, the National Socialist seizure of power in Germany in January 1933 radically changed the climate of German-Austrian relations and Austria's international position.

2

AUSTRIA — FIRST TARGET OF
THE THIRD REICH

Hitler's geostrategic objectives

The *Party Manual* of the Austrian NSDAP, issued in March 1932, details with remarkable clarity the political setting and strategy of the 'cold war' to be conducted by the German NSDAP against the Austrian state. The author of the *Manual*, Theo Habicht, was a former Communist who had been elected to the German Parliament as a National Socialist in 1931. A year later, when the Austrian NSDAP was reorganised on a national basis and placed under direct supervision from Berlin, Habicht was appointed its Inspector General. Early in 1933 he emerged as Hitler's principal intermediary in Austria.

In the preface to the *Party Manual*, Habicht marks out the Austrian party's objectives. They were 'to unite the forces which have hitherto marched alone, to launch them into an assault on Austria on the broadest possible front and, with their help, to overthrow the ruling system and effect the unification of German-Austria with the Reich.' The principal justification advanced for this assault 'on the broadest possible front' was unashamedly geostrategic: 'He who possesses Austria controls Central Europe . . . Austria, dominated by France, divides these two natural allies [Germany and Italy] and bridges the gap between France and its eastern allies. Austria thus represents a key link in the chain throttling Germany to death. This is what gives our struggle for Austria its European significance.'[1]

In the summer of 1932 Hitler, effectively cloaking his true intentions with pan-German demagogy that stressed 'self-determination', told a private circle that a Germany ruled by the NSDAP could only aspire to the global political stage when a 'granite-hard core . . . of eighty or a hundred million territorially united Germans' had been established in the centre of Europe. This he regarded as his first task. This core would secure for Germany 'once and for all, a decisive preponderance over all other European nations . . .' It went without saying that Austria would belong to this core, as would Bohemia and Moravia, parts of western Poland, and the Baltic provinces. In addition, the Czechs would have to be removed from Central Europe. Hitler was ready '. . . to accept responsibility for the renewed sacrifice of a whole generation of German youth.' He would not hesitate to burden his conscience with 'the deaths of two, even three, million Germans in the full knowledge of the gravity of the sacrifice'.[2]

At the time, very few observers appreciated the international significance of the contest over Austria, but in retrospect it is clear. On 14 October 1933, Hitler addressed a radio audience in a characteristic exercise of that well-disguised duplicity which he successfully deployed right up till 1939. Flatly contradicting his privately expressed views, he said: '. . . Nobody could demand that millions of promising human lives should be expended in order to bring about a correction of frontiers which would be of problematic extent and value.'[3] In *Mein Kampf*, however, he had scoffed at those nationalists content to make revision of the Versailles Treaty the chief goal of German foreign policy. Treaty revision, he argued, was insufficient because it could not provide Germany with the geopolitical and territorial depth it required in order to achieve the status of a world power. There was nothing immutable, he had maintained, about frontiers and divisions of territory between peoples; they were the product of warfare between peoples. The acquisition of territory by one people at the expense of another proved '. . . the strength of the conquerors and the weakness of the conquered. And in this strength alone lies justice.'[4]

The NSDAP, Hitler asserted, 'deliberately turns its back on our pre-war foreign policy'. The new German foreign policy could not be determined by dynastic considerations and still less by 'national sentimentality' (this last referred to pan-German rhetoric in the tradition of 1848–9). The colonial and foreign trade policies of the Second *Reich* would be abandoned. The primary goal of a radically new National Socialist foreign policy aspiring to world power status for Germany should be '. . . solely directed to the acquisition of a settlement area which extends the territory of the motherland, which will not only bind the new settlers in a deep sense of community with the motherland but will also confer on the whole area those advantages which naturally arise from its combined size'. National Socialist foreign policy should not seek a western or an eastern alliance, but should aim at 'the acquistion of the native soil necessary for our German *Volk*'.[5]

A major obstacle to the realisation of this policy was what Hitler perceived to be the hostile stance of France towards Germany. French European policy at this stage rested on the Little Entente (Czechoslovakia, Yugoslavia and Romania) and an alliance with Poland.

By the Versailles Treaty, Poland had acquired former German territories and frontiers which severed East Prussia from the rest of the Reich. France's hopes that German-Polish tensions would work to its advantage were rudely shaken on 26 January 1934 ~~when~~ Hitler announced the signing of a friendship and non-aggression pact with Poland. Hitler hoped that political penetration of Austria would drive a wedge between the nations of the Little Entente and thus tighten his grip on Czechoslovakia, France's chief ally in Eastern Europe.

As early as August 1933, Sir Robert Vansittart, permanent undersecretary at the British Foreign Office, had suggested in a remarkably prophetic memorandum that a contest over Austria would represent to Hitler the first trial of strength in the great struggle against the detested *status quo*. If Hitler's expansionist policy succeeded in this first round, it would be all but unstoppable. The future of Europe would therefore depend on how the other European powers confronted this challenge. Hitler had selected Austria as his first objective because he believed he could secure a takeover by political means well before German plans for rearmament matured. One possible line of action was for Germany to organise a revolt from outside Austria, followed by a seizure of power by the Austrian NSDAP. If the new National Socialist government were then prudent enough not to demand immediate *Anschluss* with Germany *de jure*, but simply effect a *de facto* alignment of Austrian and German policy, it would be extremely difficult for the League of Nations powers to intervene. Moreover, if Hitler were successful in absorbing Austria, his pursuit of further expansionist objectives in Europe would be encouraged and strengthened.[6]

Tactics of an expansionist cold war

Following his seizure of power in Germany, Hitler's unique combination of leadership roles placed him in a highly unusual political position within the context of German-Austrian relations. He united in his person the functions of Chancellor — the paramount foreign and domestic policy-maker in the Third *Reich* — with the functions of leader of the German and Austrian National Socialist parties, both of which were structured on the *Führerprinzip* ('leader principle'). Thus a foreign head of government and party leader was in a position to exercise all the intra-party powers accruing to the leadership of Austria's most radical and rapidly expanding opposition party. Riding on this nexus of powers and functions both inside and outside Austria, he was in a position to bring a great range of tactical and strategic pressures to bear on the Austrian government.

Although the powers concentrated in Hitler's hands were immense, National Socialist policy towards Austria was by no means tightly coordinated at all levels. The National Socialists were preoccupied with the fruits of victory at home, and were busily engaged in structuring and extending their newly-acquired power. There were sharply differing opinions and jurisdictional conflicts over methods and timing in the struggle for Austria both between state and party bodies and within the institutions themselves.

Before the introduction of authoritarian government in Austria and the banning of party activity, the Austrian National Socialists were confident of being able to imitate the German example and successfully exploit the parliamentary democracy they despised in order to obtain power, either alone or in coalition. The German NSDAP had very recently and in very quick time succeeded in gaining almost total control of the Reich without winning an absolute majority in any national election. The outmanoeuvring of coalition partners and use of strong-arm tactics in the right places had been enough. Why not in Austria too?

However, in 1932 the NSDAP was very much weaker in democratic Austria than in Germany. The German party emerged from the July general election the largest in the Reichstag, whereas the Austrian NSDAP, in the three provincial elections in April, obtained only one-sixth of the seats. In 1930, the German NSDAP had taken 18 per cent of the vote and 107 seats in the Reichstag, while the Austrian party had managed to secure only 3 per cent of the vote and gained no seats in parliament.

In March 1932, Theo Habicht, Hitler's principal agent in the Austrian party, noted that 'In the Reich, the movement, profiting from the break-up of the bourgeois parties whose supporters were basically nationalists, was able to mobilise a following of nearly half the voters and line them up behind it . . . In Austria . . . it faces an enemy three and a half times its size because Red and Black [Social Democrats and Christian Socialists] together command 70 per cent of the vote. Thus any gains the party makes in Austria can only come at the expense of its bitter opponents . . .'[7]

Austria was the subject of considerable policy debate at the Berlin Foreign Ministry in the lead-up to the launching of the cold war offensive against it in the early summer of 1933. While there was general agreement that in official relations with Austria Germany should seek to 'strengthen the National Socialist movement in Austria', there were strong reservations about raising the *Anschluss* question 'prematurely' lest the great powers be handed grounds for intervention. Coalition with the Christian Socialists was to be considered only if and when the Austrian Party was strong enough to hold its own.[8]

In April 1933, the Dollfuss government put out feelers, secretly at first, to the Austrian National Socialists — probably on the advice of Mussolini. Shortly afterwards, in an effort to stem their terror campaign, Dollfuss offered them two Cabinet posts. Habicht, eager to obtain control of the critical Interior Ministry for his party, demanded an upgrading of the posts and offered Dollfuss what he termed 'a concession', by which he, Dollfuss, could remain Chancellor on condition that control of the Home Defence Corps was removed from the government and autumn elections were called.[9]

The occasion fabricated by Hitler — apparently without consulting the Foreign Ministry — to justify opening his cold war against Austria was an incident involving one of his principal legal advisers, Dr Hans Frank, the Bavarian Minister of Justice. On 18 March, Frank had violently attacked the Austrian government on Munich Radio, claiming that Austria was the last part of Germany in which anyone could still dare to suppress the German national will — in other words, the NSDAP. He openly warned the Austrian government not to give cause for the German NSDAP 'to take into their own hands the safeguarding of the freedom of their compatriots in Austria'.[10] In the middle of May he arrived at Vienna airport on an official visit. He was promptly told that his presence was unwelcome, but this did not deter him from giving a press conference in Vienna. Here he held out the threat of German economic sanctions against Austria. At mass rallies he directly insulted the Austrian Chancellor and incited the Austrian people against the authorities. Following these provocative outbursts he was ordered out of the country. His expulsion failed to prompt an apology from the German side, which responded by sending a note protesting against the cold reception given to the minister.

Hitler, battening on to this contrived incident, delivered his rationale for launching a cold war against Austria at a Cabinet meeting on May 26. The Austrian government, he said, had recently 'provided opportunity enough for us to take up the struggle', and all Austrian governments to date had been essentially 'hostile to the Reich' and strongly influenced by Jews and Monarchists. No change was to be expected 'as long as

Austria remains in the hands of her present rulers'. The goal of the Austrian government was 'to drive out the German national idea and replace it with the Austrian idea'. As a result, Germany was in danger of losing 6 million people to a process of 'Switzerlandisation'. Elections in Austria would show the NSDAP to be if not the largest, then certainly the strongest, party.

Concretely, Hitler proposed the introduction of what later became known as the 'thousand-mark visa fee' (*Tausend-Mark-Sperre*), to be levied on all German travellers to Austria. He calculated that halting German tourism to Austria would prove a severe blow to Austria's weak economy given its heavy dependence on tourism for foreign exchange revenue. 'It is to be anticipated', he remarked, 'that this measure will lead to the collapse of the Dollfuss government and to new elections. These elections will result in an internal *Gleichschaltung* [unification, elimination of opposition] in Austria and there would be no need to impose *Anschluss* from outside.' The struggle, he felt, would be decided before the summer of 1933 was out, and thus, for tactical reasons, plans for formal *Anschluss* would not need to be implemented immediately.[11] For the same reasons, Hitler intervened in late 1933 to stop ratification of a German-Austrian trade agreement.[12] But Austrian resistance failed to collapse on schedule, and Hitler, after lengthy consultations with Habicht in mid-April 1934, ordered that economic pressure on the Austrian government should be stepped up. Priority was to be given to 'cutting back imports of timber, fruit and livestock'.[13] Parallel with this attempt to strangle the Austrian economy, the Third Reich used its growing monopoly of the press and radio to mount a massive propaganda campaign against the Austrian government. This campaign was kept up till Hitler's defeat in July 1934.[14] In Munich, Theo Habicht began publishing the *Österreichischer Pressedienst*, which was to become the chief organ of the Austrian NSDAP, especially after its banning in Austria in June 1933.

In southern Bavaria a so-called Austrian Legion — a task-force of professional revolutionaries — was established. Recruited from refugee National Socialists, it was deployed along the German-Austrian frontier. This SA formation, which rose to a strength of 15,000 men, underwent conventional military training and was equipped with rifles and machine-guns. Legion recruits specially trained for the purpose crossed into Austria on sabotage missions. The Legion also supervised secret shipments of weapons, explosives and propaganda material into Austria. There were sporadic exchanges of gunfire at the frontier.

A confidential memorandum prepared by the German Foreign Minister, von Neurath, notes that 'a special border guard' had been operating since February 1934 'on the German-Austrian frontier', consisting of 'Austrian refugees armed and wearing SA or NS uniforms'. The force comprised thirteen commando groups based in border towns such as Lindau, Oberstdorf, Mittenwald, Kiefersfelden, Berchtesgaden, Freilassing and Passau. Putting the Ministry view, von Neurath continued: 'The situation as described and the daily hazards it is fraught with are placing a serious burden on the foreign policy of the Reich government and have reached entirely unacceptable proportions.' The danger existed, he went on, that this state of affairs might at some point develop into a major liability to German foreign policy.[15]

When German aircraft began to make illegal sorties into Austrian airspace to release propaganda leaflets directed against the Austrian government, there were sharp official protests both from the Austrian government and from other European governments.

Dollfuss attempted to resolve what was an intolerable state of affairs by proposing negotiations on a 'government-to-government' basis to normalise Austro-German relations. Negotiations on this basis would have underlined Austria's independent statehood and formal equality of status with the *Reich*. Hitler, ignoring the urgings of the Italian Foreign Ministry, repeatedly and brusquely rejected Dollfuss' proposals.

Hitler regarded the Austrians as natural potential subjects of his Greater German *Reich*, blithely ignoring the fact that Austria had never, since the thirteenth century, been governed by rulers or governments residing in Germany. He and his supporters, and some of his critics, operated on the basis of simple-minded equations of *Deutschtum** with National Socialism, and of National Socialism with the will of the Führer. Theo Habicht's formulation of this thinking, made in a speech delivered on 12 May 1933, ran: 'The German people are like a fortress under siege. They are an encircled army forced to mobilise all its resources to survive the struggle with the outside world in order, at a later stage, to penetrate that outside world and create new *Lebensraum* [living space] . . . The new Reich . . . can only fight for and secure its freedom and future under the leadership of one man. Thus the question of the legal and political relationship is clear: Austria will become part of

---

* Because no phrase or word in English can capture the meaning of *Deutschtum* without sounding awkward — e.g. 'Germanness', 'Germandom', 'sense of German identity' — it is left untranslated.

the German Reich, of the Greater Germany to be, just like the other German states.'[16]

An Austrian protest at German interference in Austrian internal affairs elicited a reply dated 1 February 1934 which, while more cautious in tone than Habicht's speech, was still ominously pointed. Differences between Germany and Austria, the reply said, were not of the same order as differences between two states within the 'formal definition of international law', as Vienna claimed, but rather constituted a 'conflict between the Austrian government and a historic movement embracing the whole German people'.[17]

Hitler's strategy and tactics in the first year of his cold war against Austria may be summarised as follows:

1. Hitler's preferred option was to engineer, on the German pattern, a seemingly legal takeover by the NSDAP through elections and then to subvert the ensuing coalition. Although the Austrian NSDAP had failed to win a single parliamentary seat in the 1930 general election, it had moved up to third place in the party rankings as a result of the 1932 provincial elections. Hitler was doubtless correct in thinking that his seizure of power in Germany would improve the Austrian NSDAP's electoral chances. The Austrian National Socialists, stridently claiming the democratic rights which the German NSDAP was in the process of dismantling, demanded the earliest possible date for new elections. Like other totalitarian parties, the National Socialists deliberately sought to exploit the rights and freedoms of pluralist democracy to achieve their ends. The mendacity of this approach is nowhere better set out than in a chapter of the Austrian NSDAP's *Party Manual* entitled 'The National Socialist in Parliament'. It is worth quoting *in extenso*:

Parliamentary representatives of the National Socialist Party will not be elected to public bodies on the basis of the people's trust but will be appointed by the leader responsible. Public election will simply be a formality. Accordingly, the National Socialist in parliament will not be directed, in carrying out his mandate, by the wishes, opinions and beliefs of the masses but simply and solely by the orders he receives from his leader.

To ensure the proper execution of the leader's orders,

. . . every parliamentarian will, on becoming a candidate, sign an undated letter of resignation and assign to the leader who appoints him the right to make use of the letter as he sees fit. He is not sent along [to Parliament] to be a parliamentarian among parliamentarians but to stir up trouble. . . . He is not to be 'constructive' by working to prolong the life of the system. On the contrary, he should see his entire responsibility in working to eliminate these [evils of the system] along with the system they are contingent upon as quickly as possible. He is sent along to Parliament to spy out the enemy's plans right there in the centre of the enemy's position and . . . thwart them.[18]

2. In March 1933 the Dollfuss government attempted to exploit the procedural paralysis of parliament to rule without it. Riding roughshod over the law, the government began to prepare the ground for a restructuring of the political system in the direction of a corporate state. The National Socialists countered by attempting to force new elections, by mounting a terror campaign inside Austria, and by applying economic pressure from Germany. Hitler was reckoning on the collapse of the Dollfuss government under the weight of these pressures by the end of 1933.

3. When the Dollfuss government, instead of collapsing, hit back by banning the NSDAP and clamping down on Nazi terrorist activity, Hitler and Habicht lowered their sights and tried to force the government to admit National Socialists to the Cabinet.

4. The German Foreign Ministry and the National Socialists were insistent in impressing upon both the Austrian and other European governments the view that Austria was not a fully sovereign state but an integral part of the German nation. It was only the influence of foreign powers and a minority dictatorship, they maintained, that prevented Austria from espousing the will of the populace and welcoming *Anschluss* with open arms. For these reasons, Dollfuss' attempts to normalise relations with Germany as between equal and sovereign states were rebuffed.

3

SELF-DEFENCE AND THE NEW
AUSTRIAN IDENTITY

The roots of Austria's reorientation

The social, political and cultural factors impinging on the individual have at all times and in all societies created the need for local, national and international frames of reference. In most nineteenth- and twentieth-century states, loyalty to the nation was almost self-evident to the majority, and exercised a powerful influence on the shaping of their historical and political values.[1] But this was far from being the case in the Austria of the Danube Monarchy. The nationalism of the Empire's component peoples unavoidably operated in centrifugal antithesis to its supranational integrating principles.

Among those nationalities loyal to the Empire, some measure of allegiance both to the idea of Empire and to the House of Habsburg, as well as regional patriotisms, were certainly present, but the ethnically composite structure of the Empire precluded the development of any broadly-based Austrian nationalism as such. Following the collapse of the *k.u.k.* Monarchy, this produced, as we have seen, a climate of opinion which viewed the new and small German-Austrian state neither as economically viable nor as reflective of the popular will. It was widely thought that Austria was a foreign construct which, in order to survive, would eventually be compelled to join a federation of Danube states or the German Reich. Yet what was perceived as the provisional status of the Republic was long to remain a reality conditioning the socio-economic and political lives of its citizens. Consequently, the German-speaking Austrians, robbed of their role at the core of the Habsburg Empire and with no prospect of union with the German north or the Danubian southeast, embarked on a search for a new Austrian identity. This search, faltering at first, was to be taken up with increasing determination by Christian Socialist patrons.

In 1930, the poet Anton Wildgans delivered what he entitled a 'Speech on Austria'.[2] Striking in its beauty of language, the speech proved extremely influential in the search for a new concept of state-hood, although this was unlikely to have been the author's purpose.

The Austrians, Wildgans declaimed, were heirs to a supranational

19

empire whose capital, Vienna, had for centuries played a leading role in world affairs and provided the setting for outstanding cultural achievements of European and international significance — including, for example, a considerable portion of the world's legacy of classical music. The Empire and its attainments rested, he asserted, on the 'Austrian' (*der Österreichische Mensch*). The Austrian, by virtue of his Empire's political role and its position in the heart of Europe, had become accustomed to experiencing the changing fortunes of history at first hand. All this, Wildgans thought, had enabled him 'to rise above his limitations and become a European' at an early stage. His old leadership role in the supranational Empire had created in the Austrian someone 'who could think his way into alien mentalities and feelings, and indeed was compelled to do so; he thus became a connoisseur of different nationalities and a judge of human nature . . . in a word, a psychologist.' This empathy, Wildgans averred, was integral to 'the historical character of the Austrian'. Although this had made him less effective in exercising his political will than he might have wished, it had nevertheless had its advantages from a human point of view. 'It is no accident', Wildgans commented, 'that it was Grillparzer — an Austrian — who coined the phrase "from humanism through nationalism to barbarism".' Because the Austrian had lived in a multinational imperial environment, he had developed 'special abilities in the service of an idea', since in the old Empire the idea of Fatherland had only found real expression 'in the condominium of the Imperial bureaucracy and in the unity of the army'. The 'pronounced idealism' characteristic of the Imperial bureaucracy and the *esprit de corps* of the supranational army had left its mark on the Austrian people as a whole. Catholicism, the dominant confession, had also played its part 'as a school of supranational thinking, feeling and service dedicated to a universal idea'.

Three years after Wildgans gave his speech, Austria was jolted by another of history's shocks. Among the *Brudervolk* ('brother-people'), so long held in high regard, the National Socialists had been successful in establishing the first totalitarian regime on German soil. Germany's two major political parties, the Zentrum and the Social Democrats, had been destroyed, and this when their Austrian equivalents commanded fully 80 per cent of the vote. But more disturbingly, the *Bruderstaat* had turned into an antagonist engaging in economic warfare with poverty-stricken, truncated Austria, and ruthlessly conducting a hostile propaganda campaign and acts of terror against it.

Austria's Chancellor, Dr Dollfuss, faced with capitulation or confrontation following the breakdown of efforts to normalise relations with Germany, embarked on a vigorous search for a redefinition of the Austrian national identity in the hope of stiffening ideological resistance to the Third *Reich* and National Socialism. Ernst Karl Winter, a leading social theoretician in many ways highly critical of Dollfuss, has rightly observed that 'We should never forget that this first decisive break-through of the Austrian idea occurred under Dollfuss, even if we have since identified other and better reasons for the rebirth of Austria.'[3] The historian Professor Hugo Hantsch underlined the great difficulties involved in fashioning a new sense of national identity designed to underpin the state in the midst of the firestorm of National Socialist propaganda at home and abroad. The name 'Austria', intimately bound up as it was with the supranational empire of the Danube Monarchy, he wrote, had since 1919 been 'confined to the smaller state. The name had been preserved but robbed of its intellectual content: Austria had become a nation-state without its own nation.'[4]

With the intellectual climate still influenced by the *Anschluss* thinking of the immediate postwar period, Dollfuss and his supporters were not in a position to call upon nationalist feeling in the struggle with National Socialism. Nationalism was virtually non-existent in the new Austria. The state had come into being in highly unfavourable circumstances, and the majority of its inhabitants simply did not see themselves as citizens of a state. Thus those who shouldered the burden of official opposition to National Socialism were compelled to create a positive ideology to buttress the state. Spurred on by threats to Austria's existence, this ideology centred on Austrian history and the need to define the country's new role given its diminished size and an entirely new international political context. It is characteristic of the dynamics of this change of direction in the history of political thought in Austria that the leading exponents of the new 'Austria ideology', such as Dollfuss and Prince Starhemberg, had previously been supporters of Catholic pan-Germanism in its broadest sense. Starhemberg, who had earlier had direct access to Hitler, only became an active opponent of National Socialism in 1930 following a fierce quarrel with Gregor Strasser, one of Hitler's close associates.[5]

Central concepts of the new 'Austria ideology'

The chief elements of the new ideology, in so far as they were intended to serve as a weapon in the battle for independence and statehood, may be summarised as follows:

1. *The magic of Austria's past.* In an attempt to counter widespread feelings of disorientation and resignation regarding the state, the 'Austria ideology' vividly recalled the historical achievements which the Danube Monarchy, Germany and Europe owed to the small community of German-speaking Austrians. The Habsburg emperors, the Austrians were reminded, had for centuries worn the crown of the Holy Roman Empire and had later been Presidents of the German Federation; thus Austria had always been at the helm in the commonwealth of sovereign German states before 1866 and never simply one provincial state among many. As a result of their active leadership function in the multiracial Danube Monarchy, the Austrians' historical role — the supporters of the 'ideology' contended — had not only had a German dimension but also supranational and European dimensions, which indeed were more pronounced. The new Austria had inherited this dualistic role that had always been played by the central ethnic component of the Danube Monarchy. Just days before Hitler's imposition of the thousand-mark visa fee, Dollfuss said: 'It is a grave struggle that Austria now wages to alleviate her economic distress, to safeguard her freedom as a state and her thousand years of independence, to preserve above all else her Austrian character in the interests of *Deutschtum* in its entirety. Austria has a European responsibility. Lying in the middle of the continent, Austria is called upon to be the great mediator between Greater German civilisation — whose most ancient and noble pillar of support has for centuries been the Austrian people — and the other nations.'[6]

Kurt Schuschnigg, Dollfuss' successor as Chancellor, was to echo these words in a speech two years later. Austria's historical mission, he suggested, embraced 'both German and European civilisation'. Traditional Austria had been 'heir to the great principle of universality' upon which the Holy Roman Empire had once rested. By championing 'a community of European peoples founded on the bedrock of Christianity', Schuschnigg felt, smaller, independent Austria could make its contribution to a new, united Europe.[7] And Dollfuss again, looking to history as a source of inspiration in outlining his view of the 'Austria ideology', called to mind that 'For a thousand years European history has been decided on Austrian soil and for over six hundred years German Habsburg emperors ruled here in Vienna, from where they shaped world history. The Austrian citizen is rightly proud of his country, proud of being Austrian. But Austria also has the right and the will to determine her own future in freedom.'[8]

2. *Austria as a German-European synthesis.* In defining this Austrian identity (*Österreichertum*), the originators of the 'ideology' proceeded from the assumption that the qualities unique to the German-speaking Austrians were a product of their historical and cultural experience. Almost half a millennium of coexistence with Magyars, West Slavs and Italians had, they thought, created in the German-speaking Austrians a people whose mentality and outlook was quite distinct from that of the neighbouring Germans. In the pluralism of the Danube Monarchy, the German-speaking Austrians had enjoyed, they claimed, a unique leading, integrating and formative role characterised at the same time by the creative absorption of external cultural influences. This longstanding function and the wealth of experience it brought with it, they thought, was shared by no other German-speaking community. 'It is precisely the companionship of centuries with other nations', Dollfuss said in 1933, 'which has made the Austrian gentler, more tolerant and more open to foreign cultural influences, however careful he has been, and continues to be, to maintain his own culture and identity uncorrupted.'[9] Schuschnigg took up the theme in the following year: 'Austria is, to my deep conviction, a part of living European thought — at once, as it were, an accumulator, a transformer and a conductor of the steady interchange of currents which flow from west to east and from north to south.'[10] Here in this focal area of convergence among differing European cultures, Schuschnigg claimed, was the birthplace of that unique synthesis which constituted the Austrian mentality and way of life. Or, as the writer and scholar Dietrich von Hildebrand phrased it, 'what is characteristic of Austria's occidental countenance' is that, while absorbing cultural influences from many different countries, it had emerged as, and remained, 'a new and unique organic entity, quite separate from the cultures of these countries'.[11]

Nationalism, trapped in self-adulation and egocentric exclusiveness, Hildebrand argued, represented a type of 'intellectual provincialism' incompatible with the broadly-based outlook of the Austrians. This outlook had precluded the development of nationalism in Austria, he thought; the Austrian people formed a 'community of destiny' steeped in tradition and moulded by the past. This community, by its common language and the fusion of multiple cultural influences, had produced a very special 'lifestyle and variety of individual'[12] whose strong points Hildebrand characterised as humanity, magnanimity mixed with an artistic temperament, a universal and catholic outlook, and a capacity to enjoy life.

It was Anton Wildgans, again, who had, in a poem composed fifteen years earlier, evidently anticipated the prevailing nostalgic soul-searching mood and readiness for the fray in self-defence which gave rise to this consciously idealised image of the 'Austrian':*

> *Musik ist unserer jungen Menschen Schreiten,*
> *Musik, von allen Hangen jubelt sie,*
> *Und selbst der grossen Städte Nüchternheiten*
> *Berückt die allgemeine Melodie.*
>
> *Das macht das Leben wert, die Herzen weicher,*
> *Die Sinne fein, das Urteil menschlich-mild,*
> *Das macht den Künstler, macht den Österreicher*
> *Und schafft aus Träumern Helden, wenn es gilt.*
>
> *Denn immer noch, wenn des Geschickes Zeiger*
> *Die grosse Stunde der Geschichte wies,*
> *Stand dieses Volk der Tänzer und der Geiger*
> *Wie Gottes Engel vor dem Paradies.*
>
> *Und hat mit rotem Blut und blanken Waffen*
> *Zum Trotze aller Frevelgier und List*
> *Sich immer wieder dieses Land erschaffen,*
> *Das ihm der Inbegriff der Erde ist.*

3. *Austrian self-assertion and the search for peace and union in Europe.* The proponents of the 'Austria ideology' thus contended that the Austrians were quite distinct from other German-speaking peoples because of their special place in history and the dual German-European character of their cultural heritage. Once this was accepted, it was a short step to the conviction that Austria must preserve its sovereignty and not be permitted to become a dependency of the German state. The fact that Germany was under the control of a Prussian ascendancy which had been in power for a mere sixty-two years only added strength to the conviction.

Shortly after his election as Chancellor in 1932, that is before the

---

* *Translation.* Our young ones move with music's ecstasy, Resounding jubilant from mountain slopes, And even cities' grey sobriety Is thrilled by stirring melody. That makes life worthier and hearts more gentle, Makes senses fine and judgements more humane, Begets the artist, moulds the Austrian And makes of dreamers heroes When challenge and occasion come. And always yet when history's grave pointer Announced our moment of destiny, This people, dancers most and artists, Stood like God's angel before paradise. Upholding with their blood and with cold armour, In spite of cunning foes and hostile greed, A country always recreated, To which for them all roads still lead.

National Socialist seizure of power in Germany, Dollfuss began to strike a note sharply at variance with a number of public statements at the time. He declared: 'I believe in Austria and I am persuaded of its viability.'[13] He conceded that the Austrians were Germans, but Germans who insisted on the right 'to decide on their own future as a free and independent German state . . . from the depths of our own convictions'.[14]

On the question of 'nation', many leading supporters of the 'Austria ideology' postulated the existence of a German national entity bound by a common language and shared cultural values. This entity comprised the German *Reich*, Austria, the German-speaking cantons of Switzerland, the Free City of Danzig and German-speaking minorities in a number of other countries. But they did not seek to deny the fact that a number of German-speaking peoples, large and small, were resident in different states. This was because Austrian civil loyalties had centred for centuries on the state and not the nation. Thus to them there was nothing abnormal or uniquely German about the fact that there were a number of states with German-speaking populations, just as there were a number of states with English-, Spanish- and French- speaking populations. 'Austria', declared Prince Starhemberg in 1934, 'is a concept of the past, the present and the future . . . For us there will be no *Anschluss* because we know that *Anschluss* means nothing other than the degrading of Austria to the status of a colony of Prussian Berlin.'[15]

As Dollfuss viewed it, Austria's strategic position at the centre of Europe inevitably exposed the country to early involvement in any European conflict. Austria therefore cherished, 'more than any other state, understanding for, and the greatest interest in, the problem of world peace'.[16] By tenaciously holding to its 'primary objective', namely the defence of its independence, both in an international and domestic context, he said, Austria would be making 'an important contribution to the preservation of peace in Europe'.[17]

Starhemberg, clearly alluding to Austria's fierce struggle with National Socialism — which, if successful in forcing *Anschluss* on Austria, would mean ominous changes in the map of Europe —, warned in January 1935: 'It will be decided in Austria whether Europe will pass through a period of peaceful reconstruction or world war will devastate its nations and destroy its civilisation.'[18]

Schuschnigg had similarly predicted in August 1934 that the new Austria would not tire of 'proclaiming the will to peace' both in its own interest and in the interest of its neighbours, 'because we regard it as a matter of conscience to shield our younger generation from an incalculable disaster'. Without an independent Austria, he argued, the peace of Europe and the world would be very seriously endangered.[19]

But Austria's search for peace within the context of the 'Austria ideology' implied more than the promotion of cross-cultural bridge-building and opposition to National Socialist expansionism. Austria was to be 'a nucleus of a new European solidarity'.[20]

And indeed it was an Austrian — Richard Coudenhove-Kalergi, the son of a Habsburg-era diplomat — who founded the pan-European movement. Its first congress was opened in Vienna by Chancellor Seipel in 1926, with the active support of leading Social Democrats such as Karl Renner and the Burgomaster of Vienna, Karl Seitz. Dollfuss made a point of continuing this tradition and made it possible for the movement to establish its headquarters in the Hofburg, the former imperial residence in Vienna.[21] The movement, promoted by Stresemann, Briand and Thomas Masaryk among others, was a direct historical precursor of the European integration effort that followed the Second World War. Pointing to another facet of Austria's European orientation, Dollfuss made frequent reference to the country's handling of its minorities as a model for the rest of Europe. Were the Austrian example to be emulated, he claimed, it would constitute a significant contribution to peace among the nations of Europe.[22] Moulded by the supranational and universal Imperial tradition, the new Austria, centrally positioned and sharing frontiers with six other states, had a dual role to play, he suggested: first, to contribute to maintaining peace in Europe by defending its sovereignty against German expansionism, and secondly, by working to overcome self-centred nationalism, to achieve a framework for peace through the creation of a united Europe. This last is the sense in which Starhemberg's contention, cited above, was to be understood, namely that Austria stood not only for backward-looking nostalgia but for 'the past, the present and the future'.[23]

All the central ideas of this ideology were to come under violent assault in 1933 from the politico-ideological power which now controlled the full resources of the German Reich.

4. *The critique of National Socialism.*   Political ideologies not only frame values and strategies for the guidance and motivation of their followers, but also contain elements of the ideological conflict with their opponents.[24] Important aspects of the critique of National Socialism contained in the 'Austria ideology' will be briefly discussed here.

In the two-year period under review, the government of no other country bordering on Germany criticised National Socialism so openly and so energetically as the Austrian government. Dollfuss went straight to one of the core elements of National Socialism which characterised nearly everything done in its name — namely, the self-justifying nature of successes gained by the unrestrained use of force — when he said that 'People who live by power and believe themselves relieved of all moral accountability to a high authority' were gravely mistaken. 'Deep sadness overwhelms us', he continued, 'when we look at what has happened in so short a space of time under a movement which boasts and promises that it will lead the German people to a prosperous future.[25] Referring to the National Socialist propaganda and terrorist activities directed against Austria, he inquired how anybody favourably disposed towards Austria could possibly suppose that the state would be led down a better road 'with hand grenades, with bombs, with shots fired in ambushes, with a monstrous system of lies'. Let the National Socialists be under no illusions about Austria's desire for peace. Throughout its history, Austria had always been 'a bulwark of Christian-German civilisation'. Here the Avars, the Turks and the Bolshevists had run into a brick wall and 'here National Socialism will find its quietus too'.[26]

After the National Socialists had first attempted to entice Austria with cheap credits and failed, he went on, they had resorted to a systematic campaign of terror and the application of external pressure, of a kind unparalleled in modern times, in an attempt to ensure their 'participation in the affairs of state'. Austria had remained unmoved by all this. The government, Dollfuss insisted, would have to 'meet the raw violence of terror' with 'the full force of the law' in order to protect the peace-loving citizenry. 'As in the old year, so in the new year', added the Chancellor, 'neither I nor my friends will be diverted by intimidation, insults and threats to our lives from that path of duty which we see to be right.'[27] Dollfuss cautioned against the misconception that attributed the excesses of National Socialism merely to 'bad tactics and methods'. In reality, he claimed, 'we are confronted with a view of the world and society which makes such crimes possible'. He emphatically rejected the National Socialist policy of enforced intellectual uniformity in every aspect of life. This, he demanded, must be resisted 'to the last breath in one's body'.[28] The totalitarian transformation that society and culture were undergoing in neighbouring Germany imposed on Austria, he thought, a very special responsibility in its position as the second German state. 'We intend, at a time when the world stands in horror of a certain kind of *Deutschtum*, to show the world that we are the standard-bearers of traditional, Christian, German civilisation.'[29]

Dollfuss loudly inquired of those 'national circles' currently being eagerly courted by the National Socialists: 'Do you really want to have anything in common with this gangsterism? I appeal to you, whole-heartedly and unambiguously, to draw the line at their methods and at the philosophy that makes these methods possible. Only one thing can be said about these methods, and it is this: "I am against them." Anyone who cannot openly say this is an accomplice.'[30]

In December 1933, the Austrian bishops came out strongly against National Socialism. In a pastoral letter[31] read at Christmas from the pulpits of all the Catholic churches in Austria, they asserted that human-ity was a single family, and that 'We therefore condemn National Socialism's racial madness, which leads, as it must, to hatred between races and conflict between peoples . . .' Also condemned in the letter were anti-Semitism and sterilisation laws'. The bishops lauded 'the vir-tue of Christian patriotism' and condemned 'betrayal of the Fatherland'. As the state stood over the nation, they rejected 'the extremes of the principle of nationalism', defended the ancient rights of Austria, and welcomed 'the cultivation of the Austrian idea'. '. . . . Above national-ism', they claimed, 'stands religion, which is not national but supra-national.' The bishops asserted that they would therefore resist those ideas and endeavours which would unavoidably lead 'to an open break with the Catholic Church'. The key passages of this pastoral letter against racialism, anti-Semitism and chauvinism became in 1935 part of the 'state programme' of the ruling Fatherland Front.

The supporters of the 'Austria ideology' pointed to Austria's position as the one German-speaking country to stand alone against the tidal wave of National Socialism. As such, they maintained, it was Austria's mission to serve as the last refuge and bulwark of Christian German civilisation. Contrary to the ironically identical opinion of both its dazzled followers and some superficial critics, National Socialism, to the proponents of the 'Austria ideology', did not represent the culmination of a millennium of German historical and cultural development but merely a diseased perversion of *Deutschtum*. National Socialism, in their view, was as little characteristically German as the Jacobin reign of terror was characteristically French or Bolshevism characteristically Russian, for the true nature of an ancient civilisation was not manifested by sporadic derailments in its historical development. The equation of *Deutschtum* with National Socialism, they cautioned, was thus objectively untenable and dangerously propagandistic. It must be countered with trenchant criticism, because, when measured against the fundamental values of Germany's history and culture, it revealed its radical departure from those values and thus its perverted and un-German character.

Dietrich von Hildebrand saw in National Socialism the 'assault upon the intellect, the glorification of action; the noisy, insistent propaganda with which they imagine they can pull anything off and with which they think they can invent and introduce new religions; the deluge of empty phrases, the crass philistinism which leaps out of every National Socialist statement, the rule of trivial kitsch, the contempt for truth, the degrading of science to a servile handmaid of politics, the declaration of national autarky and the arrogant rejection of foreign cultural values.' With all this in mind, it would seem '. . . incomprehensible that a thousand years of German history and civilisation should be forgotten, that nobody should seem to notice that the whole thinking of National Socialism, its ethos, its cast of mind, all radically contradict what it is to be German'.[32] Therefore, he concluded, '. . . the struggle against National Socialism, unrelenting and irreconcilable, is the inescapable duty of every true German, of every man and woman who comprehends German civilisation and cherishes what it is to be German.'[33]

Starhemberg expressed himself in similar terms, arguing that *Deutschtum* would only be 'German and free' again when 'the counter-revolution of *Deutschtum* against barbarity' had succeeded. 'We Austrians wish to be the stronghold of this revolution of *Deutschtum* against barbarity. And so that we Austrians can do our duty by *Deutschtum* we must hold ourselves in all circumstances independent and free — come what may.'[34]

A former Cabinet minister, Heinrich Mataja, echoed this appeal. 'We are not fighting against, but for, the German people,' he claimed, 'and Austria is now the one great hope of millions of German compatriots in the German Reich who cannot defend themselves against the terror and who have but one wish — that we retain out independence to be able to offer them support and encouragement.'[35]

Supporters of the 'Austria ideology' sharply criticised the National Socialists for their pagan and megalomaniac self-idolatry of race, *Volk* and Führer, for isolating the Reich internationally — this was seen as catastrophic —, and for violating international law. The methods used were compared with Japan's campaign of annexation in Manchuria: in both cases 'a highly modern form of war' was being waged, 'war while maintaining a formal state of peace'. Germany, it was asserted, like Japan, aimed to obtain territory outside the jurisdiction of international law — 'not by formal annexation but by implanting and controlling an obedient domestic administration, a conformist sham regime'.[36]

The corporate state as a basis of 'legitimacy'

The 'Austria ideology' has thus far been discussed in relation to the central theme of this book, namely as an expression of Austria's self-assertion as a state and of its ideological opposition to National Social-ism. But there was a further important dimension to the ideology dictated by domestic political considerations which cannot be omitted from any examination of the political history of the period. This con-cerned the practical experiment in effecting a comprehensive restructuring of the socio-political system by replacing what was perceived to be the fragile parliamentary and constitutional framework of the First Republic with a Christian, corporate state based on the teachings of Papal Social Encyclicals — the first of its kind in history. An unexpected opportunity to make a clean break with the existing system and to introduce a major reordering of political life presented itself to Dollfuss on 4 March 1933.[37] This was the bizarre procedural paralysis that occurred in the Lower House and which, although it was by no means impossible to resolve it, effectively halted parliamentary proceedings. Under the impact of this crisis, and fearful of growing National Socialist strength as evidenced in their local election gains, the government decided that the parliamentary system, plagued by chronic strife between two parties of equal size, was to be replaced. The new system, in theory at least, was to have a strongly authoritarian — but not totalitarian — executive, allow the active participation of professional bodies organised on a corporate basis, and be strongly federal in character. Employers and employees, grouped by profession, were to share the organisation and management of the repre-sentative structure within this corporate system. The class struggle inherent in the party system would be eliminated by partnership based on Christian precepts. Political parties and direct elections to supreme legislative bodies were not envisaged. The President, appointing and dismissing the Chancellor at his discretion, was to be elected by a secret ballot of district burgomasters.[38] The new Fatherland Front was not to be an old-style political party but a mass movement embracing all patriotic Austrians committed to national independence and to reform along Christian, corporate lines.[39]

Dollfuss viewed the establishment of the first Christian, corporate state in history, opposed to both Marxism and National Socialism, as an Austrian crusade and a model for international emulation. In an important policy speech given at the first rally of the Fatherland Front on 11 September 1933, he declared that the days of the capitalist system, of Marxist materialism and of demagogic party rule were over. 'We reject *Gleichschaltung* and terrorism. We want a socially just, Christian, German state of Austria, on a corporate basis and under strong, authoritarian leadership. . . . Authority is not arbitrary power, authority is regulated power.'[40] Dollfuss went on to claim that corporate order meant rejection of class struggle, with the recognition of rights and duties for both employees and employers. People in factories and offices were to be valued in a Christian spirit as people, not as 'numbers'. His slogan 'Austria awake!' was to be the banner of the new movement for every citizen ready and willing to embrace Austria's cause and '. . . emphasises what brings us together, to reject what moves us apart and to belong to no movement which has as its aim the class struggle or *Kulturkampf* [the struggle against the Church]'.[41]

Dollfuss closed the speech with a characteristic appeal:

If I did not cherish the deep conviction that the path we have chosen has been decreed from above to be the path of duty; if I did not cherish the thought that the newly-awakened love of country was again so strong that we can withstand all adversaries, then I would not have the inner strength to address you in these words and to lead the way ahead. I am convinced that it is decreed by a higher power that we preserve our home-country Austria with its glorious history, though diminished in size today. I am convinced that this Austria will stand as an example to other peoples in the shaping of its public life . . . we now go forth from this place in the belief that we have been called upon to fulfil a higher mission. Like the crusaders before us who cherished the same faith, like one Marco d'Aviano who preached before the city walls of Vienna 'God wills it' [*Gott will es*] — so we look to the future in full confidence and in the conviction that God wills it.[42]

Psychologically, this appeal to a 'higher will' and the conjuring up of a historic mission to revive Austria's fortunes was designed to encourage the new movement in the belief that it was an agent of historic, divinely inspired change in state and society. The practical purpose of the appeal lay in the way in which it staked a claim to legitimacy, dubious though this might be. And this was a claim which the movement could not make under the constitution of the Republic since it could not command majorities in parliament. Gerhard Jagschitz, who has written extensively on Dollfuss, shows that his unconstitutional behaviour and his questionable use of religious themes did not represent a cynical political manoeuvre, but rather proceeded from a genuine and simple belief in the desirability and superiority of an authoritarian, Christian, corporate state and social order.[43]

With such radically opposed parties as the Austro-Marxists, the National Socialists and the Christian Socialists contending for power, the prospects of effectively combating foreign and internal threats were extremely poor. This, as will be shown later, provided Dollfuss and his supporters with a further motive for developing their idealistic project to restructure state and society along corporate lines. But little if anything was ever put into practice. The project remained a conceptual framework to serve as a minority government's moral defence of its authoritarian concentration of power in the critical confrontation with a brutal and powerful adversary.[44]

4

FOREIGN POLICY IN AUSTRIA'S DEFENSIVE STRATEGY

From the Lausanne Protocol to the onset of Nazi terrorism

Dramatic and significant events had occurred in the period immediately preceding the two years under review. In April 1932, regional elections in Vienna, Lower Austria and Salzburg saw the National Socialists advance from 66,000 votes (in 1930) to 336,000, giving them entry into provincial parliaments for the first time. A month later, on 20 May, Dollfuss formed his first and only administration, in which he was both Chancellor and Foreign Minister. He had a majority of one vote. Following the example of his outstanding predecessor, Chancellor Seipel, he immediately moved to obtain a League of Nations loan to boost the Austrian economy. Preliminary negotiations for such a loan had been initiated by the previous administration under Chancellor Buresch. The loan's political implications — continuation and reconfirmation of the prohibition on a customs union and *Anschluss* with Germany — sparked off a heated controversy, with Pan-German supporters, the Social Democrats and the National Socialists accusing the administration of 'treason to the nation'.

A document identified by the Hungarian historian Lajos Kerekes reveals that, before the signing of the Lausanne agreement, Hitler had prompted German industrialists and financiers to offer Dollfuss a loan of the same size and on the same terms, provided that he turned down the League of Nations credit and renounced his allegedly 'pro-French' policies. Hitler later maintained that Dollfuss, who had not entered discussions with the German side, had used their offer as a lever with which to apply pressure on France to expedite the League of Nations loan.[1]

Here perhaps lies one clue to Hitler's deepening personal hatred of Dollfuss. This young Austrian Chancellor — he had only just turned forty — had forced the League of Nations loan through parliament by the narrowest of margins (82–80) and was now effecting a profound change in the political self-perception of Austria's governing élite. On 3 September he emphatically declared: '. . . I have every confidence that we are a country with a future, and it is with this deep conviction

33

that I have undertaken to conduct Austria's affairs of state.'[2] The Geneva Protocol, he asserted, was the guarantor of 'Austria's sovereignty in the face of efforts to enmesh her, against her will, in political and economic entanglements.'[3]

Showing greater decisiveness than previous heads of government in the Republic, he had publicly defined Austria's foreign policy on 6 May: 'Our foreign policy can have but one goal: to ensure our independence on all sides and to see to it that we alone determine the future destiny of our country.'[4] A month later in London he told the press: 'We are now fighting to maintain Austria's status as an independent political and economic entity in Central Europe and we believe that, holding this goal before us, we shall be making an important contribution to preserving peace in Europe.'[5]

Theodor Hornbostel, a leading Austrian diplomat in the 1930s, described Dollfuss' foreign policy line after the successful arrangement of the Lausanne loan. As he saw it, the primary goal of Austria's foreign policy was, as before, to '. . . ensure Austria's survival by an adaptable and elastic "neutrality" in all directions, pending such time as a fundamental improvement in her conditions of existence might be expected'.[6]

The determined and multi-faceted cold war launched by the German National Socialists against Austria between March and May 1933 destroyed these hopes. What amounted to a declaration of war came, as we have seen, in the speech by the Bavarian Minister of Justice, Hans Frank, broadcast by Munich Radio on 18 March. Greeting 'persecuted fellow party members in Austria', he went on to make the statements, already quoted above, that Austria was 'the last part of Germany' in which a government still 'dared to suppress the German national will'. He warned the Austrian government against taking measures which might give German National Socialists cause 'to take into their own hands the safeguarding of the freedom of their compatriots in Austria'.[7] This speech left the Austrian government in no doubt that the German NSDAP, the Austrian National Socialists and the government of the German *Reich* would be involved in a concerted effort against Austria.

In May, Frank arrived in Vienna, made inflammatory speeches attacking Dollfuss, called on the Austrian populace openly to defy the authority of the state, and threatened to impose German sanctions, in particular a ban on travel to Austria.[8] An official Austrian request to Berlin for his recall was ignored and he was expelled. Hitler seized on his expulsion as a pretext for imposing the thousand-mark visa fee on travel to Austria, which abruptly stopped the flow of German tourists. This was the opening shot in his economic war on Austria.

Two weeks later, National Socialist gangs launched a widespread terrorist campaign such as had never previously been known in Austrian history. Its initial phase continued till the beginning of September and saw attempts — some successful — on the lives of government officials and functionaries of patriotic organisations, as well as bomb attacks on railways, public transport facilities, government offices, department stores, bridges and other targets. Following a bomb attack in June on a group of gymnasts with Christian-Socialist affiliations, in which one person was killed and twenty-nine were injured, the NSDAP was outlawed in Austria. The Austrian Nazi leadership reacted by calling for an all-out confrontation of 'unremitting brutality' for the overthrow of the Dollfuss government and the 'liberation' of Austria.[9]

Just before this, the Germans had begun a series of violently anti-Austrian broadcasts, chiefly transmitted by Munich Radio, and had started sending aircraft over Austria to drop propaganda leaflets. The complex cold war against Austria had entered a new stage.

The role of Italy and the Western Powers

To counter the internal and external dangers now threatening Austria, Dollfuss extended his defensive strategy into the field of foreign policy. Knowing that Goering (who at the time was high in Hitler's confidence) and the German Vice-Chancellor, von Papen, were to be present in Rome at the same time, and anxious at the possibility of Italian complicity in German designs on Austria, he decided to visit Mussolini over Easter. According to the account of the meeting given by Ulrich von Hassell, the German Ambassador in Rome, Goering had left the Italian dictator in no doubt that German pressure on Austria would continue, but none the less Mussolini told Dollfuss that Italy saw 'the preservation of an independent Austria as a cornerstone of its European policies'.[10] When Ulrich von Hassell warned Dollfuss that Italy might well reconsider its position in relation to Austria if the National Socialists were to score a major victory 'on the German pattern', the Chancellor confidently assured him that conditions in Austria were quite different from those in Germany, and that developments in Germany — particularly the appointment of a *Reichsstatthalter* (a representative of the National Government in Berlin) in Bavaria — had been read as a 'warning' by his party.[11]

Following his failure to appease the National Socialists and at the same time draw them into sharing the responsibilities of government by offering them two posts in the Cabinet (this was before the outbreak of the terrorist campaign), Dollfuss informed the German Ambassador to Austria, Kurt Rieth, on 1 July that he would very much like 'to restore peace with the German Reich'. He felt that with the newly-founded and rapidly expanding Fatherland Front behind him, he could deal with the Austrian NSDAP, provided that it was not supported by the Third Reich. The Ambassador bluntly stated that peaceful relations with Germany were incompatible with Vienna's hostile campaign against the Austrian NSDAP. Rieth's report of this conversation concludes that Dollfuss was not prepared to come to any kind of understanding with the Austrian NSDAP or yield in any way to its demands. Dollfuss had gone even further, the report continues, and stated his intention to use the *Heimwehr* (Home Defence Corps) to crush the National Socialists and at the same time carry out constitutional reforms 'with the Social Democrats' that would 'suspend Parliament and make new elections impossible for at least a year'.[12]

Dollfuss' robust performance for the benefit of the German Ambassador contrasted sharply with the appraisal of the situation he was concurrently communicating to the British Foreign Office through Rost van Tonningen, the League of Nations representative in Austria. British policy, Dollfuss claimed, was sympathetic to Austria but far too cautious; France was unreliable and anyway fundamentally anti-German. This being the case, he was left with little choice but to lean towards Italy — not that he was by any means convinced of Mussolini's continuing support if he should go into coalition with the Social Democrats. Hungary, he feared, would give its approval to the German annexation of Austria in exchange for the Burgenland; he was still awaiting a reply from the Hungarian government on just this matter. In his eyes, the Hungarian Prime Minister's talks with Hitler in mid-June represented a stab in the back for Austria. He was anxious too, on another score: armed National Socialist units moving into Austria from Germany could set off a major international crisis. He hoped Britain had contingency plans to be activated in the event of a full-scale Nazi invasion of Austria, and that it would join France and Italy in referring any act of aggression to the League of Nations.[13]

Speaking to the British Ambassador to Austria a few days later, Dollfuss raised the possibility of a German-organised *coup d'état* against the Austrian government.[14] On 18 July he outlined in a memorandum to the Austrian Ambassador to Germany, Stephan Tauschitz, what he felt were the two essential elements in the Austro-German conflict. First, he claimed, Germany was being high-handed and presumptuous in treating Austria 'as its own very exclusive domain' in which 'it believes it can act as it pleases, using the same methods as it does in the Reich'.[15] And secondly, Germany's support of the assault by the Austrian NSDAP on the Austrian government was so comprehensive as to encourage the Austrian Nazis to believe that they had the full force of the 60 million-strong *Reich* behind them. Austria's defensive posture was thus 'a legitimate means of resisting continued illegal terrorist acts against her and interference in her inner affairs by the German regime'.[16]

On 21 July Rieth spoke to his British counterpart deploring Dollfuss' rejection of the Austrian NSDAP's offer of cooperation, which involved what was felt to be a modest request for two Cabinet posts, and his rebuff of all other approaches on their part, despite the fact that probably one-third of the Austrian population sympathised with the Nazis. The Austrian government, he claimed, was attempting in a very unfair way to draw international attention to what was principally an internal Austrian matter.[17]

On 24 July the Austrian Ambassador to Great Britain, Georg Frankenstein, reminded the British government of its 'responsibility' to intervene in defence of Austria's independence now that it was seriously endangered.[18] Similar reminders were conveyed to the Italian and French governments with specific reference to four matters: the National Socialist bomb attacks and killings; the anti-Austrian propaganda campaign on German radio; the violation of Austrian airspace for the dropping of propaganda leaflets; and finally, the recruitment and arming of thousands of Austrian Nazi fugitives on German territory close to the Austrian border, and the use of this so-called 'Austrian Legion' for border control and sabotage activities. This 'Legion' added a new dimension to the cold war against Austria — the government feared that it could be launched across the frontier to act as a strategic reserve in a Nazi revolt.[19]

At the Riccione talks on 19–20 August, Mussolini expressly assured Dollfuss that Italy would intervene militarily in the event of an invasion of Austria from Bavaria. At the same time, he urged the Chancellor to allow the *Heimwehr* a greater degree of participation in the government and to accelerate his plans to rally Austria's patriotic support under one umbrella.[20] This advice conformed with Dollfuss' publicly-stated views. On 13 March, just nine days after the procedural breakdown ·in the

Austrian parliament, he had said that a way must be found, in hard and difficult times, of guaranteeing the government greater powers in the interests of the people. The new situation should be used to reform the Austrian political system.[21] Ten days later he appealed to loyal Austrians to join the newly-formed Fatherland Front which, standing above party and group interests, would be the buttress of the new Austrian state, both in concept and reality.[22]

The ineffectual three-power protest in Berlin

As the Great Powers prepared to deliver their formal protest to Germany over its infringements of, and threats to, Austrian sovereignty, hesitation and reluctance were much in evidence. André François-Poncet, the French Ambassador in Berlin, was actively involved and his memoirs provide a vivid account:

In order to have the desired effect, diplomatic action by the three powers should have been kept a closely guarded secret, and carried out both in concert and with resolution. The very opposite occurred, although this was probably the fault of the Paris press, which splashed the news of the three-power decision and gave it threatening overtones that had not been intended.

An unidentified leak enabled the *New York Times* to report the move on 3 August, with the result that Italy immediately distanced itself from the protest.[23] The joint basis of the protest was thus destroyed and the notes were handed in separately. François-Poncet's account continues:

On 7 August, we went to the Wilhelmstrasse to hand in our separate notes. It is still not known whether Italy even kept its promise. The British Chargé stoutly played down the remonstrations I had made earlier — with predictable results. The Reich government made a dignified reply, saying that the step being taken by the Great Powers was unfounded . . . . Difficulties between Austria and the Reich were an internal German affair and of no concern to others. The three powers accepted the rebuke and Hitler, far from being overawed, was encouraged and given the opportunity to observe for himself the hesitation, half-heartedness and disunity of the Great Powers. Never had I een involved in such a lamentable affair so patently crowned with failure.[24]

But this was not to say that some, though not many, Western statesmen fully recognised the dangerous implications of the situation and the imperative need to defend Austria's sovereignty. Sir Robert Vansittart, Permanent Under-Secretary at the Foreign Office in

London, put his thoughts to paper later in the same month in the memorandum already cited, which predicted the future with astonishing accuracy. He foresaw that Austria would not remain an isolated case but would be the point of departure for a whole series of trials of strength, each of which would further lengthen the odds against Britain. If Hitler were to conquer Austria, he would be all but unstoppable. The next victim would be Poland. If this chain of expansionist moves, each feeding on the other and escalating, were to be broken at the outset, then Hitler's first move — against Austria — would have to be checked, costly though it might be.[25]

Dollfuss and the Great Powers, summer 1933 to spring 1934

Undismayed by the unsatisfactory outcome of the protest by the Great Powers, Dollfuss continued to urge them to exert greater pressure on Berlin. As for himself, he told the British Ambassador to Austria, Sir Walford Selby, in mid-September 1933, he was determined to fight 'to the last' in the conflict with Germany, although he was under no illusion as to the gravity of the situation.[26]

Two weeks earlier, the Austrian government had sent identical notes to the signatories of the Treaty of St Germain. Pointing to the level of terrorist activity in Austria and the tensions mounting on the Austro-German frontier, the notes stated that the government was resolved to add a defence corps of up to 8,000 men to the regular army complement of 22,000 and requested the signatories' consent.[27] This move was entirely dictated by the domestic emergency, but it underlined to Germany and the other powers Austria's determination to defend her sovereignty.

Italy alone of the signatory powers was prepared to take action. Mussolini let London know that the Italian Army's headquarters had been moved up to Bolzano (in South Tirol) and Verona. This was only a signal, Mussolini pointed out, but he felt it would be correctly read by the Germans. In addition, he challenged the confidential British view that to support Dollfuss was to defend 'a lost cause'.[28]

With the exception of Italy, a special case, Dollfuss appears to have placed more confidence in Britain than in any of the other foreign powers. This is reflected in the extraordinary outspokenness he frequently displayed in conversation with Selby. He had confided to him his anxiety that Austria's independence would one day fall victim to a compromise between the Western Powers and Germany, as well as his particular concern about the future position of France. More thought should be given in the west, he urged, to the fact that the conquest of Austria would entail a very substantial accretion of power to the Third Reich. He was deeply disappointed that expressions of friendship from the Western Powers had not been followed by action. To be in a position to defend Austria's independence effectively, economic successes — without which in the long term no ideology could survive — were essential, particularly in view of the damaging effects of German economic pressure on Austria.[29]

On this and similar occasions, Dollfuss stated bluntly that he expected, where feasible, effective political and economic support from Britain and France — this not only in the interests of Austria but also in their own interests. Responding to Western concern that he was relying too heavily on Italy, Dollfuss remarked bitterly to Selby that, when it came to questions of practical aid, Italy alone could be relied on. With his back to the wall, he was resisting the National Socialist political and economic offensive on behalf of Austria and the rest of Europe. As long as no real support was forthcoming from other countries, he had no choice but to accommodate Italy's requests and interests. (see also Chapter 5, below).[30]

He reiterated this view in talks on 19 June with the French Foreign Minister, Jean-Louis Barthou. Barthou assured him that all the political parties in France would support Austria despite their reservations concerning the authoritarian character of his administration. Dollfuss disclosed his unease over the concessions he was having to make to ensure Italy's support, and appealed to France for increased economic aid.[31] He continued by saying that the ineffectiveness of the Western response to Hitler's moves to disrupt the peace settlement in Europe had been clearly demonstrated by Germany's unwarranted withdrawal from the League of Nations and from the Disarmament Conference.[32]

An official Austrian warning to Germany that, in the event of further intervention by the *Reich* in support of the NSDAP in Austria and its terrorist activities, a formal complaint would be laid before the League of Nations was peremptorily dismissed. Berlin's reply of 1 February 1934 claimed, as we have seen, that the Austro-German conflict did not fall within the purview of international law since it was deemed a matter between the Austrian government and 'a historical movement of the entire German *Volk*'.[33] The Austrian Cabinet responded to this brusque note and its implied threat to Austria's sovereignty by voting unanimously on 5 February to make good their threat and lodge a complaint with the League of Nations Council.

Cabinet minutes record Dollfuss arguing that it would be difficult for Austria to justify continued toleration of German attacks, since small countries also had their honour to defend. It was therefore imperative, he maintained, that Austria carry its threat through into action in order to demonstrate that it was determined to do all in its power to resist attacks of this nature.[34] If the League of Nations backed Austria, he suggested, then any future German moves against her would in effect be directed 'against the League of Nations'.[35]

However Italy harboured reservations about far-reaching League decisions which might restrict its own freedom of action in central and southeastern Europe. Moreover, Germany had announced its withdrawal from the League of Nations only months before. Additional complications arose from the revolt of the Socialist Defence League in mid-February against the authoritarian government's increasing suppression of Social Democracy. Fearing that the Nazis might exploit the situation, the authorities had firmly put down the revolt in a matter of days.

In view of these events, the British Foreign Secretary recommended that the Western Powers should produce a joint protest note, formulated in such a way as to preclude any possibility that it might be construed as commenting on internal developments in Austria.[36] On 16 February, the British Ambassador to Austria cabled to the Foreign Secretary, informing him that the French and Czechoslovak governments were '. . . vitally interested in maintaining Austrian independence . . . [and] unquestionably desire to continue their support of Dollfuss as the last guarantee available against danger from Germany.' Although both countries believed that the *Heimwehr* was gaining influence, neither felt that it would be reasonable to cease regarding Dollfuss as the key figure in Austrian politics.[37]

The three-power statement that emerged from these deliberations on 17 February confirmed that talks had been held on the basis of Austrian evidence of German interference in Austria's internal affairs, and that they had led to unanimous agreement on 'the necessity to maintain the independence and integrity of Austria in agreement with the respective treaties'.[38] This statement was nothing less than an Austrian foreign policy triumph. The Austrian Ambassador to Hungary explained away its careful wording by alluding to Western hopes that the German *Reich* would one day be persuaded to return to the League of Nations.[39] As will be shown, the exaggerated caution so frequently displayed in the years 1933–4 by the Western Powers with regard to the Third *Reich* in general, and its expansionist policy towards Austria in particular, was to continue until the conflict reached its dramatic climax in the assassination of Chancellor Dollfuss in July 1934.

The tripartite Rome Protocols

Italy's interest in and attitude towards the Austro-German conflict were markedly different from those of Britain and France. The fact that the three countries frequently expressed their joint support of Austria and their disapproval of German annexation points to their common interest in preserving Austria's internal and external sovereignty: but Britain and France interpreted Italy's motives for supporting Austria in terms of its desire to have a small, friendly state on its northern frontier rather than a power bloc dominated by the Third *Reich* and augmented by 6 million new citizens. By consciously assigning to Italy the main burden of obstructing German expansionism in the direction of Austria, Britain and France also hoped to sustain tensions between Rome and Berlin and thereby forestall, at least for the foreseeable future, a Rome-Berlin axis aligned against themselves. Although an attendant risk of restraint might be the strengthening of Italy's grip on Austria, Britain and France felt they could, to some degree at least, rely on the potential counter-balancing weight of Czechoslovakia and, in particular, of Yugoslavia. Yugoslavia's leaders were monitoring Italy's policies in the Danube Basin with mounting suspicion and had even threatened to intervene militarily in Austria if Italy did so. There was thus a considerable element of tactical calculation in the Western Powers' habitual caution towards the Third *Reich*. Italy, for its part, exploited Austria's increased dependence by trying to involve Austria as an ally in its overall strategy in central and southeastern Europe. Dollfuss, as noted, had repeatedly urged France and Britain to make a stronger commitment to Austria, arguing that he was loath to see a single power — Italy — burdened with the responsibility of safeguarding Austria's security. If the two Western Powers could assume a role similar to Italy's, he felt, Austria's freedom of action in the foreign policy area would be considerably augmented.

Relations between Vienna and Rome were much influenced by the powerful and autonomous *Heimwehr*. For the most part, these self-styled 'Austro-Fascist' paramilitary formations supported Dollfuss, but at times they proved extremely uncomfortable bedfellows. Mussolini's support of them caused Dollfuss serious difficulties both internally and on the international front — a dilemma which will be examined later.

In the course of a lengthy exchange in Rome in January 1934 between Mussolini and the British Foreign Secretary, Sir John Simon, the Italian leader reminded Simon that Italy had thus far shouldered the burden of containing Germany's aspirations regarding Austria. Simon pointed out that although Britain certainly supported Austrian independence in principle, 'We could not, of course, intervene more actively.'[40]

But a series of bilateral talks between Mussolini, Dollfuss and the Hungarian Prime Minister, Julius Gömbös, in which Mussolini was the prime mover, produced a number of agreements between Italy, Austria and Hungary which were signed in Rome on 17 March 1934. These later became known as the 'Rome Protocols'. Protocol I of the published version states that the three countries had reached a determination, on the basis of earlier friendship treaties and a number of common interests, to pursue 'a mutually agreed policy which shall be directed towards effective collaboration between European states and particularly between Italy, Austria, and Hungary'. For this purpose, Protocol I continued, 'the three Governments will proceed to common consultation each time that at least one of them may consider this course opportune.'[41] Cooperation would be based on 'respect for the independence and rights of every state' and would 'establish real premises for wider co-operation with other states'. The secret protocol, signed at the same time as the official version, emphasised that the problem of Austro-German relations would be central to the new tripartite association, and that while improved relations between Vienna and Berlin were desired, the Austrian Chancellor had required a guarantee that Germany should recognise Austria's autonomy — both internally and externally — as a prerequisite of cooperation with Germany.[42] Other sections of the secret protocol reflected Hungary's insistence that its position with regard to German support for its revisionist territorial claims should not be compromised.

The Rome Protocols did not establish a formal alliance, but Berlin's reaction was one of surprise and anger. State Secretary von Bülow recommended that his government pay 'very close attention' to them, 'for, where Austria is concerned, the main impression conveyed by the agreement is its anti-German character.'[43] Von Bülow instructed the German Ambassador in Budapest to issue an explicit warning to the Hungarian government to the effect that the future course of Hungarian-German relations would largely depend on the practical workings of the agreement.[44] In the history of the Republic there has been no other instance of Austria responding to political and economic pressure from a neighbouring power by entering into a form of alliance with other neighbouring powers. Shortly after the signing of the protocols, Mussolini underscored their security function by expressly stating that Austria could rely on Italian support in the defence of its independence as a sovereign state.[45]

Theo Habicht commented venomously on the protocols, claiming that Dollfuss, Prince Starhemberg* and Emil Fey† had 'succeeded in wresting Austria from the Greater German community of destiny' and had integrated it into a ring of states hostile to Germany. 'For this treachery to the German cause there can be no excuse and no pardon,' he asserted, and if Vienna imagined that the Third _Reich_ would be ready to make greater concessions to Austria as a result of the Rome Protocols, then it was labouring under a massive delusion. The goal of the National Socialist struggle was, Habicht maintained, 'a German Austria under German leadership', and the Party would not yield an inch in its pursuit of this goal. He ended with a naked threat. For Germany, he raged, the three-power pact was merely 'an episode, but for the Austrians who signed it, it means the end.'[46]

Three months later this threat was to find bloody fulfilment when Dollfuss was assassinated in the armed Nazi uprising in which Habicht was deeply involved. The revolt put the three-power pact to its first serious test — a test which it survived when Italy came out strongly in favour of the Austrian government.

The Austro-German conflict as seen from Prague and Belgrade

Dollfuss had voiced his puzzlement over the Czechoslovak government's stance as early as December 1933. Instead of offering support, he told Selby, the Czechs had presented a long list of demands. It seemed to him that the Czech leaders had no notion at all of the implications of the question of Austria's independence for their own country.[47] Shortly after the signing of the Rome Protocols, the Czech Foreign Minister, Eduard Beneš, made a remarkable speech outlining various possible solutions to

---

* Prince Ernst-Rüdiger von Starhemberg, leader of the _Heimwehr_ in Upper Austria, and subsequently the most prominent _Heimwehr_ leader.

† Emil Fey, leader of the _Heimwehr_ in Vienna.

the Austrian problem. In it he revealed that during the First World War President Masaryk and he had put forward proposals for the unification of Austria with the German *Reich* on the grounds that this would have pre-empted 'the undesirable solution, as far as we are concerned, of [the creation of] a so-called "Little Austria" '.[48] It had been the intention, he explained, to publish maps of the new Europe showing this Greater Germany. But the Great Powers had emphatically rejected the proposals. Commenting on the Rome Protocols, Beneš stated that Czechoslovakia and the Little Entente did not view them as inauspicious in principle, but would reserve definitive judgement until such time as tangible results became apparent. On the other hand, union between Austria and Hungary, supported by Italy and ruled by the Habsburgs, would mean the political division of the Danube states into two warring camps. Thus he thought the only genuinely viable solution to the Austrian question would be to obtain a Europe-wide guarantee of Austria's integrity and sovereignty. This solution, he cautioned, would of course require the agreement not only of Rome and Paris but also of Berlin and the member-states of the Little Entente.[49] Precisely how such a consensus could be reached while the Third *Reich* persisted in its ruthless cold war with Austria, Beneš did not say. He concluded darkly that 'A European war could be sparked off on Austrian soil just as it was on Serbian soil in 1914.'[50]

At about this time (it was mid-1934), Beneš frequently remarked, to the astonishment of Western observers, that Czechoslovakia still had no reason to fear *Anschluss*.[51] When the Italian Ambassador, Alfredo Rocco, urged Beneš in Czechoslovakia's interests to do something about the danger of *Anschluss*, he replied that until 1620 the Bohemian crown lands had lived 'both with and within Germany' and, in the framework of this 'symbiosis', had not fared all that badly. It was the Habsburgs who had destroyed the Kingdom of Bohemia, not Germany. Czechoslovakia therefore had no cause to fear absorption by the German *Reich*.[52] Before this, on 3 March, Beneš had assured the Austrian Ambassador in Prague, Dr Marek, that the Little Entente would find an ally in Berlin if an Austro-Hungarian customs union were established, since Berlin was even then moving 'against Italy and the Italian solution in favour of the Little Entente'.[53] The British Ambassador, Sir Joseph Addison, later recalled that on the same day Beneš had put it to him that Czechoslovakia could neither permit *Anschluss* nor enter into closer relations with Austria, since both alternatives would in their different ways lead to the break-up of Czechoslovakia. Addison notes that Beneš had contradicted this statement in the same breath by claiming that Czechoslovakia had nothing to fear from Germany.[54] As to Yugoslavia's position, the British Ambassador in Belgrade, Sir Nevile Henderson, reported from there in early March that King Alexander and the Foreign Minister, Bogoljub Jevtić were convinced that sooner or later *Anschluss* in some form was inevitable. Further expansion eastwards was thought to be 'highly improbable'. The King had a personal predilection for Germany and had told Sir Nevile as much on more than one occasion. Henderson concluded that Yugoslavia was simply waiting for a favourable opportunity to come to a closer understanding with Germany. The Foreign Minister had pointedly remarked that Germany now recognised his country as an established factor in Europe and would be willing to work with her. *Anschluss*, the Foreign Minister had continued, was a question for the Great Powers, but Yugoslavia maintained the view that a Habsburg restoration in either Austria or Hungary would be regarded by the Little Entente with very considerable suspicion.[55]

Five days later, Rieth, the German Ambassador in Vienna, reported that his Yugoslav opposite number had informed him that 'Not only Yugoslavia but Czechoslovakia, too, would mobilise if there should be a serious attempt to restore the Habsburgs to power.' The Yugoslav Ambassador had further indicated that his country hoped Germany would act as a 'counterbalancing force' against Italy and its developing friendships with Hungary and Austria.[56] Secret contacts between Yugoslav politicians and Nazi leaders — with disturbing implications for Austria — intensified in the first half of 1934. It appears that the Yugoslavs had been led to believe that in return for supporting the Austrian National Socialists they would be conceded certain border territories in Carinthia after *Anschluss*. The Yugoslav authorities turned a blind eye to secret Austrian National Socialist bases and arms caches close to the Austrian frontier.[57] Thus even among the Little Entente states bordering Austria there was little or no readiness, beyond the expression of pious hopes and the tendering of worthy advice, to become actively involved in defending Austria's sovereignty, especially in face of German opposition. The precise character of the Nazi expansionist dynamic and its potential dangers were simply far less apparent to political leaders in Prague and Belgrade than to those in Vienna, but then Austria was the immediate target.

With regard to Germany, Dollfuss, as we have seen, had made a number of approaches with a view to progressively relaxing tensions and normalising relations. Such efforts would have been expected of any leader of a small country seriously threatened by a formidable neighbour, however small the chances of success. But these attempts were doomed to founder on the fundamental incompatibility of the Austrian and German positions. While Dollfuss would not yield in his demands for recognition of Austria's sovereignty, Hitler insisted with equal obstinacy on his call for new elections, National Socialist representation in government, and political freedom of action for the Austrian NSDAP. But defence of Austria's sovereignty was simply inconsistent with allowing such accretions of power to a political group which vehemently rejected any notion of genuine Austrian independence. The conflict thus moved towards its tragic climax.

Three main foreign policy options were available to the Austrian government: it could capitulate to Germany; it could adopt an isolationist position; and it could, at a price, seek an alliance with Italy and Hungary. As we have seen, the third choice was taken. Although the active support of Britain and France in concert with Italy, such as Dollfuss had sought to encourage, would have given Austria far greater freedom of manoeuvre, both Western Powers believed that it was in their interests to have Italy take the lead against Germany in safeguarding Austria's integrity. For Austria, beset with both domestic and foreign-controlled economic pressure, propaganda activity and terrorist subversion, neutrality was not a viable short-term option if it was not to be respected by Germany. Both sides were playing for high stakes — Austria for its very existence as an independent state, and Germany for its first conquest beyond the borders of the *Reich*.

5

DEMOCRACY IN CRISIS —
CONFRONTATION ON TWO FRONTS

Government perceptions of Austro-Marxism

Impressions and realities. The cooperative relationship between the Christian Socialists and the Social Democrats in defending the state in the testing postwar years raises the question of why the forerunners of these parties in the First Republic failed to form an anti-Nazi alliance. But the imperatives of the years of tragedy, 1933–4, dictated the failure of tentative, low-level efforts to bring the parties together to halt the conflict which finally erupted in military violence and the suppression of the Social Democratic Party. Analysis of Austria's resistance to National Socialism must therefore answer the question why the Dollfuss administration chose to crack down on the country's largest party, progressively restricting the Social Democrats' freedom of action — in violation of the constitution — until finally its private army took to the barricades and the party was driven underground completely.

In order to penetrate what motivated the Dollfuss administration to undertake this seemingly unintelligible campaign, an attempt must be made to reconstruct the mental world of the Christian Socialist leadership. In any historical configuration, the protagonists are influenced by the perceptions they form and hold to be true, but it is a basic psychological insight that the realities of events are often seen and evaluated in extraordinarily different ways by different observers. And this is true of a great many perceptions that individuals and groups form of political events and processes in their immediate experience — they are frequently only true in a relative sense and thus in part false. None the less, it is this subjective notion of what is 'true' of a given situation that will be the point of departure and a controlling factor in any behaviour relating to it.[1]

Thus Neville Chamberlain and other Western politicians persisted in believing that Hitler's ambitions were confined to establishing a Greater Germany, and that if he were humoured in this, his expansionist appetite would be sated. This assessment of an important aspect of historical reality, subjectively true to those who made it at the time but later shown to have been objectively false, was to generate the policy of appeasement. This policy in turn led Hitler to overestimate his opponents' tolerance threshold and continue undeterred on his path of aggression.

The perceptions which an observer develops of a given situation, of the motives of other people, other groups or other states, are only ever partly correct, and are limited and conditioned by such factors as the information at his disposal at any given time, by personal experience and the standards of judgement derived from it (often straightforward prejudices), and by the whole bundle of both elements, rational and emotional, which go to make up his world-view and self-image. The often highly distorted nature of accounts of the early 1930s can usually be attributed to a failure to evaluate the politics of the time in the context of contemporary experiences, perceptions and values. As for the seemingly incomprehensible behaviour of the Dollfuss administration towards the Social Democrats, the only helpful analytical approach is to attempt to reconstruct the subjective perspectives of the decision-makers in terms of the experiences and evaluations that conditioned their behaviour. However, the subject-matter of the fraternal strife between left and right in Austria's First Republic is exceedingly complex, and no more than a few basic propositions can be advanced within the limited scope of this book.

Two armed parties in conflict.   As has been noted, the root-causes of the crisis of democracy in the First Republic lay in the absence of two vital areas of consensus between the two major political parties. First, there was no shared, supra-party community of interest backing the new state, the majority view being that it was provisional in character and its genesis not of their own volition. Secondly, pluralist democracy was not seen as an overriding central value in itself and certainly not as superseding party interests, but rather as a vehicle of limited use in serving those self-centred interests. It was only through painful historical experience that, in the Second Republic, a fundamental change of approach was brought about in the minds of voters and party leaders which allowed a movement towards consensus in both areas, and which accounts for the radical difference between the political climates of the First and Second Republics respectively.

The serious consequences of this absence of consensus were exacerbated by a deliberately fostered process of alienation and polarisation between the Republic's two major social groupings. This desire for clear-cut class divisions made a characteristic appearance at the first constituent meeting of the German-Austrian Provisional National

Assembly in 1918. Victor Adler, speaking for the Social Democrats, indicated willingness to cooperate with other parliamentary parties, but took a fierce stand on the issue of class struggle and the resulting polarisation of society, although he was the only speaker to do so. 'We German Social Democrats', he maintained, 'are participating in the work of this assembly simply because it is at this moment the only practicable German-Austrian parliament. *But with you, our class enemy, we shall never go into coalition, never conclude an alliance or come to a truce of any sort. We shall remain enemies — as we have always been.'* [2] Adler went on to describe the collapse of the old Austria as 'one of the signs of the general triumph of democracy . . . which will propel the working class to power all over the world and enable it to build Socialism on the ruins of the capitalist world order'.[3] Just how genuinely and deeply the leading Social Democrats were committed to the notion of class struggle is shown in the writings of Otto Bauer — Austro-Marxism's brilliant and influential theorist. In his widely-acclaimed book *Die Österreichische Revolution* (1923), he defines the political process in orthodox Marxist terms as 'the class struggle for power' and observes: 'As in every great class struggle, there is embedded in this one too . . . a contest between two different political, social, cultural and intellectual forms of life, as represented by the two classes in conflict.'[4]

The far-reaching implications of this new commitment to class struggle are detailed in Helmut Andics' excellent social history of the First Republic, with its discerning analysis of the psychological determinants involved. The Marxist goal of the Social Democratic leadership, he writes, was to turn the working class into a 'class of its own . . . in every aspect of its existence independent from and unconnected with the bourgeoisie'. 'This endeavour', he continues, 'was evident in every aspect of daily life. There was scarcely a single bourgeois institution without its rival Social Democratic counterpart. The comprehensiveness of it all stretched, as it were, from the cradle to the grave.'[5] He describes how the Austro-Marxists set up a network of parallel Socialist institutions designed to produce in their supporters a uniform ideological orientation, turn them into 'new men and women' and make them members of what was virtually a state within a state. This network embraced kindergardens, youth and student bodies, sports clubs, a 'Social Democratic Party Theatre' and a club for '*Naturfreunde*' to compete with the '*Alpenverein*'. Indeed, Socialist convictions went beyond the grave — a loyal Social Democrat was cremated, not buried. Membership of '*Die Flamme*', an organisation that defrayed the costs of cremation, rose from 20,000 in 1924 to almost 170,000 in 1932.[6] Nearly all the huge workers' housing complexes built in Vienna by the Socialist administration were provided with politically-oriented cultural facilities, and great emphasis was placed on adult education.

All these model efforts to promote the self-confidence and raise the educational standards of the electorate in working-class wards, while at the same time guiding them along party-political and ideological lines, were accompanied by a negative development which Andics, writing from a Socialist standpoint, does not seek to obscure. 'If anything was achieved by all this,' he maintains, 'then it was the widening of the gulf which had already been opened up by the political contest between the bourgeoisie and the working class. The *Gürtel* [outer ring road] literally divided Vienna into two intellectual worlds, and there were very few ways back and forth.' To the so-called 'bourgeoisie', 'the world of municipal workers' housing complexes beyond the *Gürtel* represented a sinister and impenetrable jungle of revolutionary ideas which, emblazoned on the red flags fluttering above the heads of hundreds of thousands of marching workers and conjuring up the prospect of world revolution, sent shivers down the spines of small businessmen.'[7] Thus the shadow of an organised and calculated class struggle cast a pall over the remarkable communal achievements — rightly accorded high international recognition — of Vienna's Social Democratic administration. Moreover, the Social Democratic leadership was determined not to let rising living standards and improving educational levels corrupt the proletariat and encourage them to drift off into bourgeois behaviour and lifestyles.[8]

Of greater political significance than the Austro-Marxist commitment to class struggle and the needlessly negative effect it had on the other parties' attitudes to Socialism was the Social Democrats' frontal attack on Austria's oldest, most influential and all-encompassing cultural institution — the Catholic Church. At its Party Congress in 1926, the Social Democratic Workers' Party of Austria approved a platform, later to become known as the Linz Programme, which stated that, while the Party was not antagonistic to religion *per se*, it was radically opposed to 'churches and religious organisations which exercise their power over the faithful to work against the struggle of the working class for freedom'. The Linz Programme went on to demand strict separation of Church and State, and insisted that the Church be exclusively supported by donations. Under no circumstances were 'public funds' to be used for the benefit of the Church and its purposes. Expropriation of Church land and property was also called for.

The loss of income following the implementation of these measures would have brought about the immediate and total collapse of the Church's financial infrastructure. In times of widespread poverty, public donations could only have covered a fraction of the Church's budget. In addition, the Programme insisted that religious instruction of young people should take place 'outside the framework of normal schooling', and that theological faculties were to be excluded from the universities.[9] The determination of the Austro-Marxists on this front was underlined in the following year when they stepped up their efforts to persuade the faithful to leave the Church. The results were statistically negligible but psychologically far-reaching. To the Christian Socialists — the Social Democrats' only conceivable partner in an anti-National Socialist alliance — the campaign hardened the feeling that there was something far more elemental at stake in the rivalry between the two camps than the business of winning parliamentary seats and forming governments. Chancellor Ignaz Seipel, who was also a Roman Catholic prelate, took to dubbing the Social Democrats 'adversaries of Christ'.[10] To members of the Church, the religious aspect of the contest assumed far greater proportions than any purely political antagonisms. And so the polarisation became increasingly acute. The Social Democrats' indulgence in the political luxury of a campaign against the Church could not but operate negatively on the chances that the Christian Socialists would cooperate with them. But beyond the Church question, the two parties were also deeply divided on other issues.

Rejection of traditionalism and Austrian statehood, and the attractions of Anschluss.   Recollection of the cultural and historical grandeur of traditional Austria provided Christian-Fatherland sympathisers, as we have seen, with a deeply-felt source of spiritual strength and sense of identity. The legitimacy of the new, smaller Austria was to be derived from the same source, in the hope that many of the old values could be carried over into the new context. Compared with the dynasties ruling in single-nation states elsewhere in Europe, the House of Habsburg had always played a more significant role, both emotionally and institutionally, in the lives of the loyal citizenry. Thus a positive view of Austria's history almost invariably went hand in hand with pro-Habsburg sentiment. Although it was widely recognised in Christian-Fatherland circles that a Habsburg restoration was neither feasible nor desirable, the Imperial House nevertheless retained a central place in their reading of Austrian history.

Quite the opposite was true of the Social Democratic leaders. For them, the name and myth of the Habsburgs and their Empire aroused deep hatred. This was something of a paradox in view of the fact that the bill of rights contained in the 1867 *Staatsgrundgesetz* (Basic Law) had been sufficiently acceptable to be incorporated *in toto* into the Republican Constitutions of 1920 and 1929. In 1907 universal manhood suffrage had been introduced, and the first general election held in the Cisleithanian half of the Empire. Walter Pollak, in his history of Austrian Socialism, comments: 'That day was a triumph for the Social Democrats — their fight for universal suffrage had been won. They had made a spectacular breakthrough, entering the Reichsrat with eighty-seven seats, to become the second strongest party.'[11]

No one had advanced a better solution to the pressing problem of the nationalities in the Empire than Karl Renner and Otto Bauer, Austria's leading Social Democrats. The nationalities policy of the heir to the Imperial throne, Franz Ferdinand, and of the Emperor Karl himself ran along similar lines. Nevertheless, hostility to the Habsburg Empire became an article of Social Democratic faith, so much so that Otto Bauer savaged the Treaty of St Germain for imposing upon the Republic '*the old name of Austria . . . that hated name*'.[12] In the parliamentary debate on 14 September 1922 on the League of Nations loan and its reiterated proviso regarding *Anschluss* with Germany, the Chancellor suggested that, in the national interest, the opposition should support the loan. Bauer's response on behalf of his party was vitriolic: 'One does not waste words on blatant treason: one treats it with contempt as long as it poses no risk and one strikes it down the moment it gets dangerous . . .' Renner completed the attack by asserting that German-Austria had 'no future' and that the provisional state must be kept alive only in expectation of 'the hour of liberation' when union with the German *Reich* (then the Weimar Republic) should become feasible.[13]

In an important and symptomatic policy statement issued in May 1933, the Social Democratic leadership vigorously rejected the idea of integration with the Third *Reich* but insisted that '*Anschluss* with a free and peaceful Germany of the future remains our goal . . . we shall oppose *any* restoration of Habsburg rule just as we shall steadfastly resist subjugation to Hitler's tyranny.'[14] The stress on the word 'any' was intended to underline that even restitution of a constitutional monarchy committed to the rule of law and party pluralism — should it be Habsburg-ruled — would be resisted as fiercely as what was accurately termed 'Hitler's tyranny'. Immediately after the National Socialist revolt of July 1934 and the abortive attempt to overthrow the Austrian state, Bauer commented, 'Socialist workers and National Socialist petit-bourgeois, peasants and intellectuals make up the vast majority of the Austrian people.' And then, almost as if framing a hope, he continued: 'If they could unite against it, Austro-Fascism would be swept away.' The Fatherland Front, he supposed, would attempt a Habsburg restoration as a 'last resort' and 'A proletarian revolution against the restoration of the Habsburgs would carry with it all those whose thoughts and feelings were imbued with the German national idea.' He thought that the Third *Reich* and the countries of the Little Entente would greatly welcome such a revolution.[15]

Even after the *Anschluss*, Bauer continued to belittle Austria's sover-eignty. 'The future of the Austrian working class', he maintained in 1938, 'does not lie in Austrian separatism.'[16] The response of Austrian Socialism to the fact of annexation by the Third *Reich*, he argued, 'cannot be reac-tionary but must be revolutionary'. The clock of history could not be turned back. 'But Austria is a thing of the past. Let the Austrian clericals and monarchists set up their committees abroad and dream of the resurrec-tion of an Austrian state . . . it's just a childish game.'[17]

Bauer's rejection of the 'Austrian ideology' developed by Dollfuss and his supporters was equally polemical: 'We Austrian Socialists will have nothing to do with that spectre of the 'Austrian' conjured up out of a brew of Catholicism, Habsburg tradition and Baroque culture which sets up clerical, conservative, imperial separatism in defiance of the national com-munity of the German *Volk*. . . . We have no part either in that glorifica-tion of "Little Austria" which condemns our industry to contraction and our workers to unemployment. . . .'[18]

This widespread Social Democratic belief in the coming of a Greater German Socialist Republic illuminates one aspect of the sharply-divided convictions which separated the two major parties in the First Republic as they faced the National Socialist challenge. But this belief, seen from the Christian-Fatherland perspective, only served to heighten their scepticism of any kind of cooperation built on mutual trust and consensus with sup-porters of a world view in essential points so fundamentally antagonistic to their own. When the Social Democrats in October 1933 announced their temporary abandonment of *Anschluss* — for the duration of the Third Reich — it had only a marginal effect in reducing suspicions.

— *The spectre of Bolshevism.*   As one looks back over the seven decades in which Republican Austria has existed, the Socialist Party stands out as a

pillar of Austrian democracy both in terms of its own political development and in terms of its resistance to totalitarian threats from left and
right. It is thus remarkable that non-Socialist opinion in politics and
society persistently suspected that the Socialist Party — in its Austro-
Marxist colours — represented a well-camouflaged form of Bolshevism.
Though incorrect, this view played a controlling role in non-Socialist
political behaviour and was a fateful factor in the alienation and the
development of distrust between the two major parties, whose cooperation would have been so vital to Austria's defence against National
Socialism. Helmut Andics provides a lucid account of the situation:

We know today that the Social Democrats of the First Republic had, by no
later than the 1926 'Linz Programme', jettisoned any serious hopes of carrying
out their fiery Socialist revolution. But we also know that the bourgeoisie
genuinely believed that a Social Democratic parliamentary majority of fifty-one
per cent would mean Bolshevism in Austria. And just as the *Heimwehr* was
convinced of the existence of Austrian Bolshevism because in their party jargon
the Austro-Marxist ideologues spoke loud and clear of 'revolution', the Social
Democratic working class was convinced of the existence of 'reaction' when-
ever the *Heimwehr* fantasised about a Fascist corporate state. Behind the litanies
of hate poured out by tub-thumpers at local and district meetings lay a very
humble reality.[19]

These negative stereotypes were further enhanced by a serious incident
which occurred on 30 January 1927 in the Burgenland village of
Schattendorf. Rightist veterans' organisations had arranged a reunion in
the village and, as was the practice at the time, the Socialist Defence
League arranged a counter-meeting on the same day and in the same
village as an *acte de presence*. Serious clashes developed, during which a
Socialist militiaman and a child were killed. A group of veterans had
barricaded themselves in a local inn and it was from there that the fatal
shots were fired as a large contingent of Socialist militiamen attempted
to rush it. Three men were charged with the shootings and were acquitted
on 14 July in a jury trial — an institution the Social Democrats had
fought to introduce. The acquittal moved the *Arbeiterzeitung* (Workers'
Daily) on 15 July to claim that 'civil war' was already under way, and
suggest that the shooting of innocent people by veterans appeared to be
viewed in the same light as the 'pleasures of the chase'.

In Vienna, news of the acquittal provoked a general strike and violent
mass demonstrations, both quite unprompted by the Social Democratic
party leadership. The angry crowd attempted unsuccessfully to storm
the university and parliament buildings, but managed to break into the

Palace of Justice and systematically set it on fire. There was an attempt to lynch the foreman of the jury in the Schattendorf trial. Newspaper offices were forcibly entered and looted. The Burgomaster of Vienna and other Social Democratic leaders vainly tried to calm the mob and clear a path to the building for the firemen. Police sent to the scene came under gunfire and returned it. Casualties were high: 86 dead and 118 seriously injured.[20]

In Walter Pollak's view, '15 July 1927 marked a rupture in the development of Social Democracy in Austria. But graver than this was the fact that it widened the gulf between the two political camps to such an extent that there seemed no way of ever bridging it. As for reconciliation, nobody wanted to know about it.'[21] The rabid polemics in the *Arbeiterzeitung* against the acquittal, which was branded as symptomatic of government policies, did not have the hoped-for effect of providing an outlet for outraged public opinion. The Social Democratic leaders were genuinely surprised that the acquittal had triggered off a spontaneous mass reaction and serious civil disturbances without encouragement from or direction by the party. They and the government were deeply disturbed by the events, though for different reasons. The government accused the Socialists of irresponsible demagogy, and the Socialists countered with charges of excessive use of firearms. Karl Renner gives a sombre description of the damaging effects of 15 July on the precariously balanced political cohesion of the Republic:

The antagonism which had hitherto been confined to the parliamentary arena was now — with the help, no doubt, of inflammatory polemics in the press — transformed into bitter confrontation between two armed camps. . . . Within the [Social Democratic] party, radical elements condemned the fact that violence had been stopped rather than being allowed to escalate into armed revolution, while in the bourgeois world . . . the fear of Communism (the Communists did not have a single seat in parliament) fanned by the *Heimwehr* but thus far held in check . . . took a serious turn. The least gesture of violence, calculated or not, touched on sensitive nerves among the fearful and excited the will to violence among the belligerent.[22]

Demonstrators charged with arson and violence in connection with the events of 15 July were also acquitted in jury trials. But the polarisation of the Republic's two major parties had now reached a stage where these acquittals were of minor interest.

At a Social Democratic party congress convened soon afterwards, Otto Bauer advanced the case for rejecting a coalition with the government and declared: 'This Austria is the sum of two parts which are very different but virtually equal in number.'[23] In a prescient insight into the dangers implicit in the distorted views the opposing parties held of one another, Karl Renner argued: 'It is dangerous and it is contradictory to speak of revolutions all the time and at the same time be compelled to confess that they cannot be carried out. It is a contradiction that should make us very wary of this type of propaganda . . .'[24]

In October 1932, Otto Bauer took issue with these very real misapprehensions in an article which he characteristically entitled 'We Bolsheviks. An answer to Dollfuss.'[25] He recalled that the newly-elected Chancellor had recently shouted at him in parliament: 'You're a Bolshevik! You've never honestly stated your attitude to democracy.' But, Bauer continued, when he reflected on what he knew of Soviet dictatorship in practice, he had to conclude that he simply could not go along with it. 'What divides me from Bolshevism is my regard for the intellectual freedom of the individual.' It was for the sake of this freedom, he maintained, that he was a 'democrat'. 'But for all my love of intellectual freedom', he continued, 'I detest capitalism with an ineradicable hatred.' Although he was critical of Bolshevism, he wished to tell the Soviet Union that the overthrow of 'Soviet dictatorship' in Russia would not lead to freedom but to a 'White dictatorship'. If, on the other hand, the Soviet dictatorship were to succeed in 'the task of Socialist reconstruction', and when a younger generation educated in Socialism reached maturity, 'dictatorship will have become superfluous and can be dismantled'.

Bauer's personal disavowal of Bolshevism was then followed by an essentially optimistic, though qualified, approval of it. He ended on a note which aptly reflects the contemporary mood and highly polemical character of political discussion: 'There, Mr Dollfuss, you have my stand on Bolshevism. However, I confess that it is too subtle to be grasped by those members who inanely applauded your "You're a Bolshevik" with delighted grins.'[26]

Six months later, a leading article in the *Arbeiterzeitung* renewed the charge that Dollfuss was distorting Austro-Marxist policy statements and the Party programme to conclude that the Social Democrats 'had set the dictatorship of the proletariat as their goal'. In reality, the article claimed, the aims of Social Democracy were confined to 'a struggle for freedom by the use of violence' and to the establishment of dictatorship only if their opponents destroyed the democratic forum. The *Arbeiterzeitung* reminded Dollfuss of the paradox that he had been, only two years before, one of the Christian Socialist leaders who advocated 'coalition with the Marxists'. The article ended with a call for a general election. At this stage new elections were more fervently desired by the National Socialists than by the Social Democrats.[27]

As if to confirm Social Democratic suspicions, Chancellor Dollfuss told the French newspaper *Petit Parisien* only a few days afterwards that a clear distinction had to be drawn between French and Austrian Social Democracy, because 'The Austrian Marxists have class struggle *written in large letters on their banners.* They're not statisfied with a democratic regime, they see it only as a stepping-stone to dictatorship of the proletariat.'[28] Schuschnigg echoed these doubts in his book *Dreimal Österreich* (Three Times Austria). To the Austro-Marxists, he alleged, democracy was 'only a transitional stage on the road to dictatorship of the proletariat'.[29] This would appear to be a conscious reference to Otto Bauer's *Die Österreichische Revolution*,[30] which ends on a note of caution advising fellow Social Democrats not to imitate the mistake of the petit-bourgeois democrats and view the Republic's pluralist democracy as 'the end of the road' when it was merely 'a transitional stage'.[31] The immediate need, Bauer continues, was for 'the proletariat' to defend the gains of the 1918 revolution,[32] but 'As soon as the problems that remained unresolved after the revolution of 1918 . . . ignite a new process, the temporary political and social system produced by the revolution will be destroyed in the maelstrom of a new revolution and transformed into a higher, but also provisional, stage.'[33] This chain of revolutions issuing from the class struggle would only reach its climax, he claimed, in a Socialist society which had eliminated class differences, outlawed private ownership of the means of production and realised a true, Socialist '*Volksgemeinschaft*' (people's partnership).[34]

As Karl Renner suggested (and Bruno Kreisky has since confirmed in his account of the left-right feud in February 1934), the revolutionary-sounding catchphrases bandied about by the left wing of the Austro-Marxists positively invited misunderstanding, and greatly contributed — although there were other, weightier factors — to Christian-Fatherland misconceptions of their rivals and thus to the frustration of attempts to create a united front against National Socialism. Only days after the revolt of the Socialist Defence League in February, Otto Bauer published a 'Declaration of Principles' in the name of his party. Here he claimed that what he termed the 'Austro-Fascist dictatorship' had 'deprived the Social Democrats of the democratic basis for the reconstruction of society'. Recent events in Austria, he continued, had corroborated the view that 'No real and lasting democracy can be established until economic power vested in the capitalists, the aristocracy and the Church — which they have used to destroy democracy — is seized from them. And that is why revolutionary dictatorship of the working class must first arise from a people's revolutionary uprising in Austria . . .' Only when such a dictatorship had fulfilled its task of completely socialising society would the introduction of a new 'Socialist Democracy' be possible. Bauer ended the declaration by unwittingly confirming his opponents' suspicion that the Social Democrats were tarred with the Bolshevist brush — a view genuinely held and also skilfully exploited by Dollfuss and Schuschnigg. 'Our aim is not the revival of the bourgeois democracy of old,' Bauer wrote, 'but a revolutionary dictatorship as a transitional stage in the development of genuine democracy founded on ownership by the people of the means of production and the product itself — in other words, a socialist democracy.'[35] The urgent question of how to defend Austria's sovereignty against National Socialism was not even mentioned.

Crude oversimplification also contributed to the unsustainable equation of Social Democracy with Bolshevism which was common currency in the ranks of Christian-Fatherland supporters. The equation was based on such superficial similarities between the two as the facts that they both used red flags, sang the Internationale, saluted with a clenched fist and based themselves on Marx and his teachings on class struggle — although the conclusions they drew differed sharply. This inability to distinguish between the symbols used by the two 'red' parties was compounded by memories of the regime of terror under the Communist Republic in Hungary, the rudimentary Communist republic in Bavaria, and the clumsy *coup* attempt in April 1919 by the Communist Red Guard in Austria with the aim of establishing an Austrian Soviet Republic.

Setting aside the Social Democrats' militant rhetoric and their encouragement of socio-political polarisation, the party — in and out of office — made substantial and constructive contributions to governmental and administrative development. This paradoxical contrast of radical words and moderate deeds further reduced the room for compromise between the two major parties in the crisis years of the National Socialist threat.

The widening crisis of democracy

The collapse of the First Republic's parliamentary and democratic system in the years 1933–4 clearly cannot be attributed to events occurring in those years alone. As we have seen, the survival of the democratic system was prejudiced by an absence of consensus on the issues of Austrian statehood and democratic pluralism as values overriding party interests. This had grave practical implications: a central feature of modern political systems, namely state monopoly of the means of force (Max Weber's phrase), had been seriously undermined in Austria by the existence, and gradual expansion, of paramilitary organisations under party control whose total strength greatly exceeded that of the regular armed forces.

The existence of two parties of almost equal voting strength, polarised ideologically and socially, and confronting each other with little basis of consensus, could not but adversely affect the authority and decision-making role of the legislature. Even in less testing political circumstances, a government contending with a parliament so narrowly divided and so ideologically riven would have had no easy passage.

The economic distress during the First Republic, which affected all sections of the population, was an added psychological burden. Long before the years of crisis of 1933–4, a sense of unease about and scepticism towards the democratic system had begun to pervade public opinion. Schuschnigg enumerates a number of reasons for this growing disillusionment in *Dreimal Österreich*, a revealing work. For one thing Austria could not look back on a 'great parliamentary tradition'. This was because the emotionally-charged conflicts over nationality questions fought out in the Habsburg parliaments had left a distinctly sour taste. Additionally, the infant Austrian democracy was faced with the thankless task of carrying out the provisions of the Treaty of St Germain as well as numerous other unpopular measures imposed upon the defeated state. On top of these drawbacks, the equal strength of the two major parties and frequent coalitioning set policy-making on no clear-cut, consistent path but rather on an erratic, time-consuming search for compromise. This search, Schuschnigg continued, produced half-measures that were not satisfactory to either side, while the fiercely competitive character of the party exchanges moved each side to reject sound proposals when they originated in the opposite camp. Selection of parliamentary candidates was firmly held in the hands of the leadership and members of parliament were restricted to airing their opinions at meetings of the parliamentary party. But even the decisions taken there reflected the will of individual, influential party leaders rather than genuine majorities of the members themselves. The strict voting discipline demanded by the narrowness of the majorities, Schuschnigg felt, reduced plenary sessions of parliament to a formality.[36] To this was added the undisciplined personal behaviour of the members. They traded insults, got into fist-fights and indulged in such juvenile antics as throwing inkwells and other missiles at each other.

The circumstances surrounding the parliamentary vote on the League of Nations loan — critical not only for economic recovery but also for the survival of the state — were bizarre in the extreme. Dollfuss, the newly-elected Chancellor, carried the first vote only as a result of the summary nomination of a Christian Socialist to a seat in parliament to replace Chancellor Seipel, who had recently died. In the second vote — necessitated by rejection of the bill in the *Bundesrat* (Upper House) — the replacement for Chancellor Schober, who had also recently died, came from the *Landbund*, a small party which supported Dollfuss. Such were the extraordinary and humiliating circumstances in which this crucial loan was approved. The voting was 81–80 in the first ballot and 82–80 in the second.

Karl Renner was present and later wrote, 'It is all too understandable that a majority obtained in this way and a parliament only able to function in this way were bound to produce a dramatic loss of confidence among the population at large.'[37] Renner accurately depicted the mounting scepticism of democracy as characterisitic of society as a whole, while Otto Bauer limited it to the economically distressed petit-bourgeois and peasant classes: 'They turned their backs on democracy in misery and bitterness, and sought something new, something that wasn't old, worn out and corrupt, which might save them. And so they became ripe for Fascism.'[38]

A great many political activists of all persuasions at the time were military veterans, and this was another significant factor in the sociopsychological setting. Seared by four years of fighting and their experiences in the trenches, they judged parliamentary democracy to be increasingly ineffectual, and many entertained the hope that, despite the very much greater complexity of politics, the implementation of military leadership models and crisis-handling techniques with clearly structured hierarchies and firm solidarity in the face of adversity might be a more successful alternative.

Just as conditions had become even more intractable and threatening after the Austrian NSDAP's first local election victories and Hitler's seizure of power in Germany, the Austrian parliament was struck by the self-inflicted paralysis mentioned above. As unplanned as it was unexpected, it seemed to come in dramatic vindication of the widespread scepticism of the democratic system. Faced with the prospect of a tie in an important vote, Otto Bauer resorted to the procedural ploy of persuading Karl Renner to resign as parliamentary president. This restored to Renner his voting rights as a normal member of parliament. Procedural rules stipulated that the vice-president of parliament assume the presidency. The vice-president was a Christian Socialist and his elevation deprived him of the right to vote; the Christian Socialists were thus left one vote down and the Social Democrats one vote up. However, the Christian Socialist president-designate, Dr Rudolf Ramek, a former chancellor, was fully aware of the purpose of the ploy and resigned too. Whether exasperated or scandalised at this tit-for-tat between the two major parties, the second vice-president of parliament, a member of the small Pan-German Party, followed suit and resigned the presidency that now fell to him.

The unprecedented had happened: procedural manoeuvring by the parliamentary presidents — distinguished political figures in the First Republic among them — had robbed parliament of formal direction. There was no way of adjourning the session, and members dispersed in confusion with no parliamentary officers legally empowered to convene a new session.[39]

To Chancellor Dollfuss, hard-pressed on all sides, this sudden crippling of parliament came as a stroke of extraordinary good fortune. Speaking in Villach the next day, he referred to 'rejection of the parliamentary system' and was wildly applauded.[40] He was quickly to become more explicit, declaring on 13 March: 'It is very clear to us that we must use the situation now that parliament is immobilised to carry out constitutional reforms. . . . Ways and means must be found, in these hard and difficult times, to secure stronger government leadership and legislation devised not for the sole purpose of winning votes but for the good of the people as a whole.'[41]

His administration issued a statement denying that the parliamentary crisis constituted a state crisis and asserting its claim to carry on the business of government on the basis of the wartime enabling act of 1917 *Kriegswirtschaftliches Ermächtigungsgesetz*, as restated in the provisional regulations of the Federal Constitution of 1 October 1920. On the advice of Dr Robert Hecht, under-secretary at the Ministry of Justice, this legislation was first invoked on 1 October 1932 and subsequently declared a constitutional law that could only be overridden by a two-thirds majority in parliament.[42]

Such was the legal position the administration adopted to defend its intention of governing without parliament; it caused great controversy among constitutional specialists, and came under heavy attack from both the Social Democrats and the other parties. In reality, the legislation merely provided a thin veneer of legality to the emerging authoritarian regime.

The *Nationalrat* was reconvened on 15 March by the third of the presidents to resign, Sepp Straffner, a leader of the Pan-German Party. Only Pan-Germans and Social Democrats attended. The session was hastily adjourned when plain-clothes police arrived on the scene.

The response of the party press apart, there was no public outcry at the parliamentary crisis and the government's negative reaction to it. Perhaps Rudolf Neck's comment on the crisis reflected the general view: 'The resignation of the three Presidents of the *Nationalrat* bore witness to an unbelievable degree of irresponsibility and revealed the contempt with which Parliament was treated by its own institutions.'[43]

On 2 April, Dollfuss' voice was heard ominously calling for recent events to be viewed 'in a larger and broader perspective' because, he claimed, 'at present we find ourselves in an era of reform of the totality of political and social life'.[44]

Visions on a 'march between two precipices'

On returning from a rally in Villach in early March, Dollfuss told his party colleagues Richard Schmitz and Carl Vaugoin that the peasants' enthusiastic response to what he had said about the paralysis in parliament had made a profound impression on him. During the night journey back, he had decided 'to use this unique opportunity for a fundamental restructuring and renewal of Austria'. Parliament, he asserted, should not be reactivated 'without the guarantee of thorough constitutional and procedural reform to ensure order and administrative efficacy'.[45]

A glance at the minutes of the confidential meetings of the Christian Socialist executive committee in the spring of 1933 clearly reveals the anxious climate of opinion and emotion at the head of the governing party. The psychological impact of the National Socialists' triumphal progress to seizure of power in Germany was beginning to be acutely felt in Austria. In the previous year's elections in Vienna, Lower Austria and

Salzburg, the NSDAP had advanced from insignificance to become the third strongest party. The Social Democrats — viewed with equal mistrust by the Christian Socialists — had also made gains, though these were slight. The smaller centre parties (the Pan-German Party and the *Landbund für Österreich*) had virtually been wiped out by the National Socialist electoral successes . In the previous elections, in 1930, the Social Democrats had emerged as the largest party, with 41 per cent of the vote to the Christian Socialists' 36 per cent. The implications for Austrian political life in general and the Christian Socialist Party in particular were of a very serious nature.

It is therefore not surprising to find Richard Schmitz, one of the party's leading officials, commenting on the bizarre self-inflicted paralysis of the Austrian parliament with the words: 'The Chancellor is absolutely right. We have a last, God-given opportunity to save the country and the party.'[46] Echoing these sentiments, ex-Chancellor Buresch remarked: 'The government is in the position of an army at war; the fourth of March and the hand of God have turned the tide.'[47] And Schmitz enlarged the theme: 'The existence of Austria is at stake. When the Nazi floodwaters surge over us, the southern German states will be swept away, will go to the wall. And if we get caught in these flood-waters, we're finished. We will be the future battleground. These are things of terrifying importance.' He then enquired if nothing could be done 'to counteract the disturbing influence of propaganda from the Reich'.[48]

Ex-Chancellor Ramek concurred: 'I welcome our taking up the struggle with the NS [*sic*], after what they've done in the Reich.' He urged a general ban on assemblies and demonstrations, and recommended counter-agitation. The Chancellor, members of the government and provincial leaders must, he felt, have access to the microphone and not abandon the radio and the press to the National Socialists and the Socialists. Here too, he urged, the struggle must be taken up.[49]

Dollfuss raised the question of whether new elections were practicable and advisable. The reaction was negative, Richard Schmitz saying:

New elections would cause the party very severe losses. . . . The popular mood is moving towards the same point as in Germany. . . . the people are preparing for revolution. The crucial question is whether the Nazis get their hands on Austria. If they do, they will proclaim *Anschluss* with Germany. . . . It'll be like war, with pressure all along the front. But we still hold one strongpoint. If we lose control of the government and direction of the state, we lose that strongpoint, the last we have. Painful as it is to endanger legal continuity, concern for the Fatherland comes first. The party can be sacrificed but not the Fatherland. . . . The government intends to commit all its resources to obtain a better constitution — by legal means. But to do this the balance of power must be altered to make the Socialists toe the line. It will have to be done by government *diktat*. Constitutional forms will have to be observed. We march with a precipice on either side.[50]

Dollfuss wound up the meeting with a call for resolution and firmness. Not just the future of the Christian Socialists was at stake, he said, but all of Austria; the risks were great but there was no other choice.[51] At a later meeting Schuschnigg, too, remarked that this was possibly the 'last chance': the party was agreed that constitutional and procedural reform leading to the restructuring of parliament was inevitable.[52]

At a meeting of the leaders of the governing parties on 25 March, Vice-Chancellor Winkler enquired whether the government felt capable of fighting on two fronts — against both the right and the left. He was troubled by this. Dollfuss replied that the 'Brown tide' could only be kept in check if measures were taken simultaneously to force the Marxists to their knees 'step by step'. First, he continued, they must be compelled to disband their private army, the Socialist Defence League, and before parliament could reconvene a fundamentally new constitution was required. On 30–31 March the government ordered the disbandment of the Defence League, and it went underground.

On 20 April, Dollfuss mentioned to the executive committee of his party that he would shortly be meeting Robert Danneberg, the Social Democratic Party's chief spokesman. There followed Dollfuss' report on his visit to Rome. He had arranged this, as noted, to coincide with the presence there of Goering and von Papen. Having been alerted to a German plan to conclude a deal with Italy over Austria behind Austria's back, he had intended to do everything in his power to counter the danger. 'When two powerful states negotiate,' he said, there was a clear risk that 'the third, less powerful state would be crushed.'[54] Fortunately, Mussolini had proved constructive. It was of great importance, Dollfuss remarked, that, thanks to Italy, Austria could conduct domestic and foreign policy-making without having to look over its shoulder. Italy had an active interest in Austria's independence and its current policies. In the event of a conflict with the *Heimwehr*, he said, Mussolini would support the Christian Socialists and himself, not the *Heimwehr*.[55]

All these comments clearly show how Dollfuss meant to cut the Gordian knot tied for him by the conjunction of Hitler's seizure of power in Germany and the parliamentary crisis in Austria arising from the unbridgeable differences between his party, the local NSDAP and the Austro-Marxists. Party democracy he perceived to have 'failed'. It was to be replaced by an original political and constitutional system the precise contours of which were still not clear to him, but which would have to confer on the government a greater measure of authority and on society a greater measure of public order. Concurrently with the struggle against the National Socialists, there would have to be an effort gradually to scale down the power of the Austro-Marxist Social Democrats if Austria were to survive as an independent state and if the conditions were to be created for the introduction of the new order. Only the loss of their levers of power could possibly persuade the Social Democrats to modify their ambitions and cooperate.

Thus some time before Mussolini began to harass Dollfuss with patronising proposals for the conduct of Austrian internal policy, the Chancellor had decided of his own volition to set up an authoritarian, strongly corporate system and accept the risks of a dual confrontation with National Socialism and Austro-Marxism. Mussolini later repeatedly pressed for the 'Fascistisation' of Austria,[56] but it is striking that Dollfuss himself never employed the terms 'Fascist' or even 'Austro-Fascist' in connection with Austria and its new constitution. Only the *Heimwehr* leaders spoke of 'Austro-Fascism', and while they controlled paramilitary formations, they had very little electoral support.

Following a further meeting with Mussolini on August 19–20 and the Fatherland Front rally on 11 September 1933, Dollfuss told the executive committee that while he did not want a return to 'formal democracy', neither did he want 'Fascism as a slogan'. 'No-one wants to copy Italian lawmaking,' he said. 'We want to base our corporate constitution on our own historical experience.'[57] Personality factors clearly played a role too. As shown, Dollfuss appears to have interpreted the parliamentary crisis as some kind of divine ordinance which had presented him, against all expectations, with a unique opportunity to save the Austrian state and remould it in terms of his own romantic, Christian Socialist ideals.[58] In a way which distantly points to de Gaulle, Dollfuss suddenly began to see himself as a crusader and visionary directed by a 'higher power' to create a better, Christian and socially just Austria and to defend it — if necessary, at the cost of his own life — from powerful enemies at home and abroad.

In a series of statements in the spring of 1933, Dollfuss had outlined the essential elements of the programmatic appeal he was to make at the Fatherland Front rally on 11 September. Dr Friedrich Funder, the chief editor of the Christian Socialist *Reichspost* and a close associate of his, provides an account of a meeting of Christian Socialist leaders in mid-November at which Dollfuss called for the remodelling of Austria on the basis of a new and dynamic spiritual, social and political outlook. He reports Dollfuss as saying: 'The time is now ripe to stake everything on achieving what the great Christian thinkers of the last half-century have planned and desired: the reordering of society in a corporate, Christian spirit.' The sacrifice Dollfuss demanded of his party colleagues, Funder notes, was that they 'set aside the old claims of party in order to join in and help shape the new position and, generously denying self, achieve something yet greater for Austria'. Dollfuss was clearly deeply moved, Funder continues. 'With an almost visionary expression in his eyes, glancing up, his voice lowered to a whisper . . . and measuring every syllable, he said ". . . Each one of us must do all he can. It will be an act of liberation which we owe to our people. I am aware that I am risking much in this undertaking of mine, perhaps even the welfare of my family, perhaps . . ." and here he paused for some moments . . . "perhaps even my own life. But it must be!" '[59] One can only speculate as to how far the conviction that he had been summoned to become the saviour of his Fatherland and a paladin of the faith represented a means of anaesthetising guilt feelings arising from his administration's own serious violations of the law.

The Dollfuss government was able to use wartime emergency enabling legislation, and to exploit other equally dubious legal devices, to maintain an appearance of legality by arguing that a *de facto* state of emergency similar to war conditions existed. But the opposition case put forward by the Social Democrats, based on the state and constitutional law of the First Republic then in force, was much more solidly grounded. Undeterred, the Dollfuss government pressed on with its minority dictatorship, driven forward by (1) anxiety over the shrewd misuse of democracy in neighbouring Germany by the totalitarian NSDAP; (2) deep doubts as to the real aims of the Austro-Marxists; (3) the conviction, absurd as it appears today, that parliamentary democracy had been overtaken by history; and (4) the belief that the establishment of a newer, better, Christian Socialist corporate state and society was feasible and that this new state could serve as a model and example to other countries. Taking progressively more draconian measures to control political life, the government was concerned to achieve a gradual erosion of the power of the Social Democrats.

The Constitutional Court was emasculated in the spring of 1933 by emergency decree and by bringing pressure on three of the judges to resign. The government's intention was to deprive the opposition of recourse to law in the face of its increasingly stringent control and security measures.[60] On 9 June, the *Völkischer Beobachter*, the main organ of the NSDAP, and thirteen other National Socialist publications active in the anti-Austrian propaganda campaigns were banned.[61] Finally, the National Socialist bomb attack on a group of gymnasts (see above, p. 35) led to the banning of the Austrian NSDAP on 19 June 1933. The Austrian SA, SS and similar formations were outlawed at the same time. In the same month the government, in an attempt to strengthen the organisational side of its defensive strategy, deprived the provinces of their authority in security matters and, without consultation, appointed Security Directors in each of them.[62] The decision, reached in April 1933, to raise what were termed Auxiliary Military Corps (recruited from loyal paramilitary organisations) to support the regular army and the organs of law enforcement in combating National Socialist violence, was implemented on 1 September.[63] Emergency decrees issued in May temporarily suspended district and provincial elections, and prohibited the wearing of military uniforms by members of paramilitary political organisations not earmarked for incorporation into the Auxiliary Military Corps. In June, the pro-Nazi Styrian *Heimatschutz (Heimwehr)* was disbanded. All NSDAP party assets were confiscated, and legal steps were taken to deprive Austrian Nazis who were engaged in activities against Austria outside the country of both their citizenship and their assets. One of the first cases of this kind involved the leader of the Upper Austrian NSDAP, Alfred Proksch. In September, internment camps were set up to hold Nazi activists, particularly the terrorists. Martial law was imposed in November in an attempt to check the wave of murders, bombings and acts of arson, and the death penalty was introduced for these crimes. In June, a new wave of Nazi bombings had prompted the reintroduction of the death penalty under the normal criminal code and its extension to the crime of possessing explosives. In the same month, regulations were approved for the protection of the population, especially in the villages, from Nazi terrorism by allowing communes to set up voluntary local guard forces (*Ortswehren*).[64]

As for the Social Democrats, the strongest measures introduced by the government against them — apart from the banning of their Defence League — were the highly questionable regulations which reduced the revenues of the powerful and well-funded Vienna city administration by about one-third.[65]

The Home Defence Corps (Heimwehr) — an ambivalent ally

We should here summarise the character of the three major political groupings which dominated Austrian domestic affairs at the time of the parliamentary crisis in March 1933:

1. On the left were the Social Democrats, spanning a broad ideological spectrum ranging from the reform wing under Karl Renner to the radical Marxist dogmatism of Otto Bauer and even more militant groups. The party governed the capital, Vienna, controlled a majority of the trade unions, also possessed a powerful private army in the Socialist *Schutzbund* (Defence League) and was held in high regard by social democratic and liberal opinion abroad. Its popularity was such that the Communist Party was condemned to almost total impotence.

2. On the right were the National Socialists. Their confidence formidably boosted by Hitler's recent victory in Germany, they were expanding rapidly and becoming increasingly belligerent. The party was in the process of absorbing the Pan-German Party, with which it formed a united front on 15 May 1933. This front recognised Hitler as the '*Führer*' of the entire German people (Austria included).[66] Paramilitary formations of the SA and the SS provided the party with its private army.

3. In the centre were the Christian Socialists, who had the support of two smaller parties — the *Landbund*, a peasant party, and the *Heimatblock*, a new party representing the *Heimwehr*. This third grouping did not have an integrated structure. In contrast with the Austro-Marxist Social Democrats and the National Socialists, the Christian Socialists had virtually no significant forces at their disposal. Their paramilitary support, though only on an intermittent basis, came from the *Heimwehr*, which dated back to the paramilitary formations established at the end of the First World War on a local and regional basis to defend frontier areas from incursions and, in the interior, to protect the population from violence at the hands of large groups of demobilised servicemen of the many nationalities of the Monarchy. As conditions returned to normal, most of these defence corps adopted the status of veterans' organisations. Returning veterans had frequently been greeted by the governing Socialists with derision and hostility and generally identified with the old Imperial government, and thus most of the corps developed a strongly anti-Marxist stance — those belonging to the

Socialist *Schutzbund* excepted. The heterogeneous and only loosely coordinated *Heimwehr* units in the various provinces did not affiliate themselves to any of the parliamentary parties, but they nevertheless represented a potentially important political force. Chancellor Seipel, deeply disturbed by the bloodshed of the Vienna riots of July 1927, took the first steps towards cooperation with the *Heimwehr*, and foreign powers bordering on Austria — Germany, Italy and Hungary in particular — likewise saw in these still uncommitted military formations a potentially significant political factor.

The years 1930–2 were of critical importance in determining *Heimwehr* allegiances. In 1930, informal contacts with Hitler and then with Mussolini were initiated by Prince Ernst Rüdiger von Starhemberg, a member of the Austrian nobility and leader of the *Heimwehr* in Upper Austria, and later to emerge as the outstanding *Heimwehr* leader. Hitler expatiated to him on the prospects of German expansion extending to the Adriatic, but Mussolini took the opposite line:

Austria must remain, and it must remain as Austrian Austria. . . . You must find the courage to take up the fight against a misguided national idea. Austria is politically essential to the preservation of Europe. The day Austria perishes and is swallowed up by Germany, the break-up of Europe begins. Austria must survive culturally too, because it is a bastion of Mediterranean culture.[67]

Starhemberg later commented on this conversation: 'I had always seen myself as an Austrian . . . but it was extraordinary how the words of Mussolini, an Italian, so clearly revealed to me my emotional attachment to Austria.'[68]

Shortly afterwards, Starhemberg was elected leader of the *Heimwehr*. Hitler dispatched one of his associates, Gregor Strasser, to approach him with an offer of considerable financial support and the position of Hitler's *'Unterführer* in Austria'. As his part of the bargain, Starhemberg was to mould the NSDAP and the *Heimwehr* into a united front and place it at Hitler's disposal.[69] Starhemberg, who had taken up office as Interior Minister in Vaugoin's administration, defied Strasser's threatening behaviour, which included coarse abuse of Austria, and flatly rejected the offer.[70]

The *Heimwehr* entered its first election in 1930 with Mussolini expressly recommending confrontation with the NSDAP and providing additional financial support. The chief National Socialist election slogans 'Germany awake!', and 'Long live Greater Germany!' were now countered with the *Heimwehr*'s 'Austria awake!' and 'Long live the new Austria!'.[71] The *Heimatblock* of the *Heimwehr* only managed to poll 227,197 votes, giving it eight seats in the 165-seat parliament. The NSDAP polled only 111,843 votes and failed to gain a single seat.

An amateurish attempted putsch in September 1931 led by the Styrian *Heimwehr* leader, Walter Pfrimer, and crushed in circumstances worthy of comic opera, contributed to a widening split in the *Heinwehr* between a smaller pro-National Socialist group (the Styrian *Heimwehr*) and the much larger Fatherland wing.[72] The unsuccessful putsch exposed a dangerous weakness in the Austrian democratic system. Despite much well-intentioned talk from almost all those involved, no progress had been made towards disbanding the private armies of the parties and reasserting state control. In February 1934 the Defence Ministry put the strength of the Austrian armed forces at 25,000 men and the combined strength of the gendarmerie and the police at only 14,000. The *Heimatschutz* and the Socialist Defence League were 30,000 strong. Although inferior in training and weaponry, each thus outnumbered the regular army.[73]

In April 1932 one of Hitler's deranged outbursts finally alienated Starhemberg. Shortly afterwards he came into closer contact with Dollfuss, who at the beginning of May was setting about forming his government. Dollfuss canvassed him for *Heimatschutz* support, but also emphasised that he would be seeking active Social Democratic participation in the government.[74] The majority of the *Heimwehr* leadership were initially opposed to joining the government, or wished to make their support subject to onerous conditions, but Starhemberg, by his own account, was able to persuade them to support the Chancellor. A friendly relationship, marked by occasional sharp exchanges, developed between the two men.[75] In early June Starhemberg travelled to Rome, presumably with Dollfuss' knowledge and approval, to tell Mussolini that an independent and viable Austria required his aid in the form of financial support, arms and foreign policy backing. Mussolini indicated his agreement and suggested that Dollfuss come to Rome to see him.

At the beginning of 1933, the government came under mounting pressure from the NSDAP, which was now militantly claiming that Germany belonged to it 'today', and that 'tomorrow' it would be Austria and then Europe. Starhemberg proposed to Dollfuss that the streets of Austria should no longer be abandoned to marches organised by the NSDAP or the Austro-Marxists: supporters of the Christian-Fatherland cause needed a visible demonstration of strength to give them courage and self-confidence. The new policy went into effect on 14 May with a march-past of massed Home Defence Corps units in Vienna to mark the anniversary of the liberation from the Turks. National Socialists sent in to disrupt the march were manhandled with unprecedented severity. Following the elimination of the Socialist Defence League, the *Heimwehr* remained the only militant organisation really feared by the NSDAP.[76]

As the armed Nazi revolt in July 1934 was to show, the Fatherland wing of the Home Defence Corps had become one of the major weapons in the Dollfuss government's efforts to suppress the terrorist activities and 'putschist' tendencies of the Austrian NSDAP. Dollfuss was deeply moved when Starhemberg, in his capacity as Federal leader of the Home Defence Corps, took an oath of loyalty to him in the name of 35,000 *Heimwehr* men drawn up in ranks in front of the former Imperial Palace of Schönbrunn.[77] After overcoming initial difficulties, Dollfuss managed to persuade the Home Defence Corps leadership that the movement should join the Fatherland Front, and this it did on 27 September 1933.[78] But the Home Defence Corps remained *de facto* an autonomous organisation cooperating with the government as and when it saw fit. It enjoyed excellent relations with the Italian and Hungarian governments and was, on occasions, regarded by them as a more valuable potential ally than Dollfuss and the Christian Socialist Party.[79]

An analysis of Dollfuss' comments on the Home Defence Corps at meetings of the Christian Socialist executive committee during the years 1933–4 reveals considerable ambivalence. As has been noted, he reported to the committee in April 1933 that Mussolini had given him assurances that he would support the government in any conflict with the *Heimwehr*. In early October, however, he told them that the 'main concern' was whether the *Heimwehr* was planning a putsch. While he thought highly of Emil Fey, State Secretary for Security and a radical *Heimwehr* major, it could well be that Fey was under some kind of pressure from which he could not easily escape. This, Dollfuss explained, was why he had assumed 'control of the whole security executive'. (In the government reshuffle in September, Dollfuss took over Defence and Security in addition to Foreign Affairs. Fey was retained, but only in the position of Vice-Chancellor.) Dollfuss told the committee that he had sought the support of the *Heimwehr* 'as shock-troops against the NS', but he would ensure the 'absolute predominance' of the Fatherland Front in the future. A *Heimwehr* monopoly of power must be avoided, he said, in favour of cooperation. The way was neither back to 'formal democracy' nor towards an emulation of Fascism.[80] This strongly implied that the *Heimwehr* should become a junior partner to the Father-land Front and remain so; it could not be allowed to participate in the ideological and executive leadership of the state.

On the other hand, Dollfuss responded to mounting criticism of the *Heimwehr* in the higher echelons of his party by warning on December 20:

If, in the great debate, we insist on identifying the *Heimwehr* as our opponents, what will come of it? Austria's political destiny will be settled between Rome and Berlin. We will be just an object. That's why cooperation with the *Heimwehr* makes such good sense. To engage it constructively in the struggle within Austria and against the National Socialists must remain our goal. If today we start to get rid of these people, then politics here at home will no longer be decided by us but by others. . . . If, however, the *Heimwehr* and the National Socialists get together, Austria will still be an independent country, but power politics will be the preserve of these two groups.[81]

The revelation of secret contacts between Starhemberg, Fey and the National Socialists — the police had just arrested two National Socialist and two *Heimwehr* leaders engaged in secret talks — constrained Dollfuss on 12 January to repeat the same warning to the same col-leagues. The leadership of the *Heimwehr*, he assured them, had not gone over to the opposition; only certain 'elements' had done so. The *Heimwehr* had lately come under sharper criticism, he maintained, from the ranks of the Christian Socialists than had the Socialists. But the activists were in the Home Defence Corps. In urgent tones he appealed to them: 'We have to face up to the seriousness of the situation. The struggle cannot be left to individuals. We must be eager for battle, or a police state will be upon us. Personnel changes in the administration are immaterial. The vital thing is that we hold out.' Dollfuss then reminded them of the basic Catholic values the party shared with the *Heimwehr*, particularly with its patriotic wing, despite other ideological differences: 'The *Heimwehr* is behind us on cultural affairs. It has always supported us in cultural affairs, never inconvenienced us.'[82]

The limits of Italian intervention

Politics is a business of give and take, even with partners, and Dollfuss' relations with his two principal supporters — Italy and the *Heimwehr* — in resisting the Austrian NSDAP and the Third Reich proved no exception. The *Heimwehr* attempted to put pressure on

Dollfuss for a number of purposes, both directly and indirectly with the involvement of Italy. But by adroitly tacking between its rival leaders, Starhemberg and Fey, Dollfuss was able to keep the *Heimwehr* in line without becoming over-dependent on it. This is confirmed in a report written by the British Ambassador, Sir Walford Selby, on 17 February 1934: Dr Dollfuss has undoubtedly been extremely skilful, on more than one occasion, in declining the demands of the Home Defence Corps or in evading them.'[83] But the mounting Nazi threat made resistance to the *Heimwehr*'s demands increasingly difficult. The official Austrian account of the talks between Dollfuss and Mussolini at Riccione on 19–20 August 1933 says: 'Mussolini attempted to put pressure on the Chancellor to secure greater *Heimwehr* participation [in the government]. The Chancellor, however, successfully side-stepped the attempts.'[84]

Dollfuss' readiness to compromise on other proposals put forward by Mussolini did not require any concessions on his part. As has been shown above, he had decided long before his first contacts with the Italian leader to shoulder the political responsibility of introducing a change of system in Austria based on Christian Socialist and corporate ideals. And the dismissal of two *Landbund* ministers, Franz Winkler and Vinzenz Schumy, from the Cabinet — probably at the urging of the *Heimwehr* — again represented no real compromise because the *Landbund* had challenged Dollfuss by setting up a 'National Corporate Front' to compete with his Fatherland Front.

On 15 September 1933, the Austrian Ambassador in Rome, Richard Schüller, spoke to Mussolini on Dollfuss' instructions. His report of the conversation runs: 'I said the Federal Chancellor wished to inform Signor Mussolini that serious work was being done on the constitution. . . . The Federal Chancellor had used the metaphor that he was marching swiftly but he did not appreciate it when friends tried to push him along from behind — it interfered with the progress of the march.' Mussolini, the report continues, recalled that he had expressly advised Dollfuss, before his historic programmatic speech of 11 September, to effect 'a Fascistisation of the Austrian state', and yet Dollfuss had made no mention whatsoever in his speech of importing Fascism into Austria. But Mussolini commented benignly: 'Naturally, the constitution of every state is different depending on its history and economic situation, but the principles announced by the Federal Chancellor are healthy and in keeping with the times.'[85]

Dollfuss wrote to Mussolini on 22 September referring to this conversation and restating his readiness to pursue his reform programme energetically, though 'taking into consideration Austria's special circumstances'.[86] The last direct talks between Dollfuss and Mussolini took place at Riccione on 20–21 August 1933, and Theodor Hornbostel witnessed them in his capacity as Head of the Political Department of the Austrian Foreign Ministry:

As the last surviving witness and interpreter present at the two-day talks, I can only confirm that Mussolini and his State Secretary Dr Suvich . . . were most insistent in impressing on Chancellor Dollfuss the need to take a hard line in internal affairs in view of the National Socialist threat, but that no kind of agreement, written or oral, was entered into on the Austrian side. However, it is undeniable that despite the informal atmosphere — even members of Mussolini's family were present at times — these talks exercised a powerful influence on developments in Austria. In this connenction, the often repeated assumption that Dollfuss relied on advice and instruction from Mussolini in planning his 'corporate constitution' must be laid to rest.[87]

A list of proposals to be put to Dollfuss had been prepared for Mussolini's use in the Riccione talks. Point 2*a* of this document contains a recommendation that two *Heimwehr* leaders, Steidle and Starhemberg, should be given Cabinet posts, but in the Cabinet reshuffle of 21 September, Dollfuss failed to implement the recommendation. Fey, the Vienna *Heimwehr* leader, lost the security portfolio he had held since the previous year and was appointed Vice-Chancellor. The creation of a United Front for 'The Independence of Austria and the Renewal of Austria' and the authoritarian character of the new administration (Points 2*b* and 2*c*) were fully consistent with Dollfuss' own intentions. Point 2*d*, concerning the substitution of a government commissioner for the Mayor of Vienna, was examined for its legal implications by the government law officer, Dr Hecht, in December, but not put into effect till after the Socialist Defence League revolt in February 1934. The reiterated proposal that the Austrian state and constitution be reformed on a 'Fascist basis' also fell on stony ground.[88] Assuming that the tragic bloodshed of 12 February 1934 was not the result of a calculated response to Mussolini's urgings for sweeping measures to be taken against the Austro-Marxists (and this question will be examined later), then Dollfuss' chief domestic political concessions involved the breaking-off of talks with the Social Democrats and the start of preparations for a government takeover of the Vienna City administration. This second concession was an objective energetically championed by the *Heimwehr*, in the name of which Starhemberg called out at a public meeting on 13 September 1933 at the Ballhausplatz: 'It is intolerable to the people of

Vienna that in there', and here he gestured in the direction of the City Hall, 'the Bolsheviks are in control. Mr Chancellor, throw them out, those people sitting in there. Don't delay, strike while the iron is hot!'[89]

Thus on the question of the Vienna City administration, Dollfuss was under considerable pressure from both the Italian government and the *Heimwehr*. But on the key issue of a stepped-up, joint government-*Heimwehr* defensive strategy against the Austrian NSDAP, with Italian foreign policy backing, Dollfuss, Mussolini and the two *Heimwehr* leaders were at this stage in complete agreement. Mussolini was also showing understanding for Dollfuss' insistence that normalisation of relations with the *Reich* and the NSDAP could only take place on the basis of unqualified recognition of Austrian sovereignty. In fact, from the standpoint of Austrian interests, Mussolini had done all that could possibly have been asked of him in the circumstances, namely by giving a categorical assurance that Italy would defend the independence of Austria not only in the diplomatic sphere but also militarily in the event of the use of force.

The failure of 'black-red' coalition attempts

The violent and bloody clashes of 15 July 1927, as we have seen, widened the gulf between the left and the right and deepened their mutual distrust. 'The dramatic masquerade', as Karl Renner described it, 'of the *Heimwehr* and the Socialist *Schutzbund* countermarching, challenging and outbidding each other in displays of strength' continued.[90] In 1928, Chancellor Seipel took the initiative in bringing the two sides together for talks. On the agenda were questions of disarming the party armies, a ban on marches and a 'shop-floor truce' — i.e. an end to intimidation in the factories. The talks failed.

In October 1927, Otto Bauer told the Social Democratic party congress that a pre-condition for reaching an understanding on disarming the party armies was a negotiating partner willing to reach an understanding. But this could not be said of the Seipel administration, he maintained, and therefore it was 'not profitable to talk about disarming. . . .'[91] Karl Renner, who delivered his prophetic evocation of the dangers of civil war at the same congress, called for 'a tactical understanding with that part of the bourgeois world that was still democratic'. But the call went unheeded.[92]

The last opportunity to form a grand coalition before Hitler seized power in Germany and Dollfuss became Chancellor in Austria presented itself in 1931. This was Seipel's coalition offer. (It might be interpolated here that, with the benefit of hindsight, it is easy to suggest that a grand coalition might have provided Austria with an optimum basis on which to resist the Nazi tide, but this remains an open question.) Seipel's offer embraced all the parliamentary parties, and the intention was to find a short-term solution to the political and economic crisis. The Social Democrats were to be allocated four Cabinet posts including the position of Vice-Chancellor, in which Seipel intended to install his old adversary Otto Bauer. However, the Social Democratic leaders suspected a trap; they feared that they would be used to help resolve the crisis and would have to shoulder some of the responsibility for whatever unpopular measures would be necessary, and then, once the crisis had been overcome, they would be ousted from the government. Wilhelm Ellenbogen, a Social Democratic stalwart, appealed for acceptance of the offer: 'There is no more powerful and effective way of pulling up the roots of Fascism and destroying them than by entering the government,' he said.[93] But he failed to find support. Seipel's offer was rejected — the Social Democrats' distrust of their rivals went too deep. And perhaps Andics was correct in attributing significance to the fact that a conference of the Socialist International was due to be held in Vienna a few weeks after Seipel's offer. The Socialist leaders, he suggested, very probably thought: 'Are the Austrians to play host to fellow-Socialists from all over the world as coalition partners of prelate Seipel and the Fascist *Heimwehr*? It is unthinkable!'[94]

In 1932 Dollfuss formed his cabinet with a parliamentary majority of one vote and immediately appealed for support in the crisis. Otto Bauer, responding on behalf of the Social Democrats, ended his speech with the words: 'But our first and foremost task in rescuing our country . . . we believe to be the fiercest, most determined and ruthless opposition conceivable to this government . . . which is why I now move: This Chamber resolves that it has no confidence in the federal government.'[95] In addition, the Social Democrats demanded new elections despite the NSDAP's recent electoral gains. Otto Bauer later candidly conceded that this demand had been a mistake. 'We thought new elections would be useful in getting the National Socialists into Parliament. There, they would of necessity have had to take a stand on practical economic and political issues and their demagogy would have been unmasked.'[96] The Social Democrats followed up their no-confidence motion by accusing the new Chancellor of treason for negotiating the League of Nations loan. Once the loan agreement was signed, however, they lost no time in pressing their fellow-Socialists in France for the speedy release of the funds.

Early in 1933 the Social Democratic press exposed a large-scale illegal movement of weapons from Italy to Hungary via Austria in what was later termed the 'Hirtenberg affair'. Disclosure was undoubtedly justified on ethical and legal grounds, but it caused the authorities in Vienna, Rome and Budapest, as well as the *Heimwehr*, considerable embarrassment and inconvenience, and served to deepen their animosity towards the Austrian Social Democrats.

Otto Bauer was also later to criticise his party's tactics in precipitating the parliamentary crisis of 4 March 1933. He confessed: 'With Renner's resignation we played straight into the hands of the Dollfuss government, which then had a pretext to suspend parliament. That was unquestionably a mistake.'[97] Adolf Schärf, a later president of the Republic, points out in his memoirs that Renner's gambit clearly demonstrated that the Social Democrats were placing their own interests above that of a functioning democratic system. The party, he felt, should not have sought the office of First President of the *Nationalrat* if it intended to withdraw the candidate as soon as the exercise of that office required some sacrifice.[98] What proved so corrosive of the system in this easily remediable procedural crisis was the way in which it demonstrated to the Austrian public the complete absence of consensus on the principle of placing the interests of the system above those of party. The crisis threw a harsh light on a flaw that had marred political life in Austria since the birth of the Republic; the democratic forms were present, but there was no real allegiance to the democratic idea.

Bauer also claims in his analysis of this crisis that the party erred in not having organised massive resistance when the government prevented parliament from reconvening on 15 March. He thought that the chances of success would have been high, but the party had wanted to spare the country the horrors of civil war — although when civil war did break out, conditions were much less favourable.[99] But Bauer could have been mistaken: a protracted civil war would probably not have ended in a decision favourable to the Socialists but in military intervention by Italy, the Third Reich, Hungary or even the Little Entente, each with quite different motives. Whether the Socialist Defence League — even in more propitious circumstances — would have proved a match for the combined strength of the regular army and the *Heimwehr* is highly questionable. However, an immediate and forceful protest in March

1933 calling on the full resources of the Social Democratic machine, and in concert with the other parties, might perhaps have produced a compromise on constitutional change.

The government's first priority when it had acquired its new powers was to move to disband the Socialist Defence League. The position taken by the Social Democratic party enabled the government to do so without encountering effective resistance. On 25 March, the day the decision was made, the minutes of a Christian Socialist parliamentary party meeting show Dollfuss arguing that negotiation of constitutional reform with the Social Democrats would be facilitated if they were to be deprived of control of their major instruments of power — the paramilitary *Schutzbund* and the trade unions.[100]

At another meeting of the parliamentary party on 20 April, Dollfuss mentioned that he intended to talk to Dr Robert Danneberg, a leading Social Democrat with a reputation as a mediator. Following contacts with two Christian Socialist leaders, Buresch and Reither, the Social Democratic party executive agreed to enter into formal negotiations with the Dollfuss administration. The four Social Democratic negotiators all came from Lower Austria: *Landesrat* Heinrich Schneidmadl; Oskar Helmer, a member of the Lower Austrian parliament and deputy head of the Lower Austrian government; Pius Schneeberger, a member of the *Nationalrat*; and Franz Popp, a member of the Lower Austrian parliament. Schneidmadl personally conveyed to Dollfuss the decision to negotiate, and later recorded that the Chancellor had appeared pleased and assured him that a solution would somehow be found. Initially, the government was to be represented by Dr Karwinsky, State Secretary for Security.

The talks were held in the Interior Ministry. The Social Democrats opened with an offer of support in setting up 'an effective defensive front against Nazi Fascism', and declared their readiness to make 'considerable sacrifices' in the interests of reaching a workable understanding.[101] In the following months the negotiators conferred virtually on a weekly basis. Karwinsky assured the Social Democrats that the Chancellor was following the talks 'with great interest'.[102] On 3 May, Dollfuss told the parliamentary party that elements in the government camp were pressing for harsher and speedier action against the Social Democrats. But he was against this approach, he told the meeting, because 'nothing gets on the Socialists' nerves more than tedious tactics . . .' Following this reaffirmation of his gradualist strategy of slowly wearing the Socialists down in order to make them more amenable to negotiations, he warned:

'Too much all at once will have them up in arms.'[103] The conflict between the hardliners and the moderates within the Christian Socialist party flared up again when the Social Democrats announced plans to hold a party congress on 14 October. Provincial Governor Reither informed the Social Democrats that the Vice-Chancellor, Major Fey, had intended to ban the congress, but that Dollfuss had intervened to reverse the decision, whereupon Fey had reacted by ordering police to attend the congress. Schneidmadl was quick to warn Reither of the possible serious consequences of such 'provocative action', and urged him to persuade Dollfuss to intervene once more. Reither advised him to contact Dollfuss himself. At first, Dollfuss' heavy schedule threatened to prevent a meeting, but at 4 a.m. on 14 October, the day the congress was to open, Schneidmadl was woken by a police officer and told that the Chancellor was waiting to receive him at his private apartment. The exchange with Schneidmadl persuaded Dollfuss to overrule Fey. Dollfuss, Schneidmadl records, was 'very pleased at the agreement'. 'And as I left, he shook me warmly by the hand, saying "We'll continue our talk after the party congress, and I'm convinced we'll be able to reach agreement on the other questions too".' For the second time Dollfuss had come down against Fey.[104]

Karl Renner drafted a new constitution to serve as a working paper for the Social Democratic negotiators. This envisaged an upper chamber (*Ständehaus*) of 120 members, in part to be nominated and in part to be delegated by professional organisations, and a lower chamber (*Volkshaus*) of directly elected members.[105] On 27 December, the *Arbeiterzeitung* claimed that the Social Democrats would be prepared to accept 'a corporate system and complete autonomy of professional organisations — in other words, true economic democracy'. This was quickly endorsed by Otto Bauer in an article entitled 'Class Struggle and the Corporate Constitution', published in the first issue of the Socialist journal *Der Kampf* in January 1934. Both the *Arbeiterzeitung* and Bauer added the corrective that any such corporate system would have nothing in common with the Fascist corporate system. The *Arbeiterzeitung* even spoke of an 'anti-Fascist *Quadragesimo-Anno* encyclical' which, far from destroying the workers' rights to organise and to strike, takes them for granted. . . .'[106]

Dollfuss' comments at a closed session of the parliamentary party on 12 January 1934 clearly reveal his wavering attitudes on the issue of compromise with the Social Democrats. At one point the minutes record him as saying: 'Perhaps another Socialist feeler offering participation in the struggle against the NS. I still maintain the Socialists don't want to see the Third Reich spread to Austria and that as Austrians they are conscious they have a duty to save the state from destruction.'[107] But he immediately added: 'If we entered into some form of compromise with the Socialists now, it would provide a fertile breeding ground for the NS.' Having voiced this fear that a compromise might backfire and strengthen the NSDAP, he went on to express other reservations: 'Over all these years, we've been hammering into our people's heads the need to combat Marxism. Cuddling up to them [the Socialists] now is only going to sow distrust among the population at large.'[108] Here again were evident the damaging effects of the ideological rigour with which both parties in the First Republic vilified each other. This mutual denigration went back to Victor Adler's apostrophising the opposition as 'class enemies' with whom only tactical, but never substantive, agreement was conceivable.

In the latter half of November 1933 Renner told Dr Emmerich Czermak, the general secretary of the Christian Socialist party, that the Social Democrats were ready to offer the government maximum possible cooperation. The offer, he added, stood till January 1934.

On 18 January, the same day on which the Italian Foreign Minister had chosen to pay an official visit, Dollfuss replied to the offer in a speech which was extensively reported in the *Arbeiterzeitung*. He started with what seemed to be a dramatic reversal of his previous statements by saying that he could well understand how it came about that the practice of liberal capitalism had caused the opposition to proclaim class struggle 'as the basis of organised life'. 'But', he continued, 'the Christian Socialist remodelling of state and society then under way was based on a quite new reciprocal recognition of obligations by both sides which obviated the need for class struggle as a seemingly unavoidable antithesis . . . The workers', Dollfuss urged, 'must seriously consider whether or not they too might have a duty enthusiastically to stand up for cooperation in this new form.' If this was correctly understood by 'sincere workers' leaders', he hoped that 'very soon indeed quite new opportunities will arise to draw those who have hitherto stood on the sidelines into the grand defensive front for the protection of Austria's independence and the construction of a new Austria.'[109]

The invitation could not have been more explicit. The Social Democrats were being asked to renounce that concept, which was fundamental to their programme but which had earned them nothing but distrust and hostility from all the other parties — except the Communists —

namely, the doctrine of class struggle. Dollfuss was holding out to them the prospect of equal partnership in the socio-economic field in a Christian context and entreating them to close ranks to defend Austria's independence and to build a new corporate state.

In December 1933, Dr Friedrich Funder conveyed to Dollfuss a message from Karl Seitz, the Social Democratic Burgomaster of Vienna, requesting inter-party negotiations. Dollfuss' positive reply, asking the Social Democrats to name a negotiator, reached Seitz within twenty-four hours. For reasons unknown, the Social Democrats delayed their response. On 18 January, Dollfuss made the speech excerpted above. Not till 25 January did Seitz let it be known that *Gemeinderat* Richter had been selected as the party's chief representative at the negotiations. Optimistically, Funder hurried to the Chancellery the following day, only to be met by a pessimistic Dollfuss: 'Well, Richter, he would certainly have been the right man! But it's too late!'[110] As he said this, Funder records, Dollfuss produced a sheaf of photographs from his desk. In Simmering, a Social Democratic stronghold in Vienna, the police had uncovered a large cache of explosive devices apparently designed to be placed in sewers under public buildings. Dollfuss said to Funder that he felt this represented 'a particularly fiendish criminal outrage' which clearly demonstrated that the revolutionaries had gained the upper hand in the Socialist camp. To start negotiations on defence matters in these circumstances, he said, was out of the question![111]

Since 11 January, Major Fey had been in charge of security affairs; as an extremist advocate of harsh measures against the Social Democrats, had he set up the Simmering incident in order to torpedo the planned inter-party talks? Or was the find genuine? According to the historian Professor Hugo Hantsch, Dollfuss had remarked in a conversation with Czermak before the incident on the Social Democrats' readiness to compromise and the possibility of cooperation: 'That would be excellent, but if I do it, Mussolini will throw me into Hitler's waiting jaws.'[112]

The revolt of the Socialist Defence League on 12 February 1934, though neither instigated nor encouraged by the Social Democratic party leadership and launched in defiance of its explicit orders, created an entirely new situation in which any further discussion of cooperation between the two parties was precluded.

It would thus certainly appear that Dollfuss was leaning in the direction of negotiating with a weakened Social Democratic party on its role in a new and still unspecified corporate constitution. It was unquestionably very much in his interest to win over the majority of the Austrian workforce to his plan to create a new Austria and thereby underpin his defensive strategy against National Socialism. But Social Democratic support alone would not have been sufficient. Without the backing of Italy, the only major power prepared to intervene — militarily, if need be — on its behalf, Fortress Austria had little prospect of holding out in the long term.

That was one stumbling block. The other was the Chancellor's deep-rooted personal distrust of the Social Democratic leaders. To his mind they were at best 'temporary Austrians', who looked beyond the demise of the Third *Reich* to *Anschluss* with Germany. Also, their radical doctrines caused him to view them as only 'temporary democrats' too, who regarded pluralist democracy simply as a stepping-stone towards establishing absolute and exclusive Socialist rule over state and society.[113] In addition, Dollfuss' personal experience of his opponents was negative: they had denounced him as a traitor to the nation after the Lausanne agreement, and their answer to his appeal for cooperation in 1932 had been to move a vote of no-confidence. They had called for new elections even after a dramatic increase in electoral support for the NSDAP, accepting that elections would open the door to National Socialist representation in parliament. Dollfuss also had every reason to believe that his tactics in steadily whittling down the Social Democrats had been effective. Now they were ready not only to enter into negotiations but to make concessions. But he was still faced with the question of whether an alliance on the terms set by them — which included recognition of the right to strike, complete press freedom and a general election (if only for the lower chamber of a newly structured parliament) — outweighed the risks involved. He was clearly convinced that an alliance would strengthen the position of the National Socialists and alienate his allies both at home (the *Heimwehr*) and abroad (Italy).

It appears highly unlikely, in view of the evidence cited above, that Dollfuss planned to settle accounts with the Social Democrats in the shape of a bloody military operation, such as actually occurred.

Were there alternative solutions?

It is idle to speculate, but the question of whether a defensive alliance between right and left might not have been possible continues to have a fascination fifty years later. Although other alternatives could clearly be advanced, an attempt will be made here to outline the conditions which would probably have had to be satisfied before an alliance could have been formed.

1. The Social Democrats would have had to accept that Italy's support in the foreign policy area was essential to Austria's survival. As Karl Renner correctly pointed out, the Western Powers had decided 'to push Italy forward, committing the protection of Austria to its care . . . To make Italy the policeman of Europe in Austria against Germany, in the hope that the two central European dictators, Mussolini and Hitler, would become embroiled in bitter, perhaps irreconcilable, antagonism.'[114] Italy's foreign-policy interest in having a well-disposed, small Austria and not a Greater German empire on its northern frontier was plain. Italy's imperialist foray into Abyssinia could not have been anticipated. But, as we have seen, the Social Democratic press had, with every moral and legal justification, embarrassed Italy, Hungary and the *Heimwehr* with its exposure of the 'Hirtenberg affair'. This was a tactical mistake, as Otto Bauer later conceded, because it turned Italy and Hungary against the Social Democrats.[115]

A realistic offer by the Social Democrats would not have put Dollfuss in the position of having to choose between Austria and Italy. On the contrary, they should have strongly pressed for an alliance with Italy. Even the Social Democrats in France, for far less urgent reasons of state, had advocated alliances with the dictatorships in Poland and Yugoslavia and cooperation with Italy. Moscow's alliances and agreements with Weimar Germany, France, the United States, Chiang Kai-shek and, finally, Hitler show that even highly ideological systems could enter pacts with champions of radically opposed political doctrines if and when survival was at stake. History, in both ancient and modern times, is littered with such examples. The Social Democratic proposal that Austria should declare itself a neutral country was not unreasonable, but it was inopportune at a time when the government was under severe pressure following months of economic and propaganda warfare from the Third *Reich* and the NSDAP's domestic terror campaign. Hitler had unambiguously stated that he was conducting his struggle against Austria precisely for the purpose of forestalling its 'Switzerlandisation'. If Austria had become neutralised at this stage, Italian support would have been blocked and Hitler would hardly have been deterred from continuing his assault on Austria.

2. Dollfuss' historic offer of 18 January 1934, which also included a defence of his proposed cooperation with his opponents intended for the

consumption of his supporters and allies, could have been welcomed wholeheartedly by the Social Democrats. In other words, they could publicly and unreservedly have declared their readiness to take part in an experiment to replace the class struggle with employer-employee co-determination within the framework of a new system. Instead of making demands, as Renner did, for universal suffrage and other reforms which the government was compelled at that stage to reject out of hand because of the threat from the NSDAP, the Social Democrats could have demonstrated their interest in cooperating in the development of a corporate constitutional model within a democratic framework and allowing for the election and representation of interest groups and so on. One credible source indicates that Schneidmadl proposed at the 1933 Social Democratic party congress that the Socialist trade unions be integrated into the Fatherland Front, but the proposal was defeated by the party's radical wing.[116]

3. In tandem with this, the Social Democrats could have taken an important step towards restoring public confidence in themselves — and the need to break down old suspicions was urgent — by omitting the anti-clerical language from their party programme. They would then have been in a position to cooperate with the Church in the defensive alliance against the Third *Reich*. Between March 1933 and February 1934, discoveries by the police of Socialist *Schutzbund* arms caches repeatedly heightened tensions between the government and the Social Democrats. In its parliamentary phase, the First Republic had been unable to obtain general agreement on solving the problem of the party armies, but the new Dollfuss administration tried to solve it dictatorially by conferring legal status on loyal paramilitary formations, and assigning to them an auxiliary law-enforcement role, while outlawing the others and attempting to stamp them out. As a conciliatory gesture, the Social Democrats could have turned over their secret arms caches to the regular army in anticipation of reaching an agreement on a new corporate and democratic constitution. The existence of these arms caches was a permanent cause of friction and greatly deepened the government's distrust of the Social Democrats.

4. The Social Democrats were fully aware that it would be problematic for the Dollfuss government to continue to accept the city of Vienna's Austro-Marxist administration (its term did not run out till February 1934 and, even within the framework of the new system, it governed almost one-third of the Austrian population). They could have proposed

a power-sharing administration equally divided between the Christian Socialists and themselves until such time as the new system was introduced. Fundamental changes along the lines of Dollfuss' proposals were inevitable in any event.

5. Above all, Dollfuss should at an early stage have had the political courage to spell out his 18 January proposals in detail and make the Social Democrats a comprehensive and firmly-based offer, particularly with regard to the need for Italian support. Because he was apprehensive of the negative impression that long-drawn out negotiatons with the Social Democrats would make on the *Heimwehr*, Rome and Budapest, he could have set a deadline for a clear answer one way or the other. If the Social Democrats had agreed to participate in negotiating a corporate democratic but still constitutional system, this would have given them room for manoeuvre in its final formulation. However, their attitude on the eve of 12 February showed that even after a year of temporising they had seriously misjudged their position, just as they overestimated the fighting morale not only of their membership but, more significantly, of the masses.

Given the constellation of domestic and foreign power relationships, there would seem to have been only two basic policy alternatives to the one we have outlined. The Social Democrats could have launched a carefully organised armed uprising, which would certainly have led to military defeat and then to a political defeat of far greater magnitude than if they had adopted the strategy described above. The other alternative would have been for them to submit to the repressive salami tactics of the Dollfuss government, since they lacked any effective means of intervention. This too would ultimately have been more detrimental to them than the policy suggested.

The dual revolt of the Socialist Defence League (Schutzbund)

As Austria's resistance to the Third Reich and its fifth column, the Austrian NSDAP, strengthened, elements of the Socialist *Schutzbund* rose in revolt. It was a revolt against both the Dollfuss government and the Social Democratic leadership. Preconditions for an armed revolt had been debated and decided upon at the 1933 Social Democratic party congress, and these were by no means present in February 1934. However, a section of the Linz *Schutzbund* made a determined attempt to coerce the party leadership into adopting military action. The revolt was primarily directed against the Dollfuss minority dictatorship and its campaign against the Social Democrats and operations against their underground paramilitary units and arms caches.

Karl Renner, with remarkable foresight, had made an urgent plea for restraint at the 1927 Social Democratic party congress: 'We have reached the stage in the class struggle at which the propertied and the unpropertied classes stand face to face, armed to the hilt, watchful and poised for attack. We find ourselves, figuratively, on an open battlefield. In these circumstances, lack of discipline on the part of a single group could spell certain defeat.' Renner was referring to the catastrophe of 15 July 1927, which had prompted recognition of the fact that a single group could have caused 'a shattering defeat for the entire proletariat'. Renner emphatically reiterated his call for self-discipline: 'In future only the collective as a whole, and not a part of it, will decide to act. That is a strict command. Whoever acts on his own responsibility may well endanger the whole class.'[117]

Yet this is precisely what happened on 11 February 1934. Richard Bernaschek, leader of the Linz Socialist *Schutzbund*, presented the party leadership with an ultimatum, informing them in writing that he and five other party members had decided to offer violent resistance to a police search for weapons that was due to take place the following day in Linz or one of the other Upper Austrian towns, and that this resistance would develop into an open attack. He quoted: 'This decision and its implementation are irrevocable.'[118] Otto Bauer received this communication at midnight. He commented that resistance at this moment would 'be both futile and senseless. The Governors of the Provinces are arriving in Vienna on the 12th and there is still a chance to save the constitution.'[119] An amateurishly coded telegram and telephone call were sent, informing Bernaschek that the Socialist leadership had rejected his ultimatum. The police, alerted to the secret communication by the postal censorship authorities, now decided to include the Linz headquarters of the Social Democratic party in their weapons search. An arsenal of weapons was indeed uncovered. Against instructions, Socialist militiamen opened fire on the police as they forced their way into the headquarters building on the morning of 12 February. Political tension between the government and the opposition had finally escalated into violence.

Shortly before this incident, a *Schutzbund* informer had tipped off the police about a large arms cache at Schwechat near Vienna.[120] A series of arrests of *Schutzbund* leaders had begun on 3 February. Even when the news of the fighting in Linz reached the Social Democratic party leaders they hesitated to signal a general uprising, but a number of *Schutzbund* leaders indicated before leaving the party headquarters that they might perhaps follow Bernaschek's example in Linz and take matters into their own hands.[121] Bernaschek's unauthorised action had robbed the party leaders of the element of surprise essential to any successful operation against the Dollfuss administration — such as the seizure of government buildings in the city centre. They now had to fall back on hastily improvised planning and organisation which prejudiced the chances of success from the outset, although the Socialist Defence League and government forces in Vienna were approximately equal in numerical strength. Helmut Andics' psychologically astute and balanced account of the background to the revolt and the interactive factors involved shows that neither Dollfuss nor the Social Democratic party leadership intended to unleash a conflict of this nature at this particular time.[122] The Social Democratic leaders had very reluctantly been dragged into the fray by the autonomous action of the Linz *Schutzbund*. It was thus not a revolt by the Social Democratic Party as such, and it obtained no mass backing either in Vienna or in other industrial centres. Solidarity between the party and the people, as witnessed in Czechoslovakia in 1968, or as between the Solidarity trade union and the masses in Poland in the 1980s, did not develop. One of the key unions, the railwaymen, whom Otto Bauer described as 'once the crack troops of the Austrian labour movement', did not strike — the trains ran on time. Even elements of the *Schutzbund* itself remained passive; as Otto Bauer observed, 'Some districts didn't even take up their weapons. . . . In others the local Socialist Defence League leaders evidently lacked courage and offensive spirit. But where the League did go into action, exceptional bravery, endurance and heroism were displayed. Dollfuss himself, speaking on 17 February, was compelled to acknowledge the ''heroism'' of the Socialist Defence League men who fought.'[123]

In Vienna, the *Schutzbund* was able to move on to the attack at a number of points, but because of the disorganisation caused by Bernaschek's precipitate action, it was mostly forced to remain on the defensive. Most of the militiamen barricaded themselves inside the huge, fortress-like municipal housing blocks erected by Vienna's Socialist city council on cheap land alongside the main approach roads to the city. This was a disastrous decision because it meant that the Socialist militiamen were fighting from the apartments of their own families. Women and children were not evacuated from the buildings. Government troops quickly moved in, and thus began the controversial siege and shelling of the workers' housing complexes. The government's original intention to employ tear-gas was abandoned because it would have contravened a clause in the Treaty of St Germain.[124]

Because of the unpredictable behaviour of the other armed opposition party, the NSDAP, the government was determined to end the fighting quickly. The decision was taken to deploy artillery for psychological effect and because it was felt there would be fewer casualties than in house-to-house fighting. Eye-witnesses confirm that in Vienna non-explosive practice ammunition was mostly used — as the clean, circular holes left in the masonry seemed to indicate. Before each artillery salvo, a bugle was sounded and the insurgents were called on to surrender. On the evening of 14 February, Dollfuss promised a full pardon to all insurgents who laid down their arms, the leaders excepted. All resistance came to an end on 15 February.[125]

Not until the revolt did the government issue decrees ordering the dissolution of the Social Democratic party and the replacement of the Socialist Burgomaster of Vienna by a Federal Commissioner. The assets of the party and its affiliated organisations were confiscated. It remains an open question whether the revolt eliminated the last chance of bringing about some form of agreement between the right and the left because it destroyed the Social Democratic party root and branch in a way that could have been averted — either by timely resistance in 1933 or by greater readiness to compromise in early 1934.

In human terms, the *Schutzbund*'s revolt was a heroic and principled stand, against all the odds, in defence of a political party unlawfully deprived of its constitutional rights. Apart from Spain, Austria was the only country in the 1930s where elements of the Social Democratic movement engaged in armed resistance against a dictatorship perceived as Fascist and illegal. Against the background of tragic events in 1934, the courage displayed in this struggle against domestic dictatorship stands alongside the resistance to the National Socialist assault on Austria's sovereignty as one of the memorable passages in the history of Republican Austria.

In retrospect, what was so deplorable about this domestic Austrian feud between the right and the left — which could have been prevented, albeit with great difficulty — was not the use of artillery against apartment blocks which themselves were being defended by gunfire: as Otto Bauer once remarked, the victims of violence are those who perpetrate it; those who, for the best of motives, join a revolt against the government and barricade themselves inside housing occupied by women and children will inevitably be left with the stark choice of surrendering or facing attack by government forces. What was indefensible about the revolt was the vengeance visited by the victors on the vanquished. Nine death sentences were passed and carried out. Even Starhemberg roundly denounced the unnecessary severity of the sentences and the lack of magnanimity following a total victory.[127] Speaking at the funeral of men of the *Heimatschutz* who had been killed in the action, he said: 'In a civil war there can be no winners and no losers because a civil war is a catastrophe from which all those engaged in it emerge defeated', and added that a vanquished enemy should not be the object of vengeance but be helped to recover from his despair. This earned him sharp criticism from Fey and other hardliners.[128]

A Christmas amnesty in 1935 saw the release of 1,505 of the 1,521 imprisoned insurgents.[129] The deep divide between the two major forces in Austrian politics was to be bridged only after the brutal but salutary experience of *Anschluss*, National Socialist oppression, and the shared success of the Second Republic.

6

THE ARMED NAZI UPRISING IN VIENNA
AND THE PROVINCES

The 'Lightning Coup' and the Chancellor's assassination

The stiffening of Austria's resistance to Hitler. When Hitler imposed the thousand-mark visa fee on travel to Austria in May 1933, he confidently predicted to his Cabinet that Austria would be forced to its knees by the end of the year. But by the spring of 1934 he had to concede that, despite increased economic pressure and despite the bombings, murders and hostile propaganda directed against the Dollfuss government, Austria's resistance on both the internal and the external fronts had gained strength. Hitler was incensed that, after his seizure of power in Germany, a government in another 'German' country should not only be actively opposing National Socialism but also openly criticising his policies in the name of *Deutschtum*. Moreover, the Dollfuss administration was persisting in souring his relations with Italy — the only European power friendly to the Third Reich.

Hermann Rauschning, a one-time confidant of Hitler, recalls an internal meeting in May 1933 at which the *Führer* had angrily shouted: 'I'll make short shrift of this Dollfuss. This man dares to contradict me. Just imagine it! They [the Austrian government] will come to me on bended knee yet. But I shan't flinch from having them executed as traitors.'[1] In the course of the conversation, Hitler hinted at plans to mount a *coup* in Austria, and Rauschning gained the impression that a violent *coup* was envisaged as a vehicle for the conquest of the country. Emotionally, Rauschning thought, Hitler in fact welcomed Dollfuss' resistance since he now anticipated the satisfaction he would feel from brutally crushing it. 'From the vehemence of his words', Rauschning wrote, 'one could only conclude that he was thirsting for bloody action, conspiracy, retribution in some form.' A 'hot, morbid, singeing odour' emanated from Hitler's words.[2] This emotional element is important to an understanding of the policy developed towards Austria by a party and state structured on the growing reality of the totalitarian *Führerprinzip*. It is clearly present in *Mein Kampf*: on the first page Hitler calls for *Anschluss* and, a few pages later, he reveals his deep hatred for the old Austria and everything that it represented.

In January 1934, Theo Habicht, the ex-Communist who functioned as Hitler's revolutionary chief-of-staff in Austria, had declared that 1934 would be 'the year of decision, the year of our victory' in the struggle for Austria.[3] This claim appeared in the *Österreichischer Pressedienst*, the main organ of the illegal Austrian NSDAP, which had been appearing in Munich since June 1933. A week later he was writing threateningly: 'But patience is exhausted and the desire of *Volk* for *Volk* has broken upon all Austria with elemental force . . . the revolution from below is in full swing, its victory is as certain as the collapse in ruins of the ruling system. . . .'[4] The previous September, the same publication had carried a report by Habicht on talks he had had with Dollfuss before the deterioration in German-Austrian relations. The conversation had ended with Habicht presenting Dollfuss with two choices: he could either enter German and Austrian history books as the Chancellor who had made *Anschluss* possible and had thereby 'gained immortal honour in the cause of the future of the German nation', or he could persist in the misguided belief that an idea could be resisted with bayonets and meet the same unhappy fate as General Schleicher (the last Chancellor of the Weimar Republic) in Germany.[5] Habicht was later to describe Dollfuss' policies as a last desperate attempt by destructive forces of the past 'to prevent the unification of the German people and the fulfilment of their mission in world history'.[6] Hitler himself, on the first anniversary of the Nazi seizure of power, had declared that National Socialism was an idea which embraced the entire German nation and would not be halted at Austria's frontier posts. If the Austrian government wished to stifle this movement 'by applying the full powers of the state', that was their business, but they would have to accept 'personal' responsibility for the results of this policy.[7] The warning to those promoting Austrian resistance, many of whom later found themselves in concentration camps, was unmistakable.

The Italian government's assessment of the situation in Austria at this point is outlined in a report dated 26 January 1934, written by Ulrich von Hassell, German Ambassador in Rome.[8] The Dollfuss administration was clearly being hard-pressed by the National Socialist onslaught, it was thought, but it was firmly resolved to defend itself in every possible way'. The government and the National Socialists were engaged in a contest for the loyalties of the people, but the people still appeared to be undecided. The struggle in Austria and for Austria, the Italian government felt, had reached a stage at which any chance of agreement seemed improbable at least for the foreseeable future.[9]

Parading units of the *Schutzbund* (Socialist Defence League), the party army of the Austro-Marxist Social Democratic Party. Its members were pledged to crush capitalism to establish a 'purely socialist state'. *A*

Above, Hitler reviewing SA units on the German-Austrian border, July 1932. In the foreground, wearing glasses, is Theo Habicht, his deputy in Austrian affairs. *B Below left*, Göring speaking at a Nazi rally in Vienna, 2 October 1932. *E   Below right*, Goebbels, Hitler's chief propagandist, in Vienna, 1932, with Alfred Frauenfeld, chief of the Austrian NSDAP. *A*

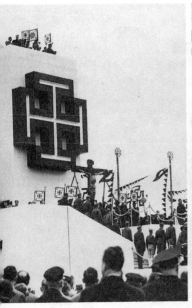

Above left, the red and white *Kruckenkreuz*; in the Dollfuss era, this Crusader cross came to symbolise Austria's independence and a controversial form of social reconstruction. B   *Above right*, Dollfuss speaking at a patriotic rally with Leopold Figl, first regular Chancellor of Austria's Second Republic (wearing glasses, to his right). B   *Below* (left to right), Kurt von Schuschnigg, Prince Starhemberg, Cardinal Innitzer and Dr Richard Steidle during a speech by Dollfuss. F

Dollfuss with, *above left*, the Italian State Secretary for Foreign Affairs, Fulvio Suvich, and, *above right*, Anton Rintelen, who conspired with the NSDAP to replace the Chancellor through an armed revolt. *C, A* *Below*, Dollfuss, who had been a First Lieutenant of the *Kaiserschützen* regiment in the First World War, seen talking with wartime comrades. *H*

Left, portrait of Dollfuss. *C
Above*, the Chancellor with his
children. *A   Below*, Dollfuss,
wounded in the first Nazi attempt
on his life in 1933, is visited by
Cardinal Innitzer. *F*

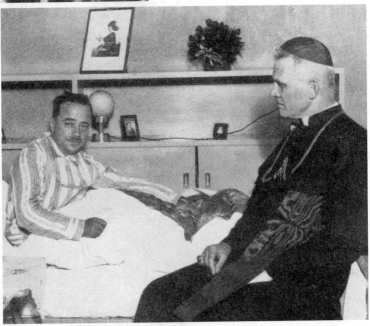

Above left, Prince
Starhemberg. *A*
Above right, Major Emil Fey,
State Secretary. *D*
Right, Benito Mussolini. *A*

Above left, a Lower Austrian *Heimwehr* unit fighting in Carinthia, July 1934. D *Above right,* a *Heimwehr* machine-gun unit. G *Below right,* Nazi rebels during their 1934 uprising in Carinthia (St Andre). G *Below left,* Nazi rebel machine-gun units in Wolfsberg, Carinthia, July 1934. B

Above, armoured police car during the assault to recapture the Vienna radio station from occupying Nazi rebels. G   *Above right*, SS rebels are arrested in Vienna, 25 July 1934. D   *Below right*, defeated Nazis escape to Yugoslavia at the end of their uprising. *A*

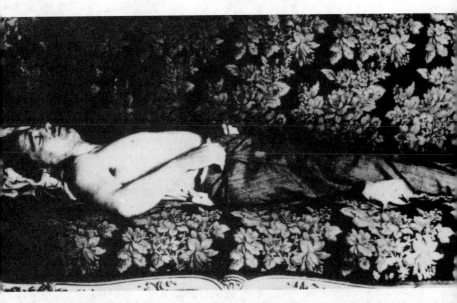

Above, the body of Dollfuss as it was found in his office on the evening of 25 July 1934. *B*   Escorted by a guard of honour, Dollfuss' coffin is borne out of the Chancellery in the Ballhausplatz. *A*

Four years before a pan-German crowd cheered Hitler in the Heldenplatz, Vienna, in 1938, an equally large crowd of Austrians gathered there (*above*) to pay their last respects to the murdered Dollfuss. *A   Left*, Nazis destr a monument to Dollfuss after the *Anschluss* in 1938 — an act curious symbolic of later attempts to disavow his heroic resistance in the cause of Austrian independence an European peace. *G*

Dollfuss, in his unsuccessful manoeuvring to extract formal recognition from Germany of Austria's sovereignty and freedom from foreign inter-ference in its internal affairs, had hoped that negotiations to reduce tension between the two countries would be conducted on a formal government-to-government basis. When Hitler, for whom Austria presented the last refractory element in the German nation, refused to cooperate, talks between Dollfuss and Habicht were arranged. The German side insisted that Habicht's status would be that of the *Führer's* 'plenipotentiary'. Dollfuss yielded on the formal point, though it was of considerable significance, but this drew such fierce criticism from Starhemberg, who was supported by Fey, that Dollfuss was compelled to cancel the talks. This he did at the last minute. Habicht's aircraft was already making its approach to Vienna's Aspern aerodrome and had to be recalled by radio.[10] Angered that Dollfuss had bowed to the *Heimwehr* leaders and that the meeting had been prevented from taking place, Habicht claimed that the *Reich* government had been 'scandalously snubbed' by the cancellation. Openly threatening Dollfuss, he went on: 'It's a question of whether Mr Dollfuss can summon up the courage and the strength to open this door [to negotiations with the Reich] before it is too late. If he cannot, then his fate too will be sealed.'[11] Habicht concluded with the sinister prophecy that 'National Socialism will come to power in Austria as in the Reich — one way or another!'[12]

On 9 February, Hitler conferred with Kurt Rieth, the German Ambassador to Austria. Rieth's report, marked 'top secret', records that Hitler discussed the 'possibility' of 'violent action' by the Austrian National Socialists and its spread across 'the whole of Austria'. Before this, Hitler had had talks with the Austrian SA leader, Hermann Reschny, in which he had indicated that violence might impede a com-promise solution. But Rieth's report concluded with the surprising comment: 'The exchange ended without the Reich Chancellor drawing any specific conclusions or giving any concrete instructions as to the position I should take in future.'[13] This suggests that while Hitler was indeed considering the possibility of a revolt by the Austrian NSDAP, he preferred to comment guardedly to a representative of the essentially more cautious Foreign Ministry.

Shortly afterwards, the Chief of Staff of the Austrian NSDAP, Rudolf Weydenhammer, recorded a conversation he had had with Rintelen, the Austrian Ambassador in Rome, who had recently and traitorously joined the NSDAP. Rintelen informed him that the Austrian government was convinced Germany would 'soon climb down' over the question of Austria, and that Italy saw this as vindicating the firm stand it had taken against Germany.[14]

On 17 March, Austria's position was further strengthened by the signing of the Rome Protocols, which paved the way for closer relations with Italy and Hungary. Berlin, as already noted, reacted angrily and was compelled to register a partial setback in the struggle for Austria. Von Hassell coldly commented: 'Austria has thus received a new, well-publicised pledge of its independence.'[15] Habicht, as spokesman for both the German and the Austrian NSDAP, wrote: 'Faced with the choice of siding with Germany or with Italy — which, after France's withdrawal, were left the only remaining antagonists in the Danube area — Dollfuss, Starhemberg and Fey have opted unreflectingly for Italy. . . . The goal of our struggle is a German Austria under German leadership. . . . For us the Rome Pact — more so than that of Lausanne — is just an episode, but for the Austrians who signed it, it means the end.'[16] Thus to the National Socialist protest against the Rome Protocols was attached a renewed threat to Dollfuss' life.

A petition addressed to Hitler through the German Embassy in Vienna at the end of March from an NSDAP party member, Hans Köhler of Hainfeld in Lower Austria, is characteristic of feeling in the party at the time. Köhler claimed that the chances of the party achieving its aims were fast disappearing in the face of the Austrian government's counter-measures. The circumstances called for 'energetic action'. He proposed that, 'following well-tried historical examples', a squad of courageous and reliable men should 'in a surprise *coup* remove the supporters and leading men of the present system without bloodshed . . . in order to clear the way for national renewal in National Socialist terms and for the return at a later date to the great Fatherland . . .' But, the petition continues, 'Without the fundamental agreement and the support of both the highest leadership [in the NSDAP] and of the regional command [for Austria], it would of course be impossible to carry out the planned undertaking . . .' For 'disciplinary reasons' alone the decision of the leadership could not be pre-empted.[17]

With the help of the German Foreign Ministry, whose views by no means coincided with those of the NSDAP, the German Embassy in Vienna attempted to intervene to obstruct plans of this kind. Two Foreign Ministry reports prepared in April reveal that, after discussions with Habicht, Hitler ordered economic pressure to be stepped up by cutting off Austria's crucial exports of timber, fruit and livestock to Germany.[18]

— *Italy and France support Dollfuss.* The first meeting between Hitler and Mussolini took place in Venice on 14–15 June 1934. Austria was high on the agenda. Hitler reassured the *Duce* that the *Anschluss* question was not of immediate interest to him, but he nevertheless wished to see the replacement of Dollfuss — the focus of the Austrian state's opposition to the Third *Reich* — by an uncommitted head of government independent of party. He would also welcome new elections in Austria and NSDAP representation in the government. The German Foreign Ministry record says: 'Furthermore, the Reich Chancellor conveyed to Mussolini his wish that he should withdraw the protective hand he had been holding out over Austria.'[19]

The meeting cannot be reconstructed in detail because Mussolini felt confident of his ability to speak German and the two dictators conversed alone on major issues. Hitler later maintained that Mussolini had agreed to his demands, but this is contradicted by the Italian record, which shows that Mussolini had said that negotiations on Austria would be dependent on the cessation of the National Socialist terror campaign — which was at that point reaching disturbing proportions.[20]

Fulvio Suvich, the Italian Under-Secretary of State for Foreign Affairs, has provided a more detailed account of the talks. On the evening of 19 July he told the British Ambassador in Rome, Sir Eric Drummond, that Mussolini in replying to Hitler's proposals had expressed the fear that Dollfuss would take his own life if he were compelled to hold elections in the present circumstances. Italy could never allow this to happen. As to the admission of Nazis into the Austrian government, Suvich's account continues, this would depend on whether they genuinely supported Austrian independence; if they were merely agents of the NSDAP or of the government in Berlin, Hitler's proposal was unacceptable. The German Foreign Minister von Neurath had been informed that Rome found the scope of the Nazi terror campaign in Austria intolerable, and that if it did not cease, Dollfuss would be constrained to take drastic measures.[21] In early July, the German Embassy in Rome had already informed its Foreign Ministry of Mussolini's position and of his belief that a signal from Berlin would be sufficient to halt Nazi terrorism in Austria.[22]

With the collapse of their hopes that the meeting between Hitler and Mussolini would bring *Gleichschaltung* of Austria a step closer, the National Socialists were forced to concede that they had sustained a serious setback in their struggle for Austria. Following the *Schutzbund* revolt and its suppression, Dollfuss' dual confrontation with

Austro-Marxism and National Socialism had been reduced to a straight-forward contest with the latter. In the short term, the National Socialists had not profited from the February 1934 revolt. Karl Renner commented:

> By dissolving the Social Democratic Party and destroying all its institutions, Dollfuss had deprived the National Socialists of one of their main propaganda weapons. Now it was utterly impossible for them to tell the bourgeoisie, the petit-bourgeoisie, the intellectuals and the peasants that the government was shielding the Communists and that, to destroy Communism, Hitler's intervention was absolutely indispensable.[23]

The opinion was also being expressed in foreign embassy situation-reports that the government's position had been strengthened, now that it could concentrate on a single opponent.[24] In addition to the unwelcome results flowing from the Rome-Vienna-Budapest agreement of March, Berlin suffered another reverse in the form of an interview given by the French Foreign Minister, Barthou, following a meeting with Dollfuss in Vienna on 19 June. 'France's entire strength', Barthou said 'stands behind Austria's independence, an independence embodied in the person of the Federal Chancellor.' As to Nazi terrorism, he remarked: 'We are wholly on the side of the Dollfuss government. Austria's freedom and peace must be guaranteed whatever the circumstances. We shall protect this freedom in every possible way.' The French Embassy added that Barthou had told Dollfuss that the French government had full confidence in his leadership.[25] Thus, following the talks, France had responded — verbally at least — in much the same way as Italy.

Starhemberg's anti-Hitler rally in Braunau. On the domestic front, the Dollfuss government remained unshaken by a new wave of National Socialist bomb attacks. In June 1934 the government responded by establishing the local defence forces described above. A good example of official attempts to stiffen resistance in the psychological and ideological area is provided by the speeches given on 17 June at a mass rally of patriotic paramilitary formations in Hitler's birthplace, Braunau am Inn. The date was deliberately chosen because it was Hitler's name day. *Landeshauptmann* Dr Heinrich Gleissner (who died in 1984) claimed that Austria was 'the last spokesman of Europe's conscience' and that it was no betrayal of the German cause if Austria refused to tread the path 'which we know leads to an abyss'. 'We German Austrians', he added, 'are the last warning voice of *Deutschtum* . . .'[26]

Starhemberg challenged the Germans in the *Reich* to rise up and 'put an end to a situation disgraceful to and unworthy of the German people'. Austria's struggle against National Socialism, he said, was not merely a defensive battle but also 'a struggle for *Deutschtum* itself, in the interests of the entire German people.' In closing, Starhemberg called for reconciliation with the opposing side in the February revolt, because 'Austria can only be rebuilt when those workers who till now have been organised along Marxist lines are to be found in the ranks of the population loyal to the Fatherland. . . .' This required a programme of 'genuine social justice and a relationship between employers and workers that reflects it'. According to the press report, he ended the speech with the words 'Austria first, because we want it!' Thousands of hands rose in the traditional salute, accompanied by a chorus of shouts of 'Austria for the Austrians!'[27]

Armed revolt as the only option. Shortly before the Hitler-Mussolini meeting in Venice, Lieutenant-General Muff, the German military attaché in Vienna, had outlined in a characteristic secret report three basic strategy options to be pursued in the drive against Austria:

1. Continuation of 'existing positional warfare'. The economic screw could be tightened further and the terror campaign intensified in the hope of eventually grinding the Austrians down. However, he added, 'Our opponents have by no means exhausted their defensive resources and continue to find support abroad, perhaps increasingly so.'

2. Removal of the government by non-violent means and by agreement with Italy, this being the simplest solution. (The meeting of the two dictators nine days later was to put an end to these hopes.)

3. Overthrow of the government by 'violent assault'. Since this would be attended by great risks, it would be advisable only 'if there is no other possibility'. Muff realistically pointed out that Austria's armed forces were still under firm government control, which had been evident in the February revolt.[28]

The logic of Muff's argument — if his reservations were ignored — would have led, even impelled, the NSDAP leadership to conclude that, after the failure of the German-Italian talks, 'violent assault' presented the only hope of achieving quick and decisive results in Austria. Given Mussolini's negative position, this option alone held out any promise of both a lightning seizure of power by the National Socialists accompanied by the installation of a puppet government, and a simultaneous popular uprising throughout Austria in support of the Greater German ideal. A quick, massive turnaround of this variety would present Mussolini with a *fait accompli*. And this could only be reversed by foreign military occupation of Austria and the suppression of the uprising.

Otto Gustav Wächter, an Austrian NSDAP leader and one of the main wire-pullers in the Nazi conspiracy, commented on the party's predicament at the time: 'The enemy [the Dollfuss government] had no intention of giving in, as was quite evident by early summer, but had hardened its policies. The mandatory death penalty, even for the possession of explosives, became law. This was certain to lead to executions of National Socialists.' The party, he maintained, would have attempted to avenge executions by bloody reprisals. This in turn would probably have prompted government counter-measures, 'and the movement would have been bludgeoned to death without even an attempt at a massed uprising against the hated regime' having been made. In order to prevent the piecemeal destruction of the Austrian NSDAP, it had been decided to grasp the nettle and examine the possibilities of a simultaneous uprising in Vienna and the provinces. Thus the growing resolution of the Austrian government was to be a causal factor in the development of plans for a *coup*.[29]

A further aspect, still unresearched and thus mentioned only peripherally, concerns claims made in a number of confidential reports that Dollfuss was negotiating at the time with 'moderates' among the outlawed Social Democrats on 'joint action against the National Socialists'. Habicht asserted in a report dated 18 June that Dollfuss and the Socialists had in fact come to a 'general agreement in principle'.[30] On 23 July Rieth reported to Berlin that he surmised that Dollfuss was working for collaboration with the Social Democrats in order to be in a position, with 'Franco-Czech assistance', to play this card even against the Italians 'if they stopped supporting him or gave him inadequate support'. He [Rieth], at any rate, had informed both Italy and Hungary of this surmise.[31] A confidential report prepared by the American Ambassador in Vienna, George Messersmith, contains a similar statement: 'He [Dollfuss] was on the point of making political peace with the Socialists, which would probably have materialised within the next few weeks.'[32] Starhemberg's speech in Braunau also contained an allusion to this effect.

The investigation into the revolt conducted by the SS Historical Commission shows that in 1933 the Austrian National Socialists were already in possession of plans for the type of uprising they attempted to carry out in July 1934. The only obstacle to putting the plans into effect in 1933 had been Hitler's refusal to give his approval. Both the 1933 plans and the actual abortive uprising the year after envisaged the following:[33]

1. Capture of the entire Cabinet in Vienna while in session; this to be carried out by armed rebels disguised as regular soldiers.

2. Seizure of the studios of Austrian Radio in Vienna, to be followed by radio announcements that the Dollfuss government had been replaced by a new government led by a well-known public figure acceptable to the National Socialists, and that all orders issued by the new government were to be obeyed.

3. Seizure of local government offices and communications centres in the provinces by use of threats or violence. This would be signalled by the radio announcements.

4. A propaganda campaign in conjunction with these operations covering the whole of Austria. It was expected that this would lead to a Greater German popular uprising against the Dollfuss government.

5. The assignment of a special commando either to arrest the Federal President and coerce him, in his constitutional role, to legitimise the new government, or to dispose of him.

Hitler's role in planning the revolt.   Interestingly, Hitler had himself outlined the strategic and tactical guidelines for a *coup* of this type in a conversation with Hermann Rauschning and others in August 1932. It emerged that he saw an operation of this kind as a form of war. 'When I go to war . . .' he said, 'I'll have troops arrive, say, in Paris, one day in peacetime. They'll be wearing French uniforms. They'll march through the streets in broad daylight. Nobody will stop them. Everything planned down to the last detail. . . . They'll seize the ministries and parliament. Within a matter of minutes, France, Poland, Austria . . . will be robbed of their leaders. . . . There will be unprecedented chaos. But I will long have been in contact with the men who will form a new government, a government that suits me.'[34] He had learnt the art of the *coup d'état*, he maintained, from the history of revolutions and in particular from the Bolsheviks.[35] His final remark is also relevant to an analysis of the 1934 revolt: 'I don't play at war. I refuse to have so-called generals ordering me about. *I* shall conduct the war. *I* shall decide the best moment to act.'[36]

It would seem highly improbable that the organisers of the revolt in

Austria would have ventured to attempt to take-over a whole country without their *Führer*'s knowledge. Slavish obedience — overriding all rivalries — characterised the relationship of all branches of the NSDAP to his person. Furthermore, in the previous month Hitler had ordered the massacre of the troublesome SA leadership in the so-called Röhm *Putsch*. Moreoever, Austria was a country in which Italy, Hitler's principal foreign ally, had a strong interest. And if in 1933 the planners of the revolt had treated Hitler's approval as a pre-condition *sine qua non* for carrying it out, they would scarcely have changed their minds following the purge of the SA and in the face of the growing importance Hitler attached to Italy.

A month before the revolt, German newspapers led by the NSDAP's main organ, the *Völkischer Beobachter*, had already begun to demand a new Austrian government headed by Rintelen, an ambitious pro-Nazi pan-German National Socialist whom the rebels intended to make Chancellor.[37] It is thus very probable that Hitler either directly ordered or, with his full knowledge and approval, authorised the organisers of the revolt to go ahead at their own risk. If the revolt had succeeded he would have supported the new 'national' government in Austria, which would have been moving towards *Gleichschaltung* with the Reich. In the event of failure, he would have had to deny any involvement. General Wilhelm Adam, commanding Military District VII in Munich, describes in his memoirs how Hitler summoned him to Bayreuth at 9 a.m. on 25 July, the day of the uprising, and told him: 'The Austrian government will be thrown out today. Rintelen will be Reich Chancellor. He will order all Austrian emigrés and members of the Legion to return to their home-country.' The legionaries, Hitler went on, would cross the frontier unarmed and be handed German weapons on Austrian territory. He instructed Adam to complete arrangements for weapons to be transported to locations, 'details of which you will receive later.'[38] At 3 p.m. Hitler rang Adam to let him know that the operation was running smoothly in Vienna, that the Chancellery had been seized and Dollfuss wounded, but that no further details were known. He assured Adam that he would ring again, but did not.[39]

The 'Lightning Coup' betrayed. According to the SS Historical Commission[40] the prime movers in the planning of the revolt were two Germans, Habicht and Weydenhammer, assisted by *Sturmbannführer* Fridolin Glass of the Austrian SS. Glass recruited the so-called 'SS *Standarte* 89' in Vienna to act as the assault party in the operation. It was largely composed of ex-Austrian Army regulars who had been discharged for engaging in National Socialist activities.

On the day of decision, 25 July, at 12.45 p.m., a convoy of trucks carrying about 150 armed men left the Siebensterngasse and headed for the Chancellery in the Ballhausplatz, where the Cabinet had been in session since 11 a.m. In order to penetrate the Chancellery guard, some had donned uniforms of the legendary Viennese *Hoch- und Deutschmeisterregiment* number 4. Others were disguised as police. Only one of the men was a serving soldier. After a seven-minute drive they drew up in front of the Chancellery, unaware that one of the conspirators, District Inspector Johann Dobler, formerly an administrative official at the NSDAP headquarters in Vienna, had had qualms of conscience and alerted the authorities. Knowing that there were National Socialist sympathisers in certain sections of the Vienna police force, he tried to arrange a meeting with officials of the Fatherland Front and, in inimitably Viennese style, fixed a café as the meeting place. Dobler's message, having travelled by a circuitous route, finally reached Fey's personal adjutant, Gendarmerie Major Robert Wrabel, at 10.45 a.m.[41] Wrabel immediately informed Fey, who had received the news from another source minutes before.[42]

Dollfuss had, as we have seen, stripped Fey of the office of Vice-Chancellor in early May and, on 10 July, removed him from his position as State Secretary for Security Affairs. At the time of the uprising, he was a Cabinet member without portfolio and carried the honorific title of State Commissioner for Extraordinary Security Measures.

Fey's fatal plan.   Rumours of an impending *putsch* had reached the Chancellery several days previously.[43] This would support Starhemberg's claim that Fey was privy to the plan for an operation directed against the Chancellery and had deliberately delayed in warning the Chancellor and the Cabinet. Instead, he had 'for no special reason' ordered an alert of units of the Vienna *Heimatschutz* under his command 'for the early hours of 25 July and ordered them to assemble at the Prater for drill'. Contrary to normal practice, live ammunition was issued. Fey, so Starhemberg argues, intended to commit these troops when the situation became critical and by so doing emerge once again as the 'saviour of the Fatherland'. He would both humiliate Dollfuss, who had ousted him from his important posts, and expose his successor in the Security Ministry, Karwinsky, as uninformed and incompetent. Fey had relished being fêted as 'saviour of the Fatherland' after the *Schutzbund* revolt, but Dollfuss had nevertheless removed him from his two key posts. He was, in Starhemberg's estimation, a man consumed with ambition and undoubtedly capable of harbouring such intentions. If this was indeed true, then Fey's irresponsible gamble was thwarted by the fact that 'everything happened much more rapidly than he had anticipated, and Planetta's fatal bullet hit the Chancellor before the Vienna *Heimwehr* battalion [under Fey] had a chance to appear on the scene.'[44]

On receiving Dobler's warning, Fey insisted that his adjutant, Wrabel, be shown the rebels' operational orders at Dobler's apartment. At 11.45 a.m. Wrabel reported to Fey that he had seen the orders.[45] At this point Fey probably telephoned instructions to the *Heimatschutz* troops at the Prater to return immediately to the city centre. Fifteen vital minutes later, at noon, he informed the Chancellor and, on the Chancellor's request, the Cabinet: 'I've just got a report, something's supposed to be going on against the Ballhausplatz. There's a gymnasium in the Siebensterngasse, it has got something to do with it.'[46] The crude and imprecise phrasing would seem to have been intentional. Twenty minutes later, Major Wrabel entered the Chancellery with the news that two policemen had reported soldiers, police and civilians pouring into a gymnasium in the Siebensterngasse and a truck being loaded with crates.

The assassination of Dollfuss. Despite the sparseness of the information given to him, Dollfuss adjourned the Cabinet meeting — contemporaries frequently remarked on this intuitive grasp — and sent the members of the Cabinet back to their ministries. According to one of the ministers, von Berger-Waldenegg, the Chancellor indicated that although he was not convinced of the authenticity of the warnings, he preferred not to have the entire government sitting in the same trap. At the same time he instructed Major-General Wilhelm Zehner, State Secretary for Defence, to place the Vienna garrison on alert. These were to be his last instructions.[47] But they blocked the main thrust of the revolt, namely the attempt to take the entire government hostage, for only Dollfuss, Karwinsky and Fey were now present in the Chancellery.

Forty minutes later the SS assault party arrived at the Ballhausplatz in its convoy of trucks, overwhelmed the guards, who mistook them for reinforcements, and quickly seized the building. The fracas could be heard on the floor above. The doorkeeper of the Chancellor's office ushered Dollfuss to a little-known spiral staircase leading to an archive, from which he could escape into the Minoritenplatz. As they hurried through the Chancellery, Dollfuss asked the doorkeeper whether he was carrying a revolver. The answer was negative. Suddenly they encountered a group of ten SS rebels who were rushing upstairs. One of them, Otto Planetta, fired at Dollfuss from close range. The bullet penetrated his spinal cord at the neck and Dollfuss fell to the ground partially paralysed and with severe internal bleeding.[48] The autopsy revealed a second relatively minor bullet wound, but it has never been completely clarified who fired the shot that inflicted it. The SS Historical Commission was not alone in concluding that the rebels, insulting and arguing with the dying Chancellor, maliciously fired at him a second time.[49]

Dollfuss regained consciousness, and his first question — characteristically — concerned the welfare of the members of the Cabinet. He told Fey that Schuschnigg should form a new government and that Mussolini be requested to look after his wife and children, who were staying as his guests in Rome. The Chancellor asked for a doctor to be called because he was having difficulty breathing. He also pleaded for a priest to attend him. Both requests were denied outright by the SS men, who tried to confuse him and place him under duress by giving him a distorted account of the situation. Contradictory statements by witnesses report Dollfuss as saying either that Rintelen should make peace or that Rintelen should become Chancellor. Characteristically, however, he was to qualify this shortly afterwards: '. . . *but I don't want to give Austria to those who don't want Austria.*'[50]

The tragedy of Dollfuss' death is poignantly summed up in the official government report. 'Whatever the final political statements made by Federal Chancellor Dr Dollfuss might have been, it is certain that he could not possibly have fully understood what was happening. In the hour of his death he must have been under the appalling illusion that the Army and police had rebelled against him and his government; he saw death approaching and was forced to conclude that his life's work lay in ruins.'[51]

To the two policemen who attended him to the end he said, 'Children, you're so good to me, why aren't the others like that? All I wanted was peace; we were never the aggressors, we were always having to defend ourselves. May God forgive them.' After sending farewells to his wife and children, Dollfuss died at about 3.45 p.m. after an ordeal of almost three hours.[52]

Hitler's principal opponent in Austria was dead. He died as he had lived and fought as Chancellor — for Austria's independence.

The revolt in Vienna fails.   At 1 p.m. an SS commando unit of about fifteen men had seized the main Austrian Radio building in Vienna. An announcer was forced at gunpoint to read a statement saying that Dollfuss had resigned and that a new government would be formed by Dr Anton Rintelen, former Ambassador to Italy and Governor of Styria. Listeners heard the playing of military marches, interrupted by the sound of shots, and then silence.[53] The management had succeeded in contacting the police by a telephone unnoticed by the rebels and had ordered the main transmitter on the Bisamberg shut down. Police shot out one of the transmitter tubes. After sharp fighting, the SS unit was overpowered at 2.45 p.m. and the radio station returned under government control.[54] The rebels' second operation had collapsed.

The third operation, designed to coerce or dispose of the Federal President, Wilhelm Miklas, who was on holiday at Velden on the Wörthersee, also failed. Miklas, as President, was constitutionally empowered to appoint the Chancellor. If he could be forced to appoint Rintelen, the change in government planned by the National Socialists would be sanctioned. If he refused, the rebels would have to remove him since he would pose a continuing risk to the successful outcome of the revolt. However, an anonymous informant had alerted the local police to this plan, and two of the commando's leaders were arrested before they could mobilise the local Carinthian SS to seize the President.[55]

At 2.30 p.m. the remaining Cabinet ministers assembled in the Defence Ministry, in front of which stands a statue of Field-Marshal Radetzky bearing the famous inscription by Grillparzer, 'Within your camp lies Austria.' Here the ministers debated counter-measures. Alarmed by the radio report that Rintelen had been installed as Chancellor, President Miklas had telephoned Vienna from Velden and been informed by Dr Skubl, Vice-President of the Vienna police, that the Chancellery had been seized and was surrounded by Army and police units. Miklas then spoke to the ministers and told them that he would not feel bound by any decisions made by members of the government who might be captives, and thus possibly under coercion in the Chancellery. He reminded them that the President alone could appoint a new Chancellor. Because the Vice-Chancellor, Starhemberg, was away in Italy, Miklas temporarily placed the government in the hands of Kurt von Schuschnigg and told him, 'Employing all the power of the state . . . you are immediately to restore legal order, arraign the rebels and, most important, free the members of the government imprisoned in the Chancellery at the Ballhausplatz. . . .'[56] After lengthy negotiations, the rebels were finally persuaded to leave the Chancellery at 7 p.m. They were promised safe conduct on condition that there were 'no fatalities

among the members of the government illegally robbed of their freedom'.[57] The rebels accepted. But they had neglected to mention that
Dollfuss was dead, and so they were arrested.

Rintelen, who had treasonably offered his support to the National
Socialists in the revolt, was staying at the Hotel Imperial in Vienna.
He records in his memoirs: 'At mid-day I was waiting anxiously for the
call to go over to the Chancellery.' But instead Wächter and
Weydenhammer, two of the chief conspirators, appeared at the hotel
and informed him of the unexpected turn of events. The three men came
to the unanimous conclusion that 'The operation had been betrayed.
The attempt to arrest the Cabinet *in toto* had failed. Elements of the
government, including the head of the Defence Ministry, Major-General
Zehner, were in undisputed control of the state's armed forces.'[58] As
Wächter and Weydenhammer were trying to persuade Rintelen to step
in to rescue the rebels besieged in the Chancellery, he received a telephone call from Schuschnigg summoning him to the Defence Ministry,
where the remainder of the Cabinet was in session.[59] Friedrich Funder
ran Rintelen to ground and virtually forced him to accompany him to the
Ministry. Following a confrontation with the ministers, he was put
under arrest and, deeply humiliated, made an unsuccessful suicide
attempt.[60] The rebels in Vienna had thus lost their final trump card.

The suppression of the revolt in the provinces

The high drama of the *coup* in the capital has drawn attention away from
concurrent events in five of the nine Austrian provinces, which have
often been overlooked by historians and commentators. As described,
the planning for the revolt was based on three main elements: first, the
immobilisation of the government by the arrest of both the Cabinet and
the President; secondly, a series of uprisings in the provinces; and
thirdly, the expectation that the first two steps would trigger off a mass
popular uprising against the Dollfuss regime and in favour of a Greater
German government. Austria was initially to retain its independence *de
jure* under this new government in order not to provoke foreign intervention. *De facto*, however, the new government was to be entirely
subordinate to the leadership of the Third Reich and the NSDAP party
leader Adolf Hitler (as head of the entire NSDAP, he was also head of the
Austrian NSDAP).

It was thought that foreign intervention, particularly by Italy, could only be prevented if the revolt effected a rapid change of government followed by a popular uprising of such sweeping dimensions that any country tempted to intervene would have to reckon with mass resistance.

The 'Kollerschlag Document',[61] so termed after the town where it was found, gives a detailed picture of the organisation and planning of the uprising. Point 1 of the document states that in the likely event of the Dollfuss government being 'forced to resign', there would follow the appointment of a new government or a struggle for power. Point 2 posits that, in either event, a temporary power vacuum would ensue during which the authorities would neither be subordinate to the ousted government nor yet be receiving instructions from the new administration. As a result, the authorities would be 'paralysed in their decision-making and their power to act'. Point 3 forcefully concludes: 'This period of inertia must be exploited.' News of the resignation of the Dollfuss administration was to be the signal for the SA throughout Austria to undertake propaganda marches'.

For public consumption, these marches would be billed as demonstrations for new elections, but in truth they would be for the purpose of 'immediately occupying public offices and buildings in the provincial capitals and local administrative centres, and seizing power'. The SA brigade leaders in the provinces were to announce that they and the regional NSDAP chiefs had assumed power as Provincial Governors and Directors of Public Safety respectively. On the principle championed by the legendary Captain of Köpenick that 'brazenness wins the day', the self-appointed Nazi functionaries would be issuing 'strict orders' in their capacity as 'new chiefs' of the provincial administration. But they were instructed, as a precaution, not to express views either for or against a possible new Chancellor, so that the bewildered population would be likely to assume that the seizure of power had his approval. For, as Point 5 explains, a change of government could have two consequences: either 'The new government will recognise the National Socialist movement and buckle under', or, if it did not, active opposition to the NSDAP by the new administration must be reckoned with; 'in short, a struggle for power will develop.' Conceding the possibility that the revolt in Vienna might fail, the document comments forcibly: 'If we succeed in seizing power in the provinces in this way, Vienna will not be able to hold out on its own but will have to follow.'

The familiar tactics of totalitarian movements — both right and left — appear in Point 6, which stresses how important it is 'that the movement appears to come spontaneously from the people'. This is why it had to be staged as a 'purely domestic' affair, and must 'under no circumstances appear as if it were directed from the outside in any way'. The clandestine nature of the operation made it imperative that only SA brigade leaders and their staff leaders should be informed of the plan. The junior leaders would only be told as much as was necessary for them to perform their duties

Point 7 concerns the *putsch* itself. What would appear to be 'propaganda marches' by unarmed National Socialists, in uniform or wearing swastika armbands, were to be organised in such a way that weapons could be secretly carried or, if this were not possible, be conveniently placed. The purpose of these marches would be to facilitate the seizure of public buildings, on which swastika flags were to be immediately hoisted. Following this, the assumption of power by the NSDAP and a general amnesty for political prisoners were to be proclaimed, and political emigrés (the Austrian Legion) would be called home. The political prisoners released would include the 'reds' (Socialists and Communists). The Austrian Legion was immediately to proceed to Vienna. Hitler had actually spelt this out to General Adam on 25 July. [62]

Point 8 in the Kollerschlag Document is also characteristic of the tactics of totalitarian movements. 'Government and defence force leaders hostile to us', it instructed, 'are to be arrested immediately and made harmless if they show any resistance. Neutrality towards the reds, as long as they don't do us any harm.'

Clashes with the Army were to be avoided if at all possible, and the same applied to the police and the gendarmerie. If combat was unavoidable, it would be essential 'to proceed with maximum vigour and force'. Once power had been seized, thoroughgoing consolidation was to follow. The SA was to be armed and 'organised as a reliable instrument of power for the new government'. Hostile defence units were to be disarmed and disbanded. Law enforcement agencies ready to put themselves under the direction of the NSDAP were to receive swastika armbands and be reinstated. Combat with the police or the gendarmerie was to be aggressive and conducted in such a way that 'the forces of the executive, which generally appear in small numbers, will find themselves pitted against superior numbers determined to fight to the last. The individual representative of the authorities', the instructions continued, 'must know that he will be risking his life if he opposes us.'

The overall tactical approach should consist of 'small-scale actions with the objective of grinding down' the law enforcement agencies. Both the idea of occupying the seat of government in Vienna by moving in from the provinces, and the order to avoid the Army wherever it appeared in large formations so that it would strike at thin air, are reminiscent of Mao Tse-tung's writings on guerrilla warfare.

In the spring months of 1934 the insurgents received secret arms shipments of machine-guns, rifles, hand-grenades, submachine-guns, revolvers, ammunition, explosives and other matériel. Some of their needs were covered by thefts from Austrian Army depots.[63]

Although there was fierce fighting in the other regions, the most serious of the uprisings occurred in the two southeastern provinces, Carinthia and Styria. The plan there was to commit the insurgents in a large number of towns and villages and overpower the local gendarmerie, police and volunteeer defence force units by surprise. These operations would serve as a preliminary show of strength, secure additional weaponry and vehicles, and provide strategic depth for an advance on the provincial capitals.[64]

The first uprising clearly to bear the stamp of the tactical directives laid down in the Kollerschlag Document took place at Wolfsberg in Carinthia. According to an official NSDAP party history, 'It was a full-scale war that was fought out in the Lavant Valley during those critical summer days of 1934.' The anticipated radio announcement reporting a change of government in Vienna put the local SA in Wolfsberg on standby until a courier arrived at noon the following day with the order to go into action. The SA assembled on the outskirts of the town and prepared to attack in three formations. The targets were the offices of the local authorities and their officials. As in numerous other towns, the railway station, post office and telegraph office were rapidly occupied in order to gain control of communications. The town was seized by about 1,500 rebels, who had previously plundered its weapons depots. The swastika was hoisted on all public buildings and at other points. The insurgents fanned out briskly to take St Leonhard, Lavamünd, St Paul and St Andrä.

By the next day the entire Lavant Valley was under rebel control. The SA leadership was now resolved to cross the Griffenberg river and attack the provincial capital, Klagenfurt. At this juncture, however, they ran into regular army units advancing down the Lavant Valley. The rebels reoccupied Lavamünd, which had in the interim been won back by government troops, and freed their prisoners. Increasingly effective Army counter-attacks forced the rebel leaders to take their troops across the frontier into Yugoslavia on 30 July.[65]

According to the official Austrian account of the July revolt:

The pattern of insurgency at Wolfsberg was faithfully repeated at most of the other locations involved in the revolt, revealing that the rebels had been well prepared and trained both for the revolt and for civil war. Mobs of National Socialist party members . . . heavily armed and issuing threats of extreme violence, seized railway stations, post offices, district government offices and other public buildings, fired on gendarmerie and Home Defence Corps barracks, disarmed and detained their occupants and arrested civil servants and known loyalists. When the population and the local administration refused to submit to their intimidatory tactics, they applied systematic terror. In Wolfsberg the rebels posted large numbers of placards which announced the takeover of power, called for compliance and calm, ordered the hoisting of flags on all houses and directed 'all able-bodied compatriots' to report to 'the nearest SA post'.[66]

Other clashes in and around Carinthia took place in St Veit on the Glan — which was temporarily occupied by the rebels — and Feldkirchen, Bleiburg and Rabenstein on the Yugoslav border. The government was forced to deploy 6,000 troops in Carinthia to end the rebellion; thirty-six were killed and sixty-two wounded.[67] In Styria the fighting was so widespread that it would be impractical to list all the towns and villages affected. Severe clashes took place in the Leoben/Donawitz area, where most of the workers in German-owned industrial companies sided with the rebels.[68] Liezen was seized by the National Socialists, as were Stainz, Radkersburg and a number of other towns. Government forces in Styria suffered losses of forty-one dead and eighty-seven wounded, the rebels eighty-eight dead and 164 wounded. The government made 3,000 arrests in the area and seized twenty heavy and five light machine-guns, 1,000 rifles, 36,000 rounds of ammunition and a large quantity of explosives.[69] In Upper Austria there was fighting in the Enns Valley and the Salzkammergut. There was bitter fighting with heavy losses on both sides around the strategic Pyhrn Pass. In the province of Salzburg, which remained relatively calm, heavy fighting broke out on 28 July in the village of Lamprechtshausen.[70]

In all, the revolt claimed 269 lives, and about 600 people were wounded. By the beginning of August, resistance in the provinces had collapsed. Nowhere had elements of the Army, gendarmerie, police or the paramilitary defence corps gone over to the rebels.

The academic question as to whether the revolt might have succeeded if the rebels had seized the entire Cabinet in Vienna is unanswerable, but what makes it unlikely is that the organisers of the revolt had overlooked the fact that the Vice-Chancellor, Starhemberg, was holidaying in Italy.

As Vice-Chancellor and as leader of the *Heimatschutz*, and not least because of his close personal relationship with Mussolini, he would undoubtedly have been successful in having himself declared the legitimate leader of the government.

In Venice, in the late morning on 25 July, Starhemberg had been informed of the uprising by telephone from Vienna and, twenty minutes later, gave the *Heimatschutz* staff officers the following order: 'The entire Austrian *Heimatschutz* is to be mobilised immediately and put on the highest state of alert. Wherever the Nazis stir, immediate offensive action is to be undertaken.'[71]

Starhemberg arrived in Austria on the evening of 26 July. The volunteer units which made up the *Heimatschutz* had mobilised as ordered the day before, and in many cases intervened in the fighting both earlier and with greater decisiveness than the regular Army.[72] No fewer than 52,820 Austrian volunteers answered the mobilisation call in defence of their country against the National Socialist revolt.[73]

7

AUSTRIA STAVES OFF HITLER'S ASSAULT

First Nazi reactions

The Austrian National Socialists' armed uprising in July 1934 marked the military culmination of the political and economic campaign conducted by Hitler, the Third *Reich* and the German and Austrian NSDAP to destroy Austria's sovereignty. Austria's successful defence blocked Hitler's hopes of exploiting its conquest to bring about decisive changes in the politico-strategic map of Europe and to give further impetus to his expansionist ambitions.

Taking first stock in a confidential report on 26 July, General Muff, the German military attaché in Vienna, wrote that he had been aware for 'a long time' of the National Socialist plan to have insurgents, disguised as soldiers, descend upon the government and arrest its members.[1] But the 'enduring success' of such an operation, Muff suggested, could only have been assured if at least one of two conditions had been fulfilled: there would have had to be either a pan-German popular uprising or 'intervention by the army on the side of the prospective new government'. The rebels had evidently been banking on Army support, but Muff had always considered any active participation by the Army to be out of the question. Although contacts were alleged to have been established between the National Socialists and individual Austrian Army officers, 'the army nevertheless remained firmly in the hands of the State Secretary for National Defence'. The NSDAP's attempt to force the issue following the failure of its efforts to undermine Austria's sovereignty had entirely miscarried. 'The moral setback suffered by the aggressor', Muff continued, 'is considerable, the initiative has passed to the other side.' This might be the beginning of a campaign to eradicate National Socialism in Austria, he thought, a campaign which would exploit popular reaction to the murder of the Chancellor, but he hoped that the Austrian NSDAP would realise that 'he who sows violence will only reap violence'.[2]

In a report dated 30 August, Muff concludes this analysis of Austro-German relations with the following passage: 'Thus the Party, i.e. its present leaders — the regional leadership in Munich — bears full and sole responsibility for the present situation. It has furnished proof of its political ineptitude.' An Austria lost to Germany's cause could turn into 'a direct threat to the Reich's internal policy', since it could become a breeding ground for any destructive forces desiring to undermine the structure of the National Socialist state from this point on. The age of the Counter-Reformation, he continued, had seen the emergence of a powerful force in Austria which had brought about the religious and political division of the German people. 'The same forces are once more at work here today,' he claimed. It was also imperative on account of Austria's immensely important strategic position that the struggle be continued, even if this meant using different methods. It had simply not yet been accepted in Austria that the 'Reich sincerely intends to alter its methods with regard to Austria'.[3]

A further confidential analysis of the Nazi defeat in Austria was that submitted to the Foreign Ministry in Berlin by Dr Hans Steinacher, the head of the National League for Germans Abroad.[4] Steinacher criticised the National Socialists for allowing themselves to be deluded into expecting cooperation from the Austrian armed forces and police. As it turned out, 'at no point did the Army and the police refuse to obey, and this sealed the fate of the military uprising'. Even two Army officers who had secretly joined the NSDAP remained loyal to the state and actively participated in combat against the insurgents. Worse still, Steinacher felt, events had confirmed the Austrian government's claim that only relatively small groups of men had engaged in the fighting: 'The "masses" are lacking. We are unable to prove that they exist. . . .' A campaign of persecution would be launched against the Austrian NSDAP, he thought, and the whole of Europe would applaud. What had now come to pass was the very opposite of what had been intended: 'The Schuschnigg era is precisely what we wanted to avoid at all costs.'

Hitler's retreat: a posthumous victory for Dollfuss

The power-politician in Hitler instantly recognised the implications of this defeat, and he drew the appropriate conclusions. He recalled Rieth, the German Ambassador, on the grounds that he had compromised the *Reich* by acceding to the pleas of the rebels under siege in the Chancellery to negotiate their release. State Secretary von Bülow recorded on 25 July that Hitler had said he would 'have the expelled conspirators taken into protective custody and transferred to a concentration camp'.[5] The

Völkischer Beobachter in Berlin gave front-page prominence to a statement that the *Reich* government did not regard the agreements between the Austrian authorities and the rebels as having legal force. 'The government of the German *Reich* has therefore ordered the immediate arrest of insurgents in the event of their entering German territory.' Condolences on the death of Chancellor Dollfuss, the statement went on, had been conveyed to the Austrian government, and the *Reich* Chancellor had, 'out of respect for the tragic events that had taken place in Austria', broken off his visit to the Bayreuth *Festspiele*.

On 1 August, Hitler told General von Reichenau in unvarnished terms that '. . . he intended to wind up the National Socialist Party in Austria and disband the Austrian Legion, merely retaining a charitable organisation for the care of Austrian refugees under the unimpeachable cover of the Red Cross'.[6] On 7 August, Brigade Leader Rodenbücher, the *Reich* German who headed the Austrian SS, passed on to the Foreign Ministry an instruction signed by Hitler's deputy, Rudolf Hess, which stated: 'The *Führer* has ordered that the Austrian regional leadership be dissolved at once. The reasons for this dissolution are ones of foreign policy.'[7] To replace the German Ambassador to Austria, Hitler asked Vice-Chancellor Franz von Papen — who had good reason to be unfavourably disposed towards the *Führer* — to take up what was now an extremely difficult post. He made this request, as he wrote to von Papen, because the already precarious situation in Europe — through no fault of Germany's — was becoming increasingly critical. Hitler said he wished to reduce tensions throughout Europe and normalise relations with Austria. Von Papen, in his new post as German Ambassador to Austria, would be directly responsible to him.[8] Hitler accordingly instructed Hess and Goebbels, the Propaganda Minister, in a letter dated 8 August, that radio and press coverage of German-Austrian relations would be subject to consultations with the Propaganda Minister and the Ambassador in Vienna.[9] On 19 August, the '*Kampfring* of Austrians in the *Reich*,' an organisation founded to support the political campaign against Austria, was prohibited by Hitler from participating in political activity 'involving interference in Austria's internal affairs'. The '*Kampfring*' was to be reconstituted as a '*Hilfsbund*' (Relief Society) exclusively concerned with the welfare of its members.[10]

On 28 September, the Foreign Ministry informed the German Embassy in Vienna that the German press had been instructed to refrain from printing statements 'which might be interpreted as one-sided interference by Germany in Austria's domestic affairs'. The Ministry then noted, grotesquely, that the German press would also 'refrain from giving the Austrian government any advice on how to overcome their domestic difficulties'. Austria's relations with Germany should now be viewed, the Ministry urged, 'as part of the general European situation and not merely in the light of specifically Austrian problems'.[11]

Hitler's retreat culminated in a letter to the *Gauleiter* of Vienna, Alfred Frauenfeld, dated 21 August and signed by Hess. It informed Frauenfeld that the *Führer* had prohibited the German NSDAP from having any contact with National Socialists in Austria. 'It is likewise strictly forbidden for Austrian leaders in Germany to exert any kind of influence on the NSDAP here.' The letter warned: 'The *Führer*'s order is not merely a formality but is definitely an order which must be obeyed unconditionally. Failure to obey this order will entail severe punishment, which, in cases where the interests of the German Reich are threatened, may even include imprisonment.'[12] Closing this extraordinary communication, Hess expressed the hope that it would be appreciated that the *Führer* and his colleagues had found it 'very hard' to adopt this 'harsh attitude', but that 'Germany's vital interests' were at stake, 'and therefore indirectly also the interests of the German-speaking peoples and not least of the Austrian NSDAP itself'. Hitler himself, Hess explained, had adopted a 'new and absolutely lawful policy' in November 1923 after the failure of his revolutionary course. It was hoped that 'despite everything' Austria would be joined to Germany in the future by perfectly legal means.[13] Hess, reflecting Hitler's own assessment, was thus drawing a parallel between the abortive Nazi revolt in Austria and the NSDAP's severest setback in Germany.

Von Papen records that his first meeting as German Ambassador with the new Austrian Chancellor and the President on 16 August had left him with the impression that he was 'visiting a churchyard instead of meeting German-Austrian statesmen at a ceremony of welcome'. On this occasion he had stated that 'The Reich Chancellor was not only determined, for the sake of *détente* in Europe, to respect Austria's formal independence, but he also recognised Austria's right to settle her own internal affairs independently.' Mixing apology with disguised threat, he added that the National Socialists' seizure of power in Germany was a revolutionary and ideological event and as such would inevitably have repercussions beyond Germany's borders. A frontier posed no barrier to the magnetism of a certain *zeitgeist* (spirit of the time). Nevertheless, he declared, Germany would from now on — and this he would vouch for — 'take all necessary measures to prevent Austrians living in Germany, or other agencies and persons, from interfering in Austria's internal affairs'. More than that Germany could not do, he claimed, in the interests of restoring normal relations. It was Vienna's responsibility to keep the peace within Austria. If the persecution and sentencing of National Socialists were to continue, 'fresh revolts might perhaps result', but in view of Germany's new position, the *Reich* must at this point disclaim all responsibility for any such developments. Von Papen quoted Chancellor Schuschnigg as saying that, despite his sympathies towards the German people, he was 'firmly resolved not to allow Austria to become a colony or province of the German *Reich*'. His new Cabinet was thus exclusively composed of ' "Austrians" in this sense'. He was pleased with the attitude the *Reich* government had adopted, but felt it remained to be seen whether this promise would be kept.[14]

The shift in Hitler's position had now brought him very close to the Foreign Ministry line on Austria. This is confirmed by his explicit endorsement of an internal policy document entitled 'Guiding Principles for German policy *vis-à-vis* Austria in the Immediate Future', dated 13 August 1934. In addition to the points just noted, this document contains the unequivocal directive: 'Easing of the atmosphere without false considerations of prestige. This entails the stopping of all aggressive press and wireless propaganda. The best thing would be for Austria to be mentioned as little as possible in the *Reich* for some time. . . .'[15]

Hitler's calculated sacrifice of the Austrian National Socialists, who had thrown themselves into battle shouting 'Heil Hitler!' and gone to their deaths with his name on their lips (the assassins of Dollfuss among them), was entirely characteristic. For the survivors he ordered the 'exclusion from the leadership of the Austrian Party of all persons compromised by having been leaders of the fight so far. Nor must such persons be "rewarded" for their "services" by being appointed to important posts in the *Reich*. . . .'[16]

Hitler's response to the failure of the revolt amounts to the most serious foreign policy retreat he conducted before 1943. In the years 1933–4, Dollfuss had repeatedly and obstinately demanded an end to National Socialist intervention in Austria and the severing of links between the Austrian NSDAP and the Nazi leadership and government in the *Reich*. Hitler's retreat thus represented a capitulation to Dollfuss' key demands. Indeed, it is not unreasonable to claim that Dollfuss, Hitler's greatly despised chief antagonist in Austria, had by his death emerged as the posthumous victor in the first trial of strength in this historic struggle for Austria and Europe.

European reactions — Rome, Paris, London

Mussolini was jolted by the National Socialist revolt in Austria and deeply shaken by the assassination of Dollfuss, who had been due to visit him the very next day and whose wife and children were already his house guests in Rome. He immediately discerned that the National Socialist plan to effect a rapid change of government backed by a nation-wide uprising was designed to present him with a *fait accompli*. But, as he had once remarked, he believed he commanded the one language that Hitler really understood and respected: he announced in an official communiqué on July 26 — while heavy fighting was still going on in a number of Austrian provinces — that on the news of Dollfuss' assassination, he had ordered open 'movements of land and air forces to the Brenner Pass and Carinthia'. These forces, Mussolini's communiqué asserted, would be 'large enough to deal with any eventuality'.[17]

On the same day Mussolini telegraphed his condolences to Starhemberg, the Austrian Vice-Chancellor, saying: 'The independence of Austria for which he died is a cause which Italy has defended and which will now be defended with all the more determination. . . . His memory will be honoured not only in Austria but throughout the civilised world, whose moral condemnation of this act has already struck home at those directly, and those indirectly, responsible.'[18] Those 'indirectly responsible' were Hitler and his henchmen in the NSDAP. During the same day, as Hitler was informed by the German Embassy in Rome, Mussolini had noticeably made a point of receiving his Under-Secretaries for War and Aviation, a number of generals, the British Ambassador Sir Eric Drummond, and the French Ambassador Count Louis-Charles de Chambrun.[19] The following day, the German Ministry of Defence reported that Italian troops at division strength had been identified at both Sterzing in South Tirol and in the Sarn Valley to the north of Bolzano. On 26 July, the divisions were issued with live ammunition.[20] To allay Hitler's agitation, von Neurath assured him that Italy could under no circumstances march into Carinthia since it would mean war with Yugoslavia.[21] The abortive revolt in Austria thus precipitated the most serious diplomatic crisis between Berlin and Rome before 1941 and severely strained relations between the two powers.

The Italian media reacted so violently to the revolt that the German Ambassador in Rome lodged a protest complaining about the 'open threats of violence' in the newspapers and the 'impudent cartoons' that were so insulting to the *Führer*.[22] Shortly after the uprising, Mussolini heatedly exclaimed to Starhemberg: 'There is no question that the National Socialist government instigated this revolt. There is no question that *Reich* Chancellor Hitler had Dollfuss murdered.' He described Hitler, Starhemberg records, as 'a despicable, sexually degenerate and dangerous fool'! Mussolini was at pains to stress that Italian Fascism, despite certain parallels, was quite different from Hitler's National Socialism; he, for example, acknowledged the rights of the individual, religious freedom and the sanctity of the family, while National Socialism embodied the barbarism of the atavistic herd mentality. But he warned Starhemberg that Italy could not continue to mass troops on the Brenner Press indefinitely without outside support. The other powers would also have to make a move; perhaps they would recognise the German threat, and it would be possible to 'organise a grand coalition against Germany'. There was no doubt in his mind that Hitler would arm Germany and go to war. 'Alone, I am not in a position to resist him,' he pleaded.[23]

In the autumn of 1934 Italy thus approached Britain and France with a view to issuing a three-power guarantee of Austria's independence. But the project foundered on disagreement over the form it should take. France envisaged a multilateral non-intervention pact involving all of Austria's neighbours and a League of Nations guarantee of Austrian neutrality. Germany was no longer a member of the League, which had demonstrated its impotence as recently as 1932 over Japanese aggression in China and its widely-condemned annexation of Manchuria. Italy proposed a French-British-Italian pact guaranteeing Austrian sovereignty, but Britain demurred, anxious to avoid binding commitments on the Continent.[24] The extremely meagre outcome of these proposals was a joint declaration issued on 27 September by France, Britain and Italy which stated that they had agreed, after reappraisal of the Austrian question, 'that the declaration of 17 February 1934 concerning the necessity to maintain the independence and integrity of Austria in accordance with the existing treaties continues to exist in full force. This declaration will also determine their joint policy in the future.'[25]

The secret Franco-Italian agreements signed by Mussolini and Laval in January 1935 were a product of their community of interest in maintaining the territorial *status quo* in Europe — an interest in which their desire to safeguard Austria's independence was a determining factor.[26] The two countries agreed to consult both with each other and with Austria should any threat to Austrian sovereignty require 'measures' necessary to protect its integrity. There was also a linked proposal for a non-intervention pact, primarily for Austria's benefit, to be signed by all its neighbours — including Germany — as well as by Poland and Romania. In the event of a renewed threat to Austria, representatives of the signatory-countries would be invited to attend Franco-Italian consultations on counter-measures.[27]

The so-called 'Stresa Front', set up on 13 April 1935, represented the last occasion on which France, Britain and Italy attempted to adopt a joint foreign policy line to contain German expansionism. The three powers reached agreement to 'consult on measures to be taken in the event of a threat to Austria's integrity and independence'. [28] On 5 May, Mussolini reiterated his concern to the other powers in a speech in which he described the problem of Austrian independence as a 'European problem' and thus also an 'Italian problem' but 'not exclusively an Italian problem'.[29]

Italy's natural self-interest in continuing to defend Austria's independence would almost certainly have led Mussolini into deeper involvement had his imperialistic adventure in Abyssinia not brought him into conflict with Britain. This clash was to drive him into Hitler's arms. It has been suggested that Italy sought to monopolise the role of Austria's protector, but this does not take account of the fact that it made a number of attempts to procure greater commitment by Britain, France and other powers. For example, two days after the Nazi revolt in Austria, the Italian Under-Secretary of State, Suvich, sounded out the British Ambassador on the possibility of Britain, Italy and France issuing a joint statement declaring that future encroachment on Austria's independence would be regarded as a *casus belli*.[30] However, Britain could not be persuaded to go beyond the point of stating that its position still accorded with the three-power agreement of 17 February 1934.[31]

Recognising that Italy was too weak to shield Austria in the long term from a rapidly rearming Third *Reich* without outside help (and this was admitted with remarkable frankness), Rome clearly endeavoured to obtain effective international guarantees to protect Austria. But shortly after the unsuccessful revolt, it emerged that those states with an interest in preserving peace in Europe were incapable of exploiting either the containment of Hitler by a new, self-assertive Austria or of comprehending the historic warning it contained. A combination of wishful thinking, disunity and irresolution were to lead to a policy of appeasing

the expansionist ambitions of the Third *Reich*. The policy was a dangerous one at the psychological level because attempts to induce Hitler to
yield in the interests of peace in Europe merely persuaded him that he
was dealing with pusillanimous opponents and thus strengthened him
in his expansionist designs.

8

EUROPE'S FIRST ACTIVE RESISTANCE TO THE THIRD REICH:
BETWEEN ANALYSIS AND PARTISAN DISAVOWAL

Implications of the 1933–4 resistance for Austria and Europe

As the evidence shows, Hitler and the NSDAP had decided to launch a 'general offensive' for the conquest of Austria by as early as 1932. Initially this was to take the form of a *Gleichschaltung* of Austrian political institutions, *de facto*. The primary motivation had very little to do with *völkische Gefühlsduselei* (national sentimentality) — as Hitler once put it — but was linked with the expectation of a dramatic enhancement of the Third *Reich's* geostrategic position and demographic resources. This enhancement was to serve as a platform for further expansion in Europe. Party members engaged in the offensive were instructed: 'Austria has the key position in the heart of Europe. Whoever possesses Austria controls Central Europe.'[1] Austria was small and weak and had no allies. Moreover, pan-German sympathisers were strongly represented among its political parties. To the National Socialists, Austria appeared to constitute the weak point within the post-war constellation of European states that they were bent on revising. Subversion of Austria's independence and integrity was to be the opening battle in a campaign to destroy the *status quo* in Europe.

Only very few active European statesmen of the time — Sir Robert Vansittart, Permanent Under-Secretary of State at the British Foreign Office, was one — discerned that what they were witnessing was not an isolated threat to the independence of an Alpine Republic but the first and unprecedented act in a large-scale effort to disrupt the peace settlement in Europe by violence. A successful assault on Austria, they realised, would be followed by further expansionist moves, with major international repercussions.

Hitler's 'general offensive' was launched in the spring of 1933 and consisted of four complementary elements: (1) a drastic reduction of both tourism to, and imports from, Austria; (2) a propaganda campaign inside Austria supported by German press and radio (now under National Socialist control); (3) a diplomatic campaign to isolate Austria

120

and undermine its integrity as an independent state; and (4) a campaign of violence carried out by Hitler's 'fifth column', the Austrian NSDAP, with the direct and indirect support of the Austrian Legion stationed on the Bavarian-Austrian frontier.

Harried by pressure from abroad and subversion from within, the Austrian government appeared to be in a desperate position. Another government clinging to power by a wafer-thin majority, without allies abroad and confronted with a serious domestic economic crisis, might have opted for capitulation by way of compromise in the face of a seemingly invincible adversary. But, after unsuccessfully attempting to restore normal relations with Germany, the Austrian government headed by Dollfuss — the youngest Chancellor in the Republic's whole history — prepared to do battle on all four fronts. Challenging both Hitler and his domestic opponents, Dollfuss did what no Republican head of government had done before him: he told the country and the world that he strongly believed in the viability of the new, small Austria and vigorously insisted that, despite its German cultural identity, it possessed unqualified rights to independence and sovereignty.

Although there was little in the way of earlier thinking on the subject to draw on by way of precedent, Dollfuss and his supporters managed, while handling this major crisis, to develop a conceptual platform known as the 'Austria ideology', a major purpose of which was to be in a position to confront National Socialism in the war of ideas. The principal concern was to refute the threatening Nazi accusation that Austria represented the last remaining German country to harbour the treasonable audacity to resist the all-embracing *zeitgeist* of Hitler's revolution heralding the new, Greater Germany. Since the idea of an Austrian 'nation' was foreign both to Dollfuss and to the electorate, he took up the idea of *Österreichertum* (Austrian identity). To him this idea embraced those attitudes and cultural values peculiar to the Austrian people which called for a political framework in the shape of an independent state. The 'Austria ideology' developed from this notion became a *leitmotiv* of Austrian state resistance to National Socialism. It was the precursor of the Austrian self-image which emerged during the Second Republic and has indirectly played a role in Austrian political thinking down to the present day. The new ideology, which with regard to Germany was sharply at variance with the policies of the other Austrian parties, served to emphasise to the international community the credibility of Austria's will to defend her endangered sovereignty. Based on Christian values and moulded by the spirit of Austria's past, the ideology also provided a springboard for a systematic refutation of National Socialism's violent totalitarian methods and racialist philosophy.

Fifty years later, it is clear that this critique was the first to expose those aspects of National Socialism which later came to be identified as the roots of its destructive character. Dollfuss and his supporters rendered the German people a signal service in drawing attention, loudly and clearly, to the extent to which National Socialism stood in crass antithesis to the ethical and cultural traditions and values of German civilisation. This was recognised abroad too. For example, the London *Times*, 30 July 1934, saw in Dollfuss' death proof of the existence of a German culture worthy of preservation. The critique of National Socialism advanced by its Austrian opponents anticipated by ten years much of the argumentation deployed, in more tragic circumstances, by its German opponents in 1944. Setting aside the dubious, failed experiment in constructing a corporate state, the supporters of the 'Austria ideology' were in some ways more progressive and farsighted than the other political parties. In rejecting the isolationism of chauvinistic nationalists and by taking up traditional Austrian concepts, they emerged as champions of the pan-European movement (a precursor of the campaign for European integration following the Second World War). The political leaders of the First Republic clearly conceived of their opposition to the Third *Reich* not only in Austrian terms but also in European terms.

On the diplomatic front, the primary objective of the government's defensive strategy was to frustrate what the National Socialists saw as the easy route to the conquest of Austria, namely the achievement of an understanding with Italy at the expense of Austrian sovereignty. Vienna was thus anxious to procure effective Italian support, but 'at minimal cost'. Dollfuss and his officials made confidential attempts to draw the Western Powers into more active support of Austria in order to avoid exclusive reliance on Italy. Dollfuss also emphasised the critical nature of Austria's strategic position in Central Europe and the need to strengthen its capacity to resist by granting economic concessions. These concessions mostly related to favourable treatment of Austrian exports.

But as Karl Renner correctly divined, the Western Powers had persuaded themselves that they could effectively counter the danger of a Berlin-Rome axis by pushing Mussolini forward into the path of Hitler's expansionist designs on Austria. On the international front, Italy, for its own reasons, proved Austria's principal backer and did not hesitate to make threatening military gestures in Germany's direction.

Well before their abortive revolt, the National Socialists, employing

novel methods of psychological warfare and engaging in more conventional terrorist activities, had reduced the country to conditions verging
on civil war. The Dollfuss government displayed great rigour and
determination in combating this campaign — so much so that by the
early summer of 1934, the NSDAP was having serious doubts about its
ability to hold out in the long term against the increasing severity of the
authorities' counter-measures. The effectiveness of these counter-
measures, coupled with Mussolini's refusal to distance himself from
Austria in June 1934, prompted the NSDAP to launch their lightning
coup against the Austrian government. This, the culmination of the Nazi
offensive, was to be the acid test of Austria's resistance.

The revolt failed when it ran into the solid opposition of the government, Army and police, backed by tens of thousands of volunteers.
Austria's agreement with Italy also proved resilient: Mussolini's military
signal to Hitler was correctly read and was probably responsible for the
cancellation of plans to commit the Austrian Legion, based over the
border in Bavaria. Foreign intervention — such as might have been
undertaken by the Little Entente, with inevitable international
complications — was made superfluous. Austria's successful resistance
to National Socialism and the solidarity demonstrated in the process
emphasised to the country itself, as well as to international opinion, a
determination and an ability to defend its claim to statehood. This
aspiration had now been sealed in blood. Hitler's propagandistic
portrayal of an Austrian populace clamouring for *Anschluss* and only
prevented from satisfying this desire by an unpopular minority dictatorship had not been without effect abroad: falsehood was now exposed.
The insurgents in fact received no support from the Austrian population
and failed to seize even a single provincial capital. 'The masses were
lacking. . .!'

Hitler had not only been defeated in this confrontation but also
personally humiliated — as his uncharacteristic reaction clearly indicated. Caught off-guard by Austria's unexpected resistance and Italy's
flanking action, Hitler turned his Austria policy diametrically around. In
a series of drastic and, in part, brutal measures against his own National
Socialist comrades, he broke off all further political interference in
Austria's internal affairs. 'Without false considerations of prestige', as
he phrased it, the propaganda campaign against Austria was halted. The
murders and bomb attacks came to an abrupt end at the same time.

Austria's effective resistance achieved at a stroke the fulfilment
of almost all Dollfuss' demands. A comparison of Hitler's original

objectives and expectations with the position he was forced to adopt after the failure of the revolt suggests that the defeat he experienced at Austria's hands in 1934 represented his most painful foreign policy setback until the disasters of 1943.

His principal adversary and the chief architect of Austria's resistance, Engelbert Dollfuss, had of course been eliminated; but even this could not be counted as a success — at least in the short term. The manner and dramatic circumstances of Dollfuss' death provoked a wave of sympathy at home and abroad which proved highly unwelcome to Hitler. The reaction of the London *Times* of 26 July 1934 was characteristic of foreign press comment:

Herr Dollfuss . . . will always be remembered as the Chancellor of Austria who, when called to lead the patriotic resistance of his country against the coercive attempts of German Nazism to assimilate it to the Third Reich, put up a fight of the utmost gallantry in the face of heavy odds. . . . [When] the Nazi storm broke loose. . . Dollfuss rose to the occasion. He was reviled and threatened by every device known to the Nazi propaganda machine. . . . But he stuck to his guns unflinchingly, declaring after a narrow escape from assassination that his motto had become *Jetzt erst recht* [Now with a vengeance]. With capable helpers he was able, not only to pursue the fight against Nazi lawlessness, conspiracy, and propaganda . . . with a vigour unlooked for in Austria, but also to conduct an intensive campaign and organise a wider following for the patriotic revival which he saw was necessary before he could hope to turn the Nazi tide.

In death more than in life, Dollfuss symbolised the Austrian people's will to resist. Karl Renner wrote of the impact of his assassination:

The victory of the authorities was complete. . . . The leadership of the victorious front honoured him in grateful devotion. The shock of his death publicised his cause and permitted the devious route by which he had risen to success to be quickly forgotten. He became a martyr and a hero to the reactionaries, and his prestige overshadowed that of Lueger and Seipel. He was buried beside Seipel in the 'Chancellor's Church', which became the Fatherland Front's foremost place of pilgrimage.[2]

His supporters and the press pronounced him a 'hero-Chancellor' and a 'martyr-Chancellor' whose trials and sufferings had opened the door to Austria's renewal and 'resurrection'. Streets and squares were named after him in many towns and villages, and plaques, chapels and memorial crosses were dedicated to his memory. The Fatherland Front encouraged the hero cult, as did the Church — after all, not many assassination victims in their moment of death call on God to forgive their assassins. But it was not this alone; in his lifetime, Dollfuss' remarkably straightforward and warmhearted personal manner had won him genuine and widespread affection among Christian Socialist voters and particularly among the peasant population. His death only served to strengthen these sympathies.

In Austria, the European implications of the successful stand against National Socialism were widely recognised. To the 'armed forces of Austria' who had rallied to suppress the revolt and thus disappointed Nazi hopes of passive acquiescence if not outright support, the new government addressed the following encomium: 'Your action and your sacrifices of blood on this occasion not only restored peace in our country but also preserved the peace in Europe. If the rebellion had succeeded, there would have followed not a new order but terrible chaos and very great danger of war. Your sacrifices have saved the world sacrifices a thousand times over!'[3]

The London *Observer* commented on 29 July 1934 that Dollfuss' death had been the historic 'price' paid for 'Austria's survival'. By his death he had 'unforgettably served both his country and Europe' and the cause of peace.

In the later European debate on ways and means of meeting the Nazi challenge, the combination of Austria's resistance and Italy's threatening moves served as a convincing example that united and determined opposition could be effective against Nazi expansionism. Austria's stand had, in addition, bought both for itself and for Europe a certain breathing space which could be exploited in anticipation of further expansionism. An opportunity had, at all events, been created. Why neither Austria nor the rest of Europe made use of it is to be explained by circumstances that lie outside the scope of this book.

How Austria's achievement was played down in a later era for political reasons

The victory of Dollfuss' fragile system over National Socialism in defence both of Austrian integrity and of the existing European peace settlement has benefited Austria to this day. It is therefore surprising and disturbing that historically-informed opinion in Austria today pays scant attention to, and indeed frequently disowns, the achievement of 1933–4.

In West Germany, all the parliamentary parties join annually in paying tribute to the members of the Bomb Plot against Hitler in 1944. No distinctions are drawn between the various groups of plotters in the light of their other domestic political aims. The Bomb Plot was heroic in stature but it involved a relatively small number of people, it came late in the day, and it failed. In France, members of democratic and anti-democratic parties and groups alike stand together at memorial services commemorating the Resistance Movement. Erstwhile Stalinist Communists are not excluded, despite the fact that, following the Nazi-Soviet Pact of 1939, they boycotted France's war with Germany until Hitler attacked Russia in 1941. This lapse was forgiven in recognition of their major contribution to the Resistance.

In Austria, by contrast, the political parties have failed to institute an appropriate form of commemoration for those large numbers of people who took part in the country's *successful* resistance to National Socialism and to whom the Austrian state and people unquestionably owe a great debt.

There are a great many reasons why this should be so. Chief among them are the Dollfuss government's violation of the constitution and abuse of parliamentary rights. However, historical analysis demands a fair and systematic balancing of the multitude of factors present at any important conjuncture: politically convenient condemnations of failings — and these continue loud and strong on the subject of the Dollfuss government — should not preclude the acknowledgement of constructive achievements on the part of those whose failings these were.

It has been suggested in previous chapters that it would not only be incorrect to hold the Dollfuss government *solely* responsible for the dismemberment of Austrian democracy but also unacceptable to evaluate the events of the time in terms of present-day political experience and conceptualisation — although the attempt is frequently made. The democratic system of the First Republic, which was very differently structured from that of the Second, had in fact destroyed itself long before the incident in March 1933 in which a handful of opposition leaders frivolously immobilised parliament — without meeting with any serious public protest. The Republic simply lacked a common commitment to state and country as well as general agreement on the primacy of the democratic process over party interests. Both the deep-rooted ideological and social gulf between the two major political camps and the failure to reach agreement on disbanding the private party armies betokened the fundamental weaknesses of the democratic system, as did the bizarre breakdown of the parliamentary machinery in March 1933.

This breakdown could of course have been remedied if the government had so desired, but its failure to do so was disconcertingly symptomatic of the organisational frailty of the parliamentary system and the general lack of confidence in it.

The year in which Dollfuss became Chancellor saw a dramatic sixfold increase in the Austrian NSDAP's share of the vote. In the following year, moreover, the German NSDAP demonstrated how parliamentary democracy could be turned to its own destruction, in particular by the toleration of 'useful idiots' prepared to extend democratic rights to totalitarian parties. In May 1933 the relatively small, but once significant, Austrian *Grossdeutsche Volkspartei* formed an alliance with the NSDAP. Spurred on by the quasi-legal victory of the National Socialists in Germany, the Austrian NSDAP proceeded to make vociferous demands for new elections, and in this were supported by the Social Democrats (Otto Bauer later conceded that this had been an error of judgement). The Social Democrats had moved a vote of no-confidence in the Dollfuss government and opposed what they regarded as 'national treason' when his government sought to revive the Austrian economy with the help of a League of Nations loan coupled with a renewed renunciation of *Anschluss*. In March 1933 the 'general offensive' of the NSDAP and the Third *Reich* got under way, while in Vienna the proceedings of the Austrian parliament ground to a halt.

Any head of government attempting to resolve a crisis of these dimensions within the framework of parliamentary democracy but without a working majority in parliament would have faced a daunting task. In fact it was virtually impossible for Dollfuss to obtain a majority without the votes of the non-democratic *Heimatblock*. This should not be read as an apologia for Dollfuss; rather it serves to point out the unsoundness of the claim frequently advanced today that the Dollfuss government wantonly crippled a functioning democratic system.

The repertoire of recent accounts of the crisis includes armchair exercises in constructing alliances between the right and the left for the years 1934 and 1938 on the assumption that they would have shielded Austria from the Nazi onslaught. The didactic intention of these exercises is laudable, but their validity is questionable. For example, Karl Renner's socialist biographer Jacques Hannak argues that the formation of a united front in Austria would probably have moved Hitler and Mussolini to reach agreement even earlier than they did to join forces to dismember Austria. In Hannak's judgement, the question as to whether an alliance 'could have helped Austria to survive' would probably have to be answered in the negative.[4] The manner of Czechoslovakia's demise four years later — with the tacit consent of the Western Powers and despite Czechoslovakia's alliances with France and the Soviet Union — points in the same direction.

Cooperation, however, requires more than good intentions, and a degree of mutual trust between the two main parties would have been essential. But for years the leaders of both sides had been slandering each other. Seipel had damned the Socialists as 'enemies of Jesus Christ' for their anti-clerical policies, and the Marxist 'reds' had denounced their 'class enemies' on the right with whom 'no alliance, no peace' was conceivable (Victor Adler). Seipel's historic coalition offer of 1931, proffered despite considerable misgivings, had been rejected by the Social Democrats a year before Dollfuss became Chancellor. The new government's basic concern was to secure Austria's long-term independence both in principle and in practice. But the Social Democrats, though they suspended their advocacy of *Anschluss* for the duration of the Third *Reich*, emphasised that '*Anschluss* with a free and peaceful Germany of the future remains our goal' (*Arbeiterzeitung*, 13 May 1933).

Dollfuss grasped the fact that only Italy was both in a position and willing — for reasons of self-interest — to provide Austria with effective backing in a major contest with Hitler. The Austro-Marxists were ideologically unable to accept support from this quarter even on a strictly pragmatic basis. But despite the many factors working against cooperation, leaders of both majority parties did intermittently put out feelers with a view to reaching an understanding. Radical elements in both camps, however, precipitated the confrontation between the Linz Socialist *Schutzbund* and the *Heimwehr* under Emil Fey. And this sparked off the courageous but ineffectual revolt of Socialist paramilitary forces against the government. The revolt was to beget another historical misconception widely current today, namely that the government, without provocation, used artillery against the insurgents' homes. In fact, the undisciplined behaviour of the Linz *Schutzbund* prevented the effective realisation of the plan of its Vienna counterpart for a surprise attack on the centre of Vienna. After Bernaschek's Socialist units in Linz had opened fire in defiance of the explicit orders from the party leadership, the Austrian government sealed off the city centre. In the confusion, the Socialist fighters retreated to their housing complexes to launch their armed battle against the Dollfuss dictatorship. The authorities responded by committing troops and artillery to besiege them. The misconception is thus an easily digestible oversimplification, but one which prejudices views of the role of the armed forces in suppressing the National Socialist uprising five months later, when it was not a matter of protecting Austria's form of government but Austria's very existence as a state.

Another misconception arises from the tendency to subsume the authoritarian corporate system in Austria under the collective term of 'Fascism', that is, assigning to it the same label as National Socialism and Italian Fascism. This is perhaps convenient shorthand, but it obscures radical dissimilarities which in reality constituted life and death differences for millions of people. The camps erected by the Dollfuss government to detain National Socialist and Marxist activists, for example, bore no comparison with the Nazi concentration camps. Not one person died in these Austrian camps, whose inmates enjoyed privileges similar to those of regular prisoners-of-war.

However, the Dollfuss government cannot be exonerated of charges that it violated the constitution, was sceptical of democratic values and conducted an experiment in minority dictatorship under the guise of introducing a corporate system. The half-heartedness and vagueness of its approaches to the Social Democrats must also be faulted, and the vengeance it meted out after the revolt of the Socialist *Schutzbund* condemned. Nine men were executed despite vigorous protests from within the ranks of the Christian Socialist Party. None of this can be lightly dismissed.

But it is also true that members of the government and tens of thousands of its supporters risked their lives — some, with Dollfuss at their head, sacrificing them — to fight and win the only battle for the survival of the Republic in its history. This achievement merits a legitimate place in the historical legacy of post-war Austria and Europe, to the same degree that the shortcomings of the Dollfuss government deserve legitimate condemnation.

Whatever view is taken of political leaders in the early years of the Second Republic, their readiness to learn from bitter experience cannot be gainsaid. Adolf Schärf, when he was Vice-Chancellor in the early 1950s, once observed: 'The miracle of Austrian politics is that today men are working together in the Austrian government who, fifteen years ago, were shooting at each other.' The ordeal of *Anschluss*, when even the use of Austria's name was banned, and the shared experience of concentration camps by many of the party leaders greatly contributed to this learning process. Richard Löwenthal once remarked with gentle irony that many Austrians had wished to become Germans until they finally did become Germans. . . . Historical experience from then on tempered dogmatism on both sides of the fence; the *Volkspartei* freed itself of political clericalism and the Socialists shook off Austro-Marxist doctrines of class struggle. Talk of the '*Ostmark*' and the 'hated name of Austria' disappeared. A leading Austrian ex-Communist, Ernst Fischer, neatly summarised the central weakness of the First Republic: 'The tragedy of Austria . . . was that the democrats had too little Austrian patriotism about them and the Austrian patriots had too little democracy about them.'[5]

It is to the great credit of the Kreisky era of the 1970s and early 1980s — historically and politically — that the Austrian past and the Habsburg achievement were re-integrated into Austria's historical heritage. However, the controversy in 1984 surrounding the fiftieth anniversary of the Socialist *Schutzbund* revolt showed that there has been no analogous development with regard to the history of the First Republic. There is little reason why historically aware and impartial Austrians, particularly young people unencumbered by the past, should fail to recognise the contribution of the Social Democrats to municipal development, the Socialist *Schutzbund*'s courageous stand, the roles of Seipel, Renner and Schober, and the country's successful defence of its independence in 1933 and 1934 under conditions of extraordinary difficulty.

The year of the Socialist *Schutzbund* revolt was also the year which saw 52,000 Austrians rally within hours to the aid of the government to oppose National Socialism. And it was the Dollfuss government's suppression of the National Socialist attempt to seize power 'from within' which underpinned Austria's claim to the status of a 'liberated' country as defined in the Allied declaration on Austria of 1943. The advantages accruing to Austria from this were manifold, not least in the area of international law.

The example set by individuals in 1934 also influenced the history of the Second Republic. In the autumn of 1950, a wave of Communist-inspired violence swept Vienna and the Soviet occupation zone. A revolt seemed to be in the making. As Communist strikers besieged the Chancellery, a security officer shouted out to the Chancellor, Leopold Figl (a concentration camp returnee), that he could no longer guarantee his safety. Other security officers urged him to leave. But he refused to do so, saying, 'Gentlemen, Dollfuss died in the next room, and I am not giving in to violence either. I will not leave this building; I would rather die. . . .'[6]

At an early stage of the four-power occupation, while Austria's status was still being debated, the grand coalition then in power mounted a campaign to secure for Austria the status of a 'liberated country'. Claiming 'justice for Austria', it published in 1946 a record of Austria's resistance to the Third Reich entitled the *Red-White-Red Book*. This was translated into several languages and given worldwide distribution.[7] On the central argument of the present book, it had this to say:

As in spite of all difficulties, in spite of the unequal proportion of forces between the aggressor and the attacked, and in spite of the absence of adequate diplomatic and economic foreign support, the Austrian Government, its executive and the vast majority of the Austrian people did not flag in their resistance against the National Socialist attempts at violation. National Socialism further augmented its terrorism, until it finally in the *July Putsch of 1934 proceeded to the first comprehensive attack* against the *existing European order*. [. . .]

The Austrian patriots killed in the defence of this National Socialist attempt are the first martyrs of the free world in the struggle against Hitler. The rapid breakdown of the 'Putsch' is the proof that not only the Austrian Government, but also the Austrian people, declined to be ruled by Hitler. . . .[8]

Is this evidence to be disparaged? It is the joint testimony of Austria's two major parties and the Communist Party. Its authors had all either taken direct part in, or been personal witnesses to, the grim contest with National Socialism which had seen the emergence of an unprecedented determination to defend the state and its independence.

Although there is clearly much to criticise about Austrian domestic affairs in 1933–4, it is none the less clear that those who supported the courageous resistance to National Socialism and fought and died for Austria in those years have been misrepresented and unjustly forgotten. It is to them that this book is dedicated.

NOTES

Chapter 1. The St Germain Treaty — An Austrian Tragedy

1. Rudolf Neck (ed.), *Österreich im Jahre 1918*, Munich, 1968, p. 79.
2. Ibid., p. 82.
3. Ibid., p. 86.
4. Walter Kleindel, *Österreich Daten zur Geschichte und Kultur*, Vienna/Heidelberg, 1978, p. 316.
5. Extracts of the German-Austrian minutes in Kleindel, op. cit., p. 319.
6. Hans Leo Mikoletzky, *Österreichische Zeitgeschichte*, Vienna, 1969, p. 71.
7. Ibid., p. 68.

Chapter 2. Austria — The Third *Reich's* First Target

1. *Dienstbuch der NSDAP Österreichs — Hitlerbewegung*, Ed. Landesleitung Österreichs der NSDAP, introduction by Theo Habicht, dated March 1932.
2. Hermann Rauschning, *Gespräche mit Hitler*, Vienna, 1973, p. 42.
3. Max Domarus (ed.), *Hitler: Reden und Proklamationen 1932–45*, Würzburg, 1962, vol. I., p. 312.
4. Adolf Hitler, *Mein Kampf*, Munich, 1934, vol. 2, pp. 737–40.
5. Ibid., pp. 471 ff. and 757.
6. Documents on British Foreign Policy, 1919–1939, 2nd Series (hereafter quoted as DBFP), vol. V (1933), no. 371, pp. 547 ff.
7. On Habicht's comments, see Introduction to *Dienstbuch der NSDAP Österreichs*, op. cit.
8. For this consideration of the German Foreign Ministry see *Akten zur Deutschen Auswärtigen Politik* (Documents on German Foreign Policy 1918–1945, Series C [1933–1937] — hereafter DGFP), vol. I., no. 256, pp. 474 ff.
9. Kurt Schuschnigg, *Dreimal Österreich*, Vienna, 1937, pp. 240 ff.; cf. also Franz Langgoth, *Kampf um Österreich. Erinnerungen.*, Wels, 1951, p. 106.
10. *Beiträge zur Vorgeschichte und Geschichte der Julirevolte*, ed. Bundeskommissariat für Heimatdienst, Vienna, 1934, p. 20 (hereafter *Beiträge zur Julirevolte*).
11. Minutes of this ministerial meeting in ADAP, vol. I, no. 262, pp. 486–90.
12. Dieter Ross, *Hitler und Dollfuss*, Hamburg, 1966, p. 32; cf. also Gerhard Jagschitz, *Der Putsch. Die Nationalsozialisten 1934 in Österreich*, Graz/Vienna/Cologne, 1976, p. 46.
13. DGFP, vol. II, no. 409, pp. 757 ff.
14. *Beiträge zur Julirevolte*, pp. 26ff.
15. DGFP, vol. I, no. 402, pp. 740 ff.; cf. also Jagschitz; *Der Putsch*. pp. 36 ff.
16. Theo Habicht, *Kampf um Österreich*, vol. 2: 'Die Rakete' der NSDAP Österreichs, Vienna, 1933, p. 13.
17. *Red-White-Red Book. Justice for Austria. Descriptions, documents and proofs to the antecedents and history of the occupation of Austria (from official sources)*, Part I, Vienna, 1947 (hereafter *Red-White-Red Book*), pp. 57–8.
18. *Dienstbuch der NSDAP Österreichs*, op. cit., pp. 178 ff.

Chapter 3. Self-Defence and the New Austrian Identity

1. Gottfried-Karl Kindermann (ed.), *Grundelemente der Weltpolitik*, 3rd edn, Munich, 1986, pp. 145–64.
2. Anton Wildgans, *Rede uber Österreich*, Vienna, 1930.
3. Quoted in Ernst Hoor, *Österreich, 1918–1938. Staat ohne Nation Republik ohne Republikaner*, Vienna/Munich, 1966, p. 75.
4. Hugo Hantsch, *Österreich. Eine Deutung seiner Geschichte und Kultur*, Innsbruck, 1934, p. 104.
5. Ernst Rüdiger Starhemberg, *Memoiren*, Vienna/Munich, 1971, pp. 85–97, 137–41 and 76–80.
6. Engelbert Dollfuss, 'Die kulturelle Bedeutung Österreichs für die Welt' (radio broadcast for the United States) in *Neue Freie Presse* (Vienna), 22 May 1933.
7. Kurt Schuschnigg, *Österreichs Erneuerung*, Klagenfurt, n.d., pp. 137 ff. (transl. from *Jour*, Paris, 18 Feb. 1935)
8. Engelbert Dollfuss, 'Die kulturelle Bedeutung Österreichs für die Welt', op. cit.
9. Ibid.
10. Schuschnigg, *Österreichs Erneuerung*, p. 146.
11. *Der Christliche Ständestaat*, 13 Dec. 1936, p. 1187.
12. Ibid., p. 1186.
13. *Kölnische Volkszeitung*, 23 Oct. 1932.
14. Ibid.
15. Ernst Rüdiger Starhemberg, *Die Reden des Vizekanzlers*, Vienna, 1935, p. 37.
16. Quoted in Tautscher, *So sprach der Kanzler: Dollfuss' Vermächtnis*, p. 88 (hereafter *Dollfuss' Vermächtnis*)
17. Said at a press conference in London, 12 June 1933; quoted in Edmund Weber, *Dollfuss an Österreich*, Vienna, 1935 (hereafter *Dollfuss an Österreich*)
18. Starhemberg, *Die Reden des Vizekanzlers*, op. cit., p. 74.
19. Schuschnigg, *Österreichs Erneuerung*, op. cit., pp. 130 ff.
20. Anton Tautscher, *Schuschnigg spricht. Das politische Gedankengut eines Österreichers*, Graz/Vienna, 1935, p. 27.
21. Richard Coudenhove-Kalergi, *Der Kampf um Europa*, Vienna, 1949, pp. 189 ff.
22. E.g. see *Dollfuss' Vermächtnis*, pp. 87 ff.
23. Starhemberg, *Die Reden des Vizekanzlers*, p. 37.
24. Kindermann, *Grundelemente der Weltpolitik*, op. cit., pp. 113–25.
25. *Dollfuss' Vermächtnis*, p. 116.
26. Ibid., p. 118.
27. *Neue Freie Presse*, 2 Jan. 1934.
28. Bundeskommissariat für Heimatdienst, *Unser Staatsprogramm — Führerworte*, Vienna, 1935, p. 31 (hereafter *Unser Staatsprogramm*).
29. Ibid., p. 29.
30. Ibid., p. 41. (See also Documents 24 and 29, pp. 164 and 167.)
31. Ibid., pp. 34 ff.
32. Dietrich von Hildebrand, 'Wahres Deutschtum' in *Der Christliche Ständestaat*, 1 Dec. 1935, pp. 1143–8.
33. Ibid.

34. *Unser Staatsprogramm*, p. 34.
35. Heinrich Mataja, 'Das europäische Problem' in *Der Christliche Ständestaat*, 17 Dec. 1933.
36. *Der Christliche Ständestaat*, 28 Jan. 1936, p. 79.
37. See Chapter V, below.
38. See Article 73 of the Constitution of the Federal State of Austria of 1 May 1934. Full text in Michael Freund (ed.), *Weltgeschichte der Gegenwart in Dokumenten, 1934/35*, vol. 2, Berlin/Essen, 1942, pp. 305–22.
39. *Dollfuss' Vermächtnis*, pp. 63–7.
40. Klaus Berchtold (ed.), *Österreichische Parteiprogramme, 1886–1966*, Munich, 1967, p. 430 (from Dollfuss' so-called 'Trabrennplatz-Rede' at the first general rally of the Fatherland Front on 11 Aug. 1933).
41. Ibid., p. 432.
42. Ibid., p. 433.
43. On Dollfuss' personal, professional and ideological background, see Jagschitz, *Die Jugend des Bundeskanzlers Dr Engelbert Dollfuss*, op. cit. This, in my view, is the most scholarly biographical work available on Dollfuss, of whom — despite general recognition of his significance for the history of Austria — no comprehensive biography exists. (The latter is also true of his successor, Kurt Schuschnigg.)
44. *Unser Staatsprogramm*. Bundeskommissariat für Heimatdienst (ed.), *Österreich Muss Sein!*, Vienna, 1934; Anton Staudinger, 'Zur Österreich-Ideologie des Ständestaates' in Ludwig Jedlicka/Rudolf Neck (eds), *Das Juliabkommen von 1936*, Munich, 1977; Rudolf Ebneth, *Die Österreichische Wochenschrift 'Der Christliche Ständestaat'*, Mainz, 1976; Heinrich Busshoff, *Das Dollfuss-Regime in Österreich in geistesgeschichtlicher Perspektive*, Berlin, 1968.

Chapter 4. Foreign Policy in Austria's Defensive Strategy

1. Lajos Kerekes, *Abenddämmerung einer Demokratie. Mussolini, Gömbös und die Heimwehr*, Vienna/Frankfurt/Zürich, 1966, p. 111.
2. *Dollfuss an Österreich*, p. 49.
3. Declaration of July 1932, in *Dollfuss' Vermächtnis*, p. 91.
4. Ibid., p. 90.
5. Ibid., pp. 86 ff.
6. Haus, Hof- und Staatsarchiv/Neues Politisches Archiv, *Hornbostel's Nachlass*, Fasc. II.
7. *Beiträge zur Julirevolte.*, op. cit., p. 19–22.
8. Ibid., p. 21.
9. Jagschitz, *Der Putsch.*, op. cit., p. 33 ff.
10. DGFP, vol. I, no. 173, pp. 318–22; cf. also Kerekes, op. cit., pp. 137 ff; Jens PETERSEN, *Hitler-Mussolini. Die Entstehung der Achse Berlin-Rom, 1933–1936*, Tübingen, 1973, pp. 168 ff.
11. DGFP, vol. I, no. 173, p. 322.
12. DGFP, vol. I, no. 346, p. 620.
13. DBFP, vol. V (1933), no. 233, pp. 395–8.
14. Ibid., no. 237, pp. 401 ff.
15. Text in *Beiträge zur Julirevolte*, op. cit., pp. 46 ff.
16. Ibid.

17. DBFP, vol. V (1933), no. 268, pp. 438 ff.
18. Ibid., no. 270, p. 445.
19. DGFP, vol. I, no. 385, pp. 708–12; cf. also *Beiträge zur Julirevolte*, op. cit., pp. 30–9; Jagschitz, *Der Putsch*, op. cit., p. 36.
20. Text of the official Austrian memorandum on the Dollfuss-Mussolini talks of 19/20 Aug. 1933 in *Geheimer Briefwechsel Mussolini-Dollfuss*.
21. *Dollfuss' Vermächtnis*, pp. 44 ff.
22. Ibid., p. 63.
23. Petersen, op. cit., pp. 197 ff.
24. André François-Poncet, *Als Botschafter im Dritten Reich*, Mainz/ Berlin, 1980, pp. 231 ff.
25. DBFP, vol. V, 1933, no. 371, pp. 547–59.
26. Ibid., no. 390, p. 586 ff.
27. *Documents on International Affairs, 1933*, Wheeler-Bennett and Heald, London, 1934, pp. 388–91.
28. DBFP, vol. VI (1933/4), pp. 254 and 256–7.
29. Ibid., pp. 154–6; cf. ibid., no. 541, pp. 748 ff.
30. Ibid., no. 332, pp. 524 and 528 ff.
31. Ibid., p. 772.
32. Arnold J. Toynbee, *Survey of International Affairs, 1933*, London, 1934, pp. 306–14; *Archiv der Gegenwart 1933*, p. 1089.
33. Reproduced in *Red-White-Red Book*, pp. 50 ff.
34. Minutes of the ministerial meeting of 2 May 1934 in *Protokolle des Ministerrats der Ersten Republik*, vol. 5: Kabinett Dr Engelbert Dollfuss, 3.11.1933 – 17.2.1934, pp. 533–45, esp. p. 537.
35. Ibid.
36. DBFP, vol. VI, no. 277 (14 Feb. 1934) and no. 280 (15 Feb. 1934).
37. Ibid., no. 286 (16 Feb. 1934).
38. *Weltgeschichte in Dokumenten*, op. cit., vol. I, pp. 252 ff.
39. Dieter A. Binder, *Dollfuss und Hitler — Über die Aussenpolitik des autoritären Ständestaates in den Jahren 1933/34*, Graz, 1979, p. 209, note 17.
40. DBFP, vol. VI, no. 164, (4 Jan. 1934); cf. also Petersen, op. cit., p. 294; DBFP, ibid., no. 194 (20 Jan. 1934).
41. Text in *Weltgeschichte in Dokumenten*, vol. I, p. 253.
42. Text of the concurrent secret agreements in Kerekes, op. cit., pp. 187 ff.
43. DGFP, vol. II, no. 333 (19 Mar. 1934), p. 636.
44. Ibid., no. 334 (19 Mar. 1934), p. 637.
45. Petersen, op. cit., p. 323.
46. Österreichischer Pressedienst (Munich), no. 51, 24 Mar. 1934, p. 3.
47. DBFP, vol. VI, no. 100, pp. 154 ff.
48. Text in *Weltgeschichte in Dokumenten*, op. cit., vol. I, p. 259.
49. Ibid., pp. 261 ff.
50. Ibid., p. 263.
51. DBFP, vol. VI, no. 194 (20 Jan. 1934).
52. Walter Hummelberger, 'Österreich und die Kleine Entente um die Jahresmitte 1934' in *Das Jahr 1934: 25. Juli* (= Veroffentlichungen der Wissenschaftlichen Kommission des Körner-Stiftungsfonds und des Kunschak-Preises, ed. Ludwig Jedlicka, Rudolf Neck, Munich, 1975, p. 61.

53. Ibid., p. 60.
54. DBFP, vol. VI, no. 328, pp. 514–17.
55. Ibid., no. 331 (5 Mar. 1934).
56. DGFP, vol. II, no. 316 (10 Mar. 1934), pp. 586–9.
57. Erwin Steinböck, 'Kärnten', in Weinzierl/Skalnik, *Österreich 1918 bis 1938*, vol. II, Graz/Vienna/Cologne, 1983, p. 820; cf. also Erwin Steinböck, 'Die Verhandlungen zwischen den Nationalsozialisten und jugoslawischen Stellen vor dem Juliputsch 1934' in *Österreich in Geschichte und Literatur*, vol. 12, no. 10, December 1968, pp. 533–8.

Chapter 5. Democracy in Crisis and Confrontation on Two Fronts

1. Kindermann, op. cit., pp. 87–8 and 109–13.
2. Neck, op. cit., p. 81.
3. Ibid., pp. 81 ff.
4. Otto Bauer, *Die Österreichische Revolution*, Vienna, 1923, p. 287.
5. Hellmut Andics, *Der Staat, den keiner wollte. Österreich 1918–1938*, Vienna, 1962, p. 300.
6. Ibid., p. 302
7. Ibid., pp. 302 ff.
8. Jacques Hannak, *Karl Renner und seine Zeit,* Vienna, 1965, pp. 504 ff.
9. Text of the 'Linz Programme' in Berchtold, op. cit., pp. 247–64. On the Socialists' stance towards the Church see ibid., pp. 258 ff.
10. 'Der Staat, den keiner wollte', *Neue Freie Presse* (morning edn), Oct. 18, 1927.
11. Walter Pollak, *Sozialismus in Österreich: Von der Donaumonarchie bis zur Ära Kreisky*, Vienna/Düsseldorf, 1979, pp. 95 ff.
12. Bauer, op. cit., pp. 159.
13. Shorthand minutes of the 134th session of the *Nationalrat* (Lower House) of Sept.14, 1922, 1st Legislative period.
14. *Arbeiterzeitung* (Vienna), 13 May 1933. See also Document 31, pp. 169–70.
15. Otto Bauer, '*Der Austrofaschismus nach dem Naziputsch*' in *Der Kampf*, August 1934.
16. *Der Kampf*, April 1938.
17. Ibid.
18. *Der Kampf*, January 1937.
19. Andics, op. cit., pp. 249 ff.
20. Ibid., pp. 208–21; Mikoletzky, *Österreichische Zeitgeschichte*, pp. 116–21; Ludwig Jedlicka, Rudolf Neck (eds), *Vom Justizpalast zum Heldenplatz. Studien und Dokumentation 1927–1938*, Vienna, 1975, Documents 1–4, pp. 283–88.
21. Pollak, op. cit., p. 190.
22. Karl Renner, *Nachgelassene Werke*. vol. II: *Österreich von der Ersten zur Zweiten Republik*, Vienna, 1953, p. 78.
23. Quoted in Hannak, op. cit., p. 487.
24. Ibid., p. 483.
25. *Arbeiterzeitung* (Vienna), 23 Oct. 1932.
26. Ibid.
27. *Arbeiterzeitung*, 4 April 1933.
28. *Wiener Zeitung*, 10 April 1933.

29. Schuschnigg, *Dreimal Österreich*, op.cit., p. 214.
30. Bauer, *Die Österreichische Revolution*, op. cit., pp. 290 ff.
31. Ibid.
32. Ibid.
33. Ibid.
34. Ibid.
35. Text in Berchtold, *Österreichische Parteiprogramme*, op. cit., p. 267.
36. Schuschnigg, *Dreimal Österreich*, op. cit., ch. VII, pp. 104–25.
37 Quoted in Hannak, *Karl Renner und seine Zeit*, op. cit., p. 563.
38. Otto Bauer, *Der Aufstand der Österreichischen Arbeiter*, repr. Vienna, 1947, p. 26.
39. Kleindel, *Österreich Daten zur Geschichte und Kultur*, op. cit., p. 341.
40. Ibid., p. 340.
41. *Dollfuss Vermächtnis*, pp. 44 ff.
42. Peter Huemer, *Sektionschef Robert Hecht und die Zerstorung der Demokratie in Österreich*, Vienna, 1975, pp. 150–6.
43. Ludwig Jedlicka, Rudolf Neck, *Das Jahr 1934: 12. Februar* (= Vol. 2, Veröffentlichungen der Wissenschaftlichen Kommission des Körner Stiftungsfonds und des Kunschak-Preises), Vienna, 1975, p. 17.
44. *Dollfuss' Vermächtnis*, p. 44.
45. Friedrich Funder, *Als Österreich den Sturm bestand*, Vienna/Munich, 1957, pp. 65 ff.
46. *Protokolle des Klubvorstandes der Christlichsozialen Partei 1932–1934*, ed. Walter Goldinger, Vienna, 1980, p. 133 (hereafter *CS Protokolle*).
47. Ibid., p. 210.
48. Ibid., p. 133.
49. Ibid., p. 136.
50. Ibid., pp. 153 ff.
51. Ibid., pp. 156 ff.
52. Ibid., pp. 183 ff.
53. Ibid., p. 212.
54. Ibid., p. 228.
55. Ibid., pp. 230 ff.
56. *Geheimer Briefwechsel*, pp. 37 and 32.
57. *CS Protokolle*, p. 271.
58 Gerhard Jagschitz, 'Die Jugend des Bundeskanzlers Dr Engelbert Dollfuss', unpubl. Ph. D. diss., University of Vienna, 1967.
59. Funder, op. cit., pp. 79 ff.
60. Huemer, op. cit., pp. 178 ff.
61. Ludwig Reichold, *Kampf um Österreich*, Vienna, 1984, pp. 101 ff.
62. Ibid., pp. 111 ff.
63. Ibid., pp. 112–15.
64. Ibid., pp. 115–18.
65. Huemer, op. cit., pp. 261 ff.
66. See Isabella Ackerl's excellent essay 'Das Kampfbündnis der National-sozialistischen Deutschen Arbeiterpartei mit der Grossdeutschen Volkspartei vom 15. Mai 1933' in Jedlicka/Neck (eds), *Das Jahr 1934: 25. Juli*, op. cit., pp. 21–35.

67. Starhemberg, *Memoiren*, Vienna/Munich, 1971, pp. 74–8.
68. Ibid., p. 80.
69. Ibid., pp. 87 ff.
70. Ibid., pp. 93 ff.
71. Ibid., pp. 94 ff. and 96 ff.
72. Heinrich Benedikt (ed.), *Geschichte der Republik Österreich*. ch. 3: 'Die Heimwehrbewegung', Munich, 1954, pp. 359–68.
73. Walter Wiltschegg, *Die Heimwehr. Eine unwiderstehliche Volksbewegung*. Munich, 1985, p. 415.
74. Starhemberg, *Memoiren*, op. cit., pp. 125 ff.
75. Ibid., pp. 130 ff.
76. Ibid., pp. 145–52.
77. Wiltschegg, op. cit., pp. 88 ff.
78. Kleindel, op. cit., p. 343.
79. See Kerekes, op. cit., pp. 87–161.
80. *CS Protokolle*, p. 271.
81. Quoted in Rainer Stepan, 'Dollfuss, die Parlamentsausschaltung 1933 und das Jahr 1934' in *Christliche Demokratie*, vol 2, no. 1 (Feb. 1984), p. 127.
82. *CS Protokolle*, p. 325.
83. Quoted in Hannak, *Karl Renner und seine Zeit*, p. 583.
84. *Geheimer Briefwechsel*, p. 35.
85. See Schüller's report in ibid., pp. 40 ff.
86. Ibid., p. 43.
87. Theodor von Hornbostel, 'Fremde Einflusse auf die Politik der I. Republik Österreichs' in ÖGL 2 (1958), p. 136.
88. *Geheimer Briefwechsel*, p. 32.
89. Quoted in Kerekes, op. cit., p. 158.
90. Renner, op. cit., p. 81.
91. Hannak, op. cit., p. 488.
92. Ibid., p. 485.
93. Norbert Leser, 'Ignaz Seipel und Otto Bauer' in *Geschichte und Gegenwart*, vol. 1, 12 April 1982, p. 278. On this question, see also 'Österreichs Demokratie am 19. Juli 1931', op. cit., pp. 52–62; cf. Wilhelm Ellenbogen, *Ausgewählte Schriften* (ed. Norbert Leser/Georg Rundel), Vienna, 1983, pp. 111–27.
94. Andics, op. cit., p. 346.
95. Shorthand minutes of the 81st session of the *Nationalrat* of the Austrian Republic, 27 May 1932.
96. Bauer, *Der Aufstand*, p. 24.
97. Ibid.
98. Quoted in Norbert Leser, *Zwischen Reformismus und Bolschewismus — Der Austromarxismus als Theorie und Praxis*, Vienna/Frankfurt/Zürich, 1968, pp. 463 ff.
99. Bauer, *Der Aufstand*, p. 25.
100. *CS Protokolle*, p. 212.
101. Hannak, *Karl Renner und seine Zeit*, pp. 584 ff.
102. Ibid.
103. *CS Protokolle*, p. 248.

104. Heinrich Schneidmadl, *Über Dollfuss zu Hitler*, Vienna, 1964, pp. 30 ff.
105. Hannak, op. cit., p. 603.
106. *Arbeiterzeitung* (Vienna), 27 Dec. 1933.
107. *CS Protokolle*, pp. 324 ff.
108. Ibid., p. 325.
109. *Arbeiterzeitung* (Vienna), 20 Jan. 1934.
110. Funder, op. cit., p. 128.
111. Ibid.
112. Hannak, op. cit., p. 587.
113. On this question see Leser, *Zwischen Reformismus und Bolschewismus*, pp. 149–67; Bauer; *Die Österreichische Revolution*, pp. 286–91; Schuschnigg, *Dreimal Österreich*, p. 214.
114. Renner, *Nachgelassene Werke*, p. 131.
115. Bauer, *Der Aufstand*, p. 14.
116. Funder, op. cit., pp. 138 and 136.
117. Quoted in Hannak, op. cit., p. 49.
118. Reproduced as Document 46 in Jedlicka/Neck, *Vom Justizpalast zum Heldenplatz*, p. 385.
119. Ibid.
120. Otto Leichter, *Glanz und Ende der Ersten Republik*, Vienna, 1964, p. 235; cf. *Ministerratsprotokoll*, no. 922 of 12 Feb. 1934 in *Protokolle des Ministerrats*, Part VIII, vol. 5, p. 580.
121. Kurt Peball, *Die Kämpfe in Wien im Februar 1934*, 3rd edn, Vienna, 1983, p. 21.
122. Andics, op. cit., pp. 431–7.
123. Bauer, *Der Aufstand*, op. cit., p. 19.
124. On the plan to employ tear gas, see Andics, *Der Staat den keiner wollte*, pp. 441 ff., and G. Brook-Shepherd, *Dollfuss*, London, 1961, pp. 140–3.
125. A confidential report by the American chargé d'affaires at the US Embassy in Vienna (Kliefoth) records that he and the US military attaché visited the buildings in question and spoke to some of the occupants. A number of women claimed they had been locked in their flats by government troops. The women are said to have expressed anger at being locked in their flats by socialists so that they could be 'used as a screen against attacking forces', but not against the socialist cause as a whole. *Foreign Relations of the United States: Diplomatic Papers 1934*, vol. II, Washington, DC, 1951, pp. 16–17.
126. Starhemberg, op. cit., p. 169.
127. Ibid., p. 171.
128. Kurt Schuschnigg, *Im Kampf gegen Hitler*, Vienna, 1969, p. 153.

Chapter 6. The Nazi Armed Uprising in Vienna and the Provinces

1. Rauschning, op. cit., p. 84.
2. Ibid., p. 86.
3. *Österreichischer Pressedienst* (Munich), 5 Jan. 1934.
4. Ibid., Jan. 13, 1934.
5. Ibid., Sept. 26, 1933.
6. Ibid., Nov. 8, 1933.
7. Ibid., Feb. 3, 1934.

8.   DGFP, op. cit., vol. II, no. 225 (26 Jan. 1934), pp. 431–4.

9.   Ibid.

10. Report on this: ibid., vol. II, no. 166 (8 Jan. 1934), cf. Starhemberg, op. cit., pp. 154–7.

11. *Österreichischer Pressedienst* (Munich), 8 Feb. 1934

12. Ibid.

13. DGFP, vol. II, no. 247 (10 Feb. 1934), pp. 466–7

14. Ibid., vol. II, no. 308, pp. 575–7 (approx. mid-March 1934; no date given in this document).

15. Ibid., no. 332 (17 Mar. 1934), p. 625.

16. *Österreichischer Pressedienst* (Munich), 24 Mar. 1934.

17. DGFP, vol. II, no. 369 (29 Mar. 1934), p. 692. See also Köhler's petition, esp. pp. 4 and 5, in no. E 452740 Archives of the Foreign Ministry, Bonn, G.A. II FM 29, vol. 2.

18. DGFP, vol. II, no. 409 (19 April 1934), pp. 757–8 and no. 431 (30 April 1934), pp. 789–90.

19. Petersen, op. cit., p. 349.

20. Ibid., p. 359.

21. DBFP, vol. VI, no. 462 (20 June 1934).

22. Petersen, op. cit., p. 359.

23. Renner, *Nachgelassene Werke*, p. 139.

24. See Franz Goldner, *Dollfuss im Spiegel der US-Akten*, St Polten, 1979, pp. 117 ff.; cf. also DGFP, vol. II, no. 328 (15 Mar. 1934).

25. Text in *Foreign Relations of the United States. Diplomatic Papers, 1934*, vol. II, Report from Messersmith, 21 June 1934, p. 28.

26. *Der Heimatschützer* (Vienna), 23 June 1934, pp. 3 ff.

27. Ibid., p. 4.

28. Report of the German Embassy (Vienna). Der Militärattaché no. Geh./ 246 5.6.1934 (No. E 452851, Archives of the Foreign Ministry, Bonn).

29. Confidential report by SS-*Standartenführer* Dr Otto Gustav Wächter. Text with commentary by Helmuth Auerbach in *Vierteljahreshefte für Zeitgeschichte*, vol. 12 (1964), pp. 200–18.

30. DGFP, vol. III, no. 17 (18 June 1934), pp. 46–7.

31. Rieth's exact words were: 'A similar effect might be achieved by the fact that Dollfuss, behind an innocuous façade, is attempting to reorganise the Social Democratic Party and its leader, Renner — who is hostile in the extreme to the new Defence League — in order, with the aid of France and Czechoslovakia, to be able to play them off against Italy, should the latter withdraw its support or not provide it in adequate measure.' DGFP, vol. III, no. 112 (23 July 1934), p. 226

32. *Foreign Relations of the United States, Dipl. Papers 1934*, vol. II, Report by Ambassador Messersmith to Under Secretary Phillips of 1 Aug. 1934, p. 42.

33. *Files of the Historical Commission of the Reichsführer of the SS: The Uprising of the Austrian National Socialists July 1934*, Vienna/Frankfurt/Zurich 1965. Reprinted 1984, pp. 71–8 (hereafter *SS Historical Commission*); cf. Jagschitz, *Der Putsch*, pp. 80–8

34. Rauschning, *Gespräche mit Hitler*, p. 13.

35. Ibid., p. 16.

36. Ibid.

37. Ralf Richard Koerner, *So haben sie es damals gemacht … Die Propaganda-vorbereitungen zum Österreich-Anschluss durch das Hitler-Regime 1933 bis 1938*, Vienna, 1958, p. 50. Outwardly, Rintelen remained in the Chancellor's party.

38. Quoted in Anton Hoch/Hermann Weiss, 'Die Erinnerungen des General-obersten Wilhelm Adam' in *Miscellania — Festschrift für Helmut Krausnick zum 75. Geburtstag*, Stuttgart, 1980, p. 47.

39. Ibid., pp. 47 ff.

40. *SS Historical Commission*, op. cit., pp. 71–9.

41. Ibid., p. 84.

42. Jagschitz, *Der Putsch*, pp. 89–98. Text of evidence given by Major Wrabel before the investigating committee and their assessment of it in Jedlicka/ Neck (eds), *Vom Justizpalast zum Heldenplatz*, Doc. 57, pp. 429–35.

43. Ibid., pp. 91–8.

44. Starhemberg, *Memoiren*, op. cit., pp. 196 ff.

45. *SS Historical Commission*, pp. 84 ff.

46. Ibid., p. 260; Jagschitz, *Der Putsch*, p. 106.

47. *Vorgeschichte zur Julirevolte*, pp. 64 ff; Jedlicka/Neck (eds), *Vom Justizpalast zum Heldenplatz*, Doc. 57, p. 425.

48. According to the autopsy report, extracts of which are contained in *SS Historical Commission*, pp. 171 ff. and 180.

49. Ibid., pp. 102 and 142.

50. *Beiträge zur Julirevolte*, p. 72; *SS Historical Commission*, p. 112.

51. *Beiträge zur Julirevolte*, p. 72.

52. Ibid.

53. Andics, *Der Staat den keiner wollte*, p. 471.

54. *SS Historical Commission*, pp. 109 ff. and pp. 128 ff; Jagschitz, *Der Putsch*, pp. 128 ff.

55. *SS Historical Commission*, op. cit., pp. 130 ff.

56. Ibid., pp. 202–6.

57. *Beiträge zur Julirevolte*, p. 77.

58. Anton Rintelen, *Erinnerungen an Österreichs Weg*, Munich, 1941, pp. 305–11.

59. Funder, op. cit., pp. 214 ff.

60. ibid.

61. The text of this revealing document is reproduced in *Beiträge zur Julirevolte*, pp. 54 ff. See also below, appended documents, pp. 352 ff.

62. Hock/Weiss, 'Die Erinnerungen des Generalobersten Wilhelm Adam', op. cit., pp. 47 ff. See also appended documents, pp. 248 ff.

63. Jagschitz, *Der Putsch*, p. 140.

64. Steinböck, 'Kärnten', op. cit., p. 821.

65. Otto Reich von Rohrwig, *Der Freiheitskampf der Ostmarkdeutschen*, op. cit., pp. 157–65 (cf. Steinböck, 'Kärnten', p. 824). On the official government account see *Die Julirevolte, 1934. Das Eingreifen des Österreichischen Bundesheeres zu ihrer Niederwerfung*, ed. Bundesministerium für Landesverteidigung, Vienna, 1936, pp. 56–61 (hereafter *Das Eingreifen des Österreichischen Bundesheeres*).

66. *Beiträge zur Julirevolte*, op. cit., pp. 88 ff.

67. Ibid., p. 93; cf. also *Das Eingreifen des Österreichischen Bundesheeres*, op. cit., ch. II, pp. 23–84.

68. *Der Heimatschützer* (Vienna), 11 Aug. 1934, p. 4.

69. *Beiträge zur Julirevolte*, op. cit., pp. 93 and 107. The best overall account of the fighting in Styria is in *Das Eingreifen des Österreichischen Bundesheeres*, op. cit., ch. III, pp. 87–128.

70. Ibid., pp. 166–72, cf. *Beiträge zur Julirevolte*, op. cit., p. 115.

71. Starhemberg, *Memoiren*, op. cit., p. 186.

72. This view is also reflected in the official National Socialist reports in Reich von Rohrwig, op. cit.; cf. Starhemberg, op. cit., p. 189.

73. *Heimatschutz in Österreich. Die Juliereignisse*, Vienna, 1935, p. 11; Ministerratsprotokoll no. 960 of 3 Aug. 1934, p. 7.

Chapter 7. Austria Staves off Hitler's Assault

1. DGFP, vol. III, no. 125 (26 July 1934), pp. 255–7.

2. Ibid. See also Documents 73 and 75, pp. 204–7.

3. Ibid., no. 186 (30 Aug. 1934), pp. 372–4.

4. Ibid., no. 143 (2 Aug. 1934), pp. 283–8.

5. Ibid., no. 115 (26 July 1934), pp. 236–7.

6. Ibid., no. 141 (1 Aug. 1934), p. 281.

7. Ibid., no. 149 (7 Aug. 1934), p. 293.

8. Ibid., no. 123 (26 July 1934), pp. 252–3.

9. Ibid., no. 151 (8 Aug. 1934), p. 299.

10. Ibid., no. 165 (19 Aug. 1934), p. 333.

11. Ibid., no. 222 (28 Sept. 1934), pp. 430–1.

12. Ibid., no. 173 (21 Aug. 1934), pp. 352–3.

13. Ibid. See also Document 84, p. 212.

14. Ibid., no. 167 (19 Aug. 1934), pp. 342–3.

15. These 'Guidelines' are appended to von Papen's report (see note 10, above).

16. Point 2b of the 'Guidelines' (loc. cit.).

17. Text in *Weltgeschichte in Dokumenten*, vol. I, p. 276.

18. Ibid., pp. 256–66.

19. DGFP, vol. III, no. 122 (27 July, 1934), pp. 251–2.

20. Ibid., no. 128 (27 July 1934), p. 259.

21. Ibid., no. 134 (30 July 1934), pp. 271–2.

22. Ibid., no. 132 (29 July 1934), pp. 268–9.

23. Starhemberg, *Memoiren*, pp. 204–5. Mussolini expressed himself along the same lines in a public speech of 25 May 1935.

24. Petersen, op. cit., pp. 365–79.

25. *Weltgeschichte der Gegenwart in Dokumenten*, 5 vols, ed. Michael Freund, Essen, 1944, vol. I, pp. 269 ff.; *Red-White-Red Book*, op. cit., pp. 52 ff.

26. On the secret agreement between France and Italy see *Survey of International Affairs 1935*, vol. I, London, 1936., pp. 107–18.

27. *Red-White-Red Book*, op. cit., p. 53.

28. Ibid.

29. *Weltgeschichte in Dokumenten*, vol. I, p. 273.

30. DBFP, vol. VI, no. 539 (27 July 1934).

31. Ibid., no. 546 (31 July 1934). In June 1935, a secret agreement was signed by

France and Italy which envisaged combined military countermeasures in the event of a German invasion of Austria. See also Petersen, op. cit., pp. 401 ff.

Chapter 8. Europe's First Active Resistance to the Third *Reich*

1. *Dienstbuch der NSDAP Österreichs*, Introduction by Theo Habicht.
2. Renner, *Nachgelassene Werke*, vol. II, p. 142.
3. *Das Eingreifen des Österreichischen Bundesheeres*, op. cit., p. 190.
4. Hannak, *Karl Renner und seine Zeit*, p. 552.
5. Ernst Fischer, *Das Ende einer Illusion*, Vienna/Munich, 1972, p. 89.
6. Ernst Trost, *Figl von Österreich*, 3rd edn, Vienna, 1972, p. 246. On the events of Autumn 1950 see also Oskar Helmer, *50 Jahre Erlebte Geschichte*, Vienna, 1957, pp. 287–301; Karl Stadler, *Adolf Schärf*, Vienna, 1982, pp. 341–6.
7. The aim of this volume of documents, presented to the public in the summer of 1946 by the ÖVP–SPÖ (Österreichische Volkspartei-Sozialistische Partei Österreichs) coalition government, is described in the preface as being to justify Austria's claim to the status of a 'liberated state' as defined in the Moscow Declaration. National Socialist propaganda, it maintains, had successfully depicted Austria as being pro-*Anschluss*, but the historical facts of the period 1933–9 reveal an entirely different state of affairs. 'During this time, the Austrian people wrote the first chapter of their resistance in blood . . . which was all the more momentous for the fact that they were forced to fight their battle alone.' *Red-White-Red Book*, p. 3.
8. Ibid., p. 26.

APPENDIX

DOCUMENTS

Part I

HITLER'S 'GENERAL OFFENSIVE' AGAINST AUSTRIA

1. Motives and objectives of the 'general offensive'

The foreword of the 'Party Manual of the Austrian NSDAP', written by the Inspector-General of the Austrian NSDAP, Habicht, begins as follows:

By a party order of 11 July 1931, the Supreme Leader [Hitler] has fundamentally restructured the party organisation in Austria. In place of six district directorates, each of which was subordinate to the administration in Berlin, there will henceforth be an 'integration of all Austrian districts to form a single organisational unit known as "Austria" and headed by the senior party official of the newly established regional leadership.'

. . . . In the Reich, the movement, profiting from the break-up of the bourgeois parties whose supporters were basically nationalists, was able to mobilise a following of nearly half the voters and line them up behind it before having to face up to an equally strong opponent in the November regime.

In Austria, where conditions are similar, *it faces an enemy three and a half times its size*, because Red and Black [the Social Democrats and the Christian Socialists] together command 78 per cent of the vote.

Thus any gains the party makes in Austria can only come at the expense of its irreconcilable opponents, and if it wants to win, it will have to recruit support from the enemy camp.

. . . . *Austria maintains a key position in the heart of Europe. Whoever possesses Austria controls Central Europe.* . . . Austria, dominated by France, divides these two natural allies [Germany and Italy] and bridges the gap between France and its Eastern allies. Austria thus represents a key link in the deadly chain around Germany. This is what gives our struggle for Austria its European significance. With this in mind, we enter the decisive battle — one against three.

Source: Theo Habicht (ed.), *Dienstbuch der NSDAP Österreichs — Hitler Bewegung Landesleitung Österreichs der NSDAP*, n.d. (March 1932 — Foreword dated 1 March 1932). Emphasis added.

2. Hitler declares his cold war on Austria

Extracts from the Minutes of the Conference of Ministers (26 May 1933, 4.15 p.m.)

. . .

The Reich Chancellor [Hitler]:

The situation in Austria today was one where 6 million Austrians were for the most part subject to the influence of the half-Jews of Vienna and the Legitimists. The Austrian Governments in the past had stressed their pro-Anschluss sentiments only when they needed more money from France. In their hearts they were hostile to the Reich. This would not change as long as Austria remained in the hands of her present rulers. If elections were held in Austria today, the NSDAP would emerge not as the largest party, to be sure, but certainly as the most powerful one. National Germany must steer an unequivocal course. He would therefore propose that the same method be applied to Austria which had brought prompt success in Bavaria. An accommodating attitude or willingness to negotiate on our part would be exploited by the present Austrian regime merely to take the wind out of the sails of the national-minded opposition in Austria. *Its goal is the expulsion of the idea of German nationalism from Austria and to replace it by the Austrian idea. There is great danger that Germany might thereby definitively lose 6 million people*, who are in the process of becoming something like the Swiss [*Verschweizerungsprozess*]. The Austrian Government had in recent times furnished enough grounds for us to take up the battle. Of course, this would have to be done in the form which was most adroit from the political point of view, that is, by issuing a statement to the effect that the measures against German tourists taken by the Austrian Government in recent times had unfortunately brought about a situation where the German Government, mindful of its desire to live on friendly and peaceful terms with the Austrian Government, felt constrained to inaugurate a visa requirement for German tourists going abroad, in order 'to preclude visits by German guests, not wanted by Austria, which might possibly lead to diplomatic complications.' Visas for travel to Austria will be issued only on payment of 1,000 reichsmarks. This measure will presumably lead to the collapse of the Dollfuss Government and bring new elections. Such new elections will result in Austria's internal *Gleichschaltung*, which will obviate the need for actual Anschluss. Italy's position on the Anschluss is entirely understandable. Her consent will have to be paid for with concessions in other areas. But this [question] is not acute at present because such consent to the Anschluss depends also on the agreement of the other signatory Powers of the Peace Treaty and is not to be expected.

. . .

The contest will be decided before the end of the summer. The sacrifices which Germany must make now are nothing compared to the sacrifices which would have to be borne if the development in Austria continued in its present course. The Little Entente was only waiting for the moment when Austria would fall into its lap. Italy, too, could not remain indifferent to this prospect, because Italy would likewise be threatened by such an increase in the power of the Little Entente.

Source: ADAP 1918–1945, Series C, vol. I, no. 262 (26 May 1933). Emphasis added.

3. Dollfuss' stance as seen by the German embassy in Vienna

Minister Rieth to State Secretary Bülow

Vienna, 1 July 1933

. . .

Nevertheless I was forced to note that the struggle which has been carried on here in recent weeks* with unprecedented severity has after all had the result that, at least at the present moment, Herr Dollfuss is not yet ready for an understanding with the National Socialists here, to say nothing of yielding to their demands. On the other hand, he would obviously like very much to restore peace with the German Reich. I believe, however, that after our conversation it has become clearer to him that the one would hardly be possible without the other . . .

However, a considerable effort will still be required to dissuade Herr Dollfuss from the illusion he still cherishes, that he will be able on the one hand with the help of the Heimwehr to suppress National Socialism forcefully and on the other hand to put through a constitutional reform together with the Social Democrats by parliamentary methods — he admitted this plan to me — which would in practice eliminate the Parliament and make new elections impossible for at least 1 year.

*Following a series of terrorist acts by National Socialists the Austrian Government issued a decree on June 19, banning the Austrian National Socialist party and all its auxilliary organizations.

Source: ADAP 1918–1945, Series C, vol. I, no. 346 (1 July 1933).

4. German embassy report on the potential danger of the 'Austrian Legion'

Minister Rieth to State Secretary Bülow

Vienna, 17 August 1933

Dear Herr von Bülow: In the top secret report of July 26, 1933 — A 918 — I recorded under number II (page 9) the rumor that an SA formation made up of Austrians was being trained and readied in Bavaria for use in Austria when the occasion arises, with September 6 being rumored as the date on which such an action would be launched.

. . .

Actually, however, a part of the National Socialists here counts on an intervention by this force that has been trained in Bavaria, especially since leading party figures here are convinced that the SA in Austria is too weak to prevail against the armed power of the State if the moment should arrive.

. . .

It surely requires no further amplification that the political repercussions of intervention — in case it should actually be planned — by an SA force consisting of Austrians, yet trained and equipped with arms in Germany, could be disastrous. One of the consequences that could certainly be anticipated is that the Austrian question would be raised on the broadest front against us, not to speak of possible military moves by other powers. Even a Hapsburg restoration might perhaps appear not impossible after the failure of such a venture, and it might then perhaps receive the approval of powers which might otherwise seek to prevent it.

Source: ADAP 1918–1945, Series C, vol. I, no. 407 (7 Aug. 1933).

5. Habicht's enticement of and threat to Dollfuss

Theo Habicht, Hitler's Inspector-General of the NSDAP in Austria, reported on a conversation with Dollfuss, among other things:

. . .

And in ending the conversation I said the following:

'Herr Chancellor, you have two opportunities of going down in the history of Austria and the German people — either as the Chancellor who helped a new era towards breakthrough and thereby gained immortal honour in the cause of the future of the German nation, or as the General Schleicher of Austria, who believed he could resist an idea with bayonets and in the attempt came to a pitiful end. You have the choice.'

That applies today as it did then.

And perhaps more so today than then!

Source: Österreichischer [NSDAP] Pressedienst (Munich), no. 13 (26 Sept. 1933).

6. From the appeal for support for the *Kampfring* of Austrians in the *Reich*

The German people find themselves at a turning point in their destiny and their history.

. . .

At this time of upheaval in the German nation, the Dollfuss government's policy of violence comes as a last attempt of the destructive forces of the past to prevent the unification of the German people and the fulfilment of their historical mission.

. . .

In this hour of great peril for the German people in Austria, we call the German Austrians in the Reich to battle.

. . .

Source: Österreichischer [NSDAP] Pressedienst (Munich), no. 25 (8 Nov. 1933).

7. The determination for revolution

The National Socialist rallies throughout Austria's cities and villages, mountains and valleys, are increasing at such a pace that it has become impossible to report on all the noteworthy manifestations of opposition by the Austrian National Socialists against the ruling system.

. . .

But patience is exhausted and the demand of *Volk* for *Volk* has broken upon all Austria with elemental force.

. . .

The revolution from below is in full swing, its victory is as certain as the collapse in ruins of the ruling system, that is only just kept alive by financial support from the world Jewry, the Catholic element in politics, and those foreign nations who are hostile to Germany.

Source: Österreichischer [NSDAP] Pressedienst (Munich), no. 41 (18 Jan. 1934).

8. International law not valid for the German-Austrian conflict

From a reply by the German Reich Government of 17 January 1934, to Austrian protests

It is not a question of a conflict between the two German states as such, which would come under the formal ideas of the law of actions which the Austrian Government sets forth, but of a controversy of the Austrian Government with a historical movement of the whole German nation.

National Socialism which has overwhelmed the population of the Reich with elementary force and which for a long time has subjected the German population of Austria to its influence, is being hampered by force by the Austrian Government in its legal development and free unfolding. It goes without saying that by the political frontier between the Reich and Austria the feeling of national afinity cannot be removed and the penetration of ideas which move the people cannot be stopped.

Source: *Rot-Weiss-Rot-Buch* (Red-White-Red-Book), Vienna, 1946, p. 57.

9. Hitler's threat to the Austrian resistance

From a speech before the Reichstag on the first anniversary of the Third Reich

If the present Austrian government believes that it is necessary to suppress this [Nazi] movement by applying the full powers of the state, this is of course their own concern. They must then, however, be prepared to accept personal responsibility for the consequences.

Source: Österreichischer [NSDAP] Pressedienst (Munich), no. 46 (3 Feb. 1934).

10. Hitler steps up economic pressures against Austria

Report by Counsellor of Legation Hüffer

Berlin, 19 April 1934

Landesinspekteur Habicht informed me this morning before flying to Munich that yesterday after the Cabinet meeting, he had again thoroughly discussed all aspects of the Austrian question with the Reich Chancellor in a conference lasting several hours. The Reich Chancellor had in conclusion stated with the greatest emphasis that he would not consider yielding in the Austrian question, even if the conflict were to last 10 years more. Above all, he had no intention of yielding to Italian pressure and possibly making concessions which the Austrian National Socialist party might regard as a surrender. And particularly, abolition of the 1000-reichsmark restriction or of the other coercive measures was out of the question.

The Reich Chancellor desired, on the contrary, also in the economic field to take all possible measures which might, without denouncement of the commercial treaty, result in a curtailment of the imports of all those Austrian articles of export which were of particular importance to the Dollfuss Government in its domestic political struggle. With respect to this matter, Herr Habicht had last evening submitted to the Chancellor the enclosed memorandum on the development of Austrian exports to Germany, and pointed out that for Austrian domestic reasons, above all, the exports of lumber and the buying up of the forthcoming fruit crop had to be prevented. According to Herr Habicht's statements, the Reich Chancellor allegedly entirely approved this request, and is going to speak to the Reich Minister of Economics today in order to have him initiate the necessary action.

Source: ADAP 1918–1945, Series C, vol. II, no. 409 (19 April 1934).

11. Austria's independence presents a danger to the *Reich*

From a confidential analysis presented to Hitler by the German military
attaché in Vienna, 1 June 1934 (Secret Doc. no. 240)

. . .

The only possibility for peaceful expansion lies in the direction of the south and the southeast. Control of Austria would fundamentally alter the Reich's position with regard to these areas. From then on, Czechoslovakia would be encircled. The path to Hungary and the Balkans would be free, and German-Italian cooperation, which might be desirable in the future, would become a possibility. This [conquest of Austria] would provide us with a point of departure for a variety of combinations. . . . An 'independent' Austria is thus not simply a hindrance to the Reich's defence, it is a positive threat.

Source: Archives of the Foreign Office, Bonn.

12. Habicht reckons with Dollfuss' imminent overthrow

The Inspector of the National Socialist Party in Austria, Habicht, to Counsellor of
Legation Hüffer

Munich, 18 June 1934

. . .

In the most diverse circles in Austria the opinion may be heard that the next few weeks may possibly already decide the fate of the Dollfuss Government. In the endeavours made to bring about a national development in Austria, Rintelen, the Austrian Minister in Rome, is once again the centre of interest. Rintelen is said to be expecting Dollfuss to fall soon after the Hitler-Mussolini conversation.

. . .

In this event — and this is being seriously discussed — Rintelen would form a provisional Cabinet composed of "Moderate Nationalists" and "Nationalist Christians" which would be authorized to hold an election after six months.

. . .

Incidentally, the Dollfuss Government are at present carrying on negotiations with the moderate Social Democrat leaders, in the first place with Renner, on the basis of joint action against the National Socialists and against the *Anschluss* of Austria to the Reich. The negotiations are supposed already to have led to far-reaching agreements in principle between the two parties.

Source: ADAP 1918–1945, Series C, vol. III, no. 17 (18 June 1934).

13. Bombing terror in Austria

Report from the National Socialist daily, Völkische Beobachter

112 bomb attempts in fourteen days
A confidential report from the Director of Security in Salzburg (from our correspondent in Vienna)

Vienna, 5 July

According to reports, 112 bombing incidents occurred between June 15 and 30. The following is a list of those that occurred in the last few days of the month:

29 June. A railway section between Mürzzuschlag and Neuburg. Detonation of a reinforced concrete bridge.

29 June. Regional bridge of Seeboden-Spittal detonated. The bridge collapsed into the river.

29 June. Bomb attack on the Elisabeth Bridge in Graz.

29 June. Viaduct on the Leitendorf-Hinterberg line seriously damaged.

28 June. Rail explosion near Vöcklabruck.

28 June. Rail explosion near Judenburg (900 schillings worth of damage).

28 June. Rail explosion on the Mittenwald line (2,000 schillings worth of damage).

28 June. Water supply lines at the electric power station in Kufstein (2,000 schillings worth of damage).

28 June. Salzburg: Market-place and country-house (considerable damage)

28 June. Three masts of the Tiwag works in Mutters (Tirol)

28 June. Tiwag works near Achenkirch (Tirol).

28 June. Bridge near Achenkirch (Tirol) bombed.

28 June. Railway near Ederbauer (Salzburg) bombed.

28 June. Railway near Steindorf (Salzburg) bombed.

28 June. Railway near Seekirchen (Salzburg) bombed.

28 June. Railway near Hohenems-Dornbirn bombed.

28 June. Railway near Bregenz-Lindau bombed.

28 June. Railway near Ebelsberg-St. Florian bombed.

28 June. Langenegger Bridge in the Bregenzwald burnt down (200,000 schillings worth of damage).

29 June. Salzburg water supply lines near Leopoldskron bombed.

28 June. Water pipelines of the Hall works in Tirol bombed.

28 June. Water pipelines of the Mühlau works in Tirol bombed.

The government claims, however, that Austria is the most peaceful country in the world!

Source: *Völkischer Beobachter*, no. 187 (6 July 1934).

14. The death penalty for criminal bombing outrages

Announcement by the Federal Government

Criminal elements continue to seek ways of hindering the favourable economic development of our Fatherland through bomb attacks. They neither respect public property nor are they concerned about human life.

The responsibility for the well-being of all honest citizens imposes upon the Federal Government the obligation of taking firm measures against violators who seek to hide their brutality and cowardice behind deceitful political slogans, in order to wipe them out once and for all. Calls for a return to reason have not been lacking. These have not been without effect. Many citizens who had fallen victim to the incitement have found their way back to a peaceful existence in society. There is a small minority, however, which persists in criminal activity. From this point on they will experience the extreme severity of state authority.

With this in view, a federal law for the suppression of political violence will come into force on 14 July 1934.

From that time on, the death penalty will be imposed on:

1. Those who, with the perpetration of criminal bomb attacks in mind, manufacture explosives, materials or equipment for bomb attacks, or obtain, order, possess or transfer these to other persons.
2. Those who conspire with others for the purpose of carrying out criminal bombings.
3. Those who associate with others for the purpose of carrying out criminal bombings.
4. Those who commit bomb attacks or murder, or attempt to commit murder, or through criminal activities endanger the security of public transportation or public utilities supplying water, light or electricity.

This law will be enforced without leniency.

Enemies of the state who, despite repeated warning, continue their criminal and inhumane fight against the Fatherland and against the life and possessions of the loyal citizenry, forfeit every right and every moral claim to leniency or clemency.

A final deadline for the renunciation of criminal acts is now offered to the guilty parties:

Anyone who possesses explosives, materials for explosives, or equipment for bomb attacks, or has access to such materials, and, at a time when their possession is still secret and damage can be averted, delivers this material to the authorities by 12 o'clock midnight on 18 July 1934, or reveals its whereabouts to them, will not be punished or prosecuted in any way for their illegal possession. . . .

With effect from 12 o'clock midnight, 18 July 1934, all guilty persons shall incur the death penalty.

Vienna, 12 July 1934   THE FEDERAL GOVERNMENT

Source: *Der Heimatschützer*, 21 July 1934, pp. 2ff.

Part II

THE 'AUSTRIA IDEOLOGY' AS A WEAPON IN THE STRUGGLE FOR SELF-PRESERVATION

15. Dollfuss on the historical character of Austria

From the Chancellor's radio address to the United States

It was with genuine joy that the Austrian government and the people of Austria received Roosevelt's appeal to the conscience of the world at large.

. . .

Austria, situated in the heart of Europe and the first to be affected by any conflict, has, more than any other nation, an appreciation of and immense interest in the problem of world peace.

. . .

Austria has a European responsibility. Lying in the middle of the continent, Austria is called upon to be the great mediator between Greater German civilisation — whose most ancient and noble pillar of support has for centuries been the Austrian people — and the other nations. It is precisely the companionship of centuries with other nations which has made the Austrian gentler, more tolerant and more open to foreign cultural influences, however careful he has been, and continues to be, to maintain his own culture and identity uncorrupted.

. . .

Austria is hereby making a conscious appeal to the other nations for understanding of its nature and its mission. Austria, this small, German, Danubian-Alpine country steeped in tradition, has for centuries played a decisive role in world events.

. . .

For a thousand years European history has been decided on Austrian soil, and for over six hundred years German Habsburg emperors ruled here in Vienna, from where they shaped world history.

The Austrian citizen is rightly proud of his country, proud of being Austrian. But *Austria also has the right and the will to determine its own future in freedom.*

Source: *Neue Freie Presse* (Vienna), 27 May 1933. Emphasis added.

16. 'The psychology of the Austrian character'

By Joseph August Lux

. . .

The crucial and indisputable aspect lies in the fact that a people is capable of producing a vivid image and ideal of its own character to serve as a model by which individuals and entire generations may mould themselves. The Austrian as an ideal and a reality is much more than a national political construct of a party: he is, rather, a historical and cultural entity of which every era has produced outstanding examples . . .

. . .

This is how he presents himself, outwardly unaffected, uncomplicated, simple and engaging. But this simplicity turns out to be something far more complex when we recall that the Austrian has co-existed with many nations and has assimilated them all into his subconscious memory. The synthesis of this has been his rich individuality, inextricably tied up with so many peoples and yet of a consistent distinctiveness that enables one legitimately to speak not only of the Austrian individual and the Austrian people, but — by virtue of its distinct culture and statehood — of the Austrian nation, too.

Such emphasis on self is not an Austrian characteristic as such; on the contrary, the Austrian is a victim of the very opposite, namely excessive modesty and self-denial to the dangerous point of self-irony; what is self-evident need not be articulated, and if it is, then it is not out of arrogance or self-conceit but almost invariably in self-defence.

But out of this self-defence something else has grown — the *revival of Austria's self-awareness as a state.*

Source: *Der Christliche Ständestaat*, no. 46, 21 Oct. 1934, pp. 5ff. Emphasis added.

17. 'Austria awake!. . . . God wills it!'

From Dollfuss' so-called 'Trabrennplatz' speech at the general rally of the Fatherland Front of 11 September 1933

. . .

Friends, today we have called the Fatherland Front to its first mass rally. In hundreds of gatherings, the words 'Austria awake!' — first uttered by me in Innsbruck — have been taken up to become our banner! And at hundreds of rallies, transcending party differences, the idea of unity, of Fatherland, of what unites us, is being proclaimed. Today the Fatherland Front is a movement and not just the sum of two or three parties. It is an internally independent, vast patriotic movement that is open to all who declare Austria to be their German homeland, a movement that places an obligation on everyone . . . to emphasise what brings us together, to reject what moves us apart and to belong to no movement which has as its aim class struggle or *Kulturkampf* . . .

. . .

If I did not cherish the deep conviction that the path we have chosen has been decreed from above to be the path of duty; if I did not cherish the thought that the newly-awakened love of country was again so strong that we can withstand all adversaries, then I would not have the inner strength to address you in these words and to lead the way ahead. I am convinced that it is decreed by a higher power that we preserve our home-country Austria with its glorious history, though diminished in size today. I am convinced that this Austria will stand as an example to other peoples in the shaping of its public life and that in Austria we have a great and invaluable service to render to *Deutschtum* as a whole . . .

. . .

We now go forth from this place in the belief that we have been called upon to fulfil a higher mission. As the crusaders before us who, too, cherished the same faith, as one Marco d'Aviano, who preached before the city walls of Vienna 'God wills it' — so we look to the future in full confidence and in the conviction that God wills it!

Source: Klaus Berchtold (ed.), *Österreichische Parteiprogramme 1868 bis 1966*, Munich, 1967, pp. 427 and 432–3.

18. Vienna as a bulwark Against National Socialism

From a speech by Dollfuss, 10 May 1934

Here [in Vienna] the Avars and the Turks ran into a brick wall, here Bolshevism found an impenetrable barrier, and here National Socialism will find its quietus too. This country has always been a bulwark of Christian German culture, and will always remain so.

Source: Anton Tautscher (ed.), *So Sprach der Kanzler. Dollfuss' Vermächtnis*, Vienna, 1935, p. 118.

19. Austria as the heart of Europe

From a speech by Schuschnigg before the League of Nations, 12 September 1934

We firmly believe that Austria cannot be evaluated purely in terms of its territorial dimensions and population figures, its economic capacity and military strength. Austria is, to my deep conviction, a part of living European thought, at once, as it were, an accumulator, a transformer and a conductor of the steady interchange of currents which flow from west to east and from north to south.

. . .

Source: *Unser Staatsprogramm — Führerworte*, Bundeskommissariat für Heimatdienst, Vienna, 1935, p. 57.

20. Austria as a messenger of peace

From a speech by Schuschnigg, 29 August 1934

For the new Austria it is a point of honour, in the interests of its people at every social level and in the self-understood interests of its European neighbours and the world, never to tire of proclaiming the will to peace, because we regard it as a matter of conscience to shield our younger generation from an incalculable disaster. And so, as ever, we proclaim to the world: Austria wishes to be able, by its own resources, to ensure that its freedom is respected. [Mariazell, 29.8.34]

Source: Kurt Schuschnigg, *Österreichs Erneuerung*, Klagenfurt (n.d.), p. 126.

21. Austria — representative of European universalism

From an interview with Schuschnigg, 18 February 1935

. . .

Austria's mission, as it has developed from its history, encompasses both German and the whole of European civilization. If we insist that our political independence be unconditionally preserved, we are not motivated — as certain circles would have the world believe — by particularist considerations. Through the centuries, the German-speaking population in the Danube area has been able to maintain its traditions intact while living side by side with multiple other nationalities within the framework of the Dual Monarchy. It is as a result of this that old Austria inherited the great principle of universalism on which the Holy Roman Empire once rested. The Austrians preserved the fundamental concept of a European community of nations based on shared Christian values.

. . .

Without going so far as to suggest that Austria is the nucleus of a new European solidarity, we cannot, however, shut our eyes to the fact that Austria is an element of Europe that is not only prepared but also more than capable of organising and stabilising our part of the world. The fact that the guiding principles we hold before us are in perfect accord with the exigencies of the moment gives us the courage to continue on this path.

Source: *Jour* (Paris), 18 Feb. 1935.

22. Austria and the destiny of Europe

From a speech by Prince Starhemberg, 5 January 1935

In Austria we are fighting for our freedom and independence, for a state as we envisage it, for something which may only be recognised in centuries to come: *We are fighting for a new Europe. The decision will fall in Austria as to whether Europe passes through a period of peaceful reconstruction or whether a world war devastates its nations and destroys its civilisation.* This is the goal we are pursuing on Austrian soil by championing the cause of Austria's honour, freedom and independence and Austria's influence on the affairs of the world.

Source: Ernst Rüdiger Starhemberg, *Die Reden* (ed.) Österreichischer Bundespressedienst, Vienna, 1935, pp. 73ff. Emphasis added.

23. For us there will be no *Anschluss*!

From a speech by Prince Starhemberg, 9 December 1934

. . . Austria is a concept of the past, the present and the future. It is not just a by-product of the peace settlements. For us, Austria must remain independent and autonomous, even at such a time as Berlin might have the power to bring about *Anschluss* of Austria with Germany. For us there will be no *Anschluss* because we know that *Anschluss* means nothing other than the degrading of Austria to the status of a colony of Prussian Berlin.

Source: Ernst Rüdiger Starhemberg, *Die Reden* (ed.) Österreichischer Bundespressedienst, Vienna, 1935, p. 37.

Part III

THE AUSTRIAN CRITIQUE OF NATIONAL SOCIALISM

24. Anyone who is not against it is an accomplice

Dollfuss on National Socialism in the month before his death

'Draw the line! I am appealing to all "decidedly national" circles and ask them: Do you really want to have anything in common with this gangsterism? I appeal to you, wholeheartedly and unambiguously, to draw the line at their methods and at the philosophy that makes these methods possible. Only one thing can be said about these methods, and it is this: "I am against them." Anyone who cannot unequivocally say this is an accomplice. We wish all those who want to serve this German country as their independent fatherland to be united in the patriotic movement.'

Source: *Unser Staatsprogramm — Führerworte*, Bundeskommissariat für Heimatdienst, Vienna, 1935, p. 41. The above is extracted from a speech given at a patriotic rally in Mauer, near Vienna, 17 June 1934.

25. Against National Socialism and anti-Semitism

From a joint pastoral letter of the Austrian Bishops denouncing National Socialism

We oppose the ideology of National Socialism on the basis of four fundamental truths:

First basic truth: Mankind is a homogeneous family that thrives on justice and love. We therefore condemn National Socialism's racial madness, which leads, as it must, to hatred between races and conflict between peoples; for this reason we also reject the unchristian sterilisation laws, which stand in irreconcilable contradiction to natural law and Catholicism.

Second basic truth: True Christian nationalism is divinely sanctioned and has the blessing of the Church, because it is in the nature of man to love his own people and to be devoted to his fatherland. That is why we preach the virtue of Christian patriotism, condemn betrayal of the fatherland, and deplore racial anti-semitism.

Third basic truth: Nation and state are not equal; the state comes before the nation. That is why we reject the extremes of the principle of nationalism, defend the historically anchored rights of our fatherland and welcome the cultivation of the Austrian idea.

164

Fourth basic truth: Above nationalism of any kind stands religion, which is not national but supranational. Religion has the power to ennoble every nation, and is therefore a blessing for all peoples. It is the origin of true civilisation and the vehicle of its advancement among every nation. But it is not confined to any particular nation; its mission is to spread the Gospel to all peoples and at the same time to help create well-being on earth. That is why we condemn all those ideas and endeavours which would unavoidably lead to the establishment of a national church and ultimately to an open break with the Catholic Church.

Source: Unser Staatsprogramm — Führerworte, Bundeskommissariat für Heimatdienst, Vienna, 1935, pp. 34ff. The above was read at Christmas 1933 from the pulpits of all Catholic churches in Austria. In 1935, these excerpts were incorporated in full into the party platform of the ruling Fatherland Front, which thus became Europe's first governing party to include an explicit denunciation of racism and anti-Semitism in its official platform.

26. U.S. evaluation of the Bishops' stand for Dollfuss and against National Socialism

The Minister in Austria (Earle) to the Secretary of State

Vienna, 23 December 1933 — noon
[Received 23 December — 11.20 a.m.]

72. On December 5th all Catholic clergy in Austria were ordered by the Church to withdraw from active politics. This action was interpreted by the critics of Dollfuss as meaning that the Church feared a rising tide of Nazism. Tomorrow the Church clarifies this situation by the issuance of a Christmas pastoral letter in which it comes out solidly:

1st, supporting the Dollfuss regime;

2nd, condemning Nazism because it (*a*) works with measures inconsistent with the principles of Christianity (*b*) fails to promote peace and international understanding and (*c*) promotes race hatred and international discord;

3rd, condemning anti-Semitism;

4th, placing blame on Germany for Austro-German strained relations.

Inasmuch as Catholicism embraces 90 per cent of Austrian population this action is most significant. It greatly strengthens Dollfuss' position.

EARLE

Source: Foreign Relations of the United States, Diplomatic Papers, vol. II, Washington, DC, 1951, p. 5.

27. Against terror and *Anschluss*

From Dollfuss' New Year message, 31 December 1933

The struggle against National Socialist terror. . . . The National Socialist movement was of the opinion that the conflict between the government and the Marxist opposition party presented a suitable juncture at which to enforce a participation in affairs of state which went far beyond its factual significance in Austria. When this was refused with calm resolution, there began seemingly unorganised acts of terror which, as it turned out, were carefully planned, and external pressure of an intensity unknown in recent years and accompanied by incitement, abuse of the responsible leaders of the state, and even official reprisals.

In the interests of the peace-loving population, it was necessary for the government to meet the raw violence of terror with the full force of the law.

The National Socialists' struggle against Austria, which initially confined itself to promises such as that of interest-free loans and so on, developed more and more into a systematic campaign towards the integration of Austria into the Third Reich and thereby into an attack on Austria's independence as a state; this became increasingly perceptible both within Austria and abroad. It was in this way that the value of sovereignty, the right to self-determination and commitment to their historical past became firmly implanted in the Austrians' conscience: Austria, the Fatherland, became the very essence of the lives of millions of this beautiful country's citizens . . .

. . .

As in the old year, so in the new year, neither I nor my friends will be diverted by intimidation, insults and threats to our lives from that path of duty which we see to be right.

Source: *Neue Freie Presse*, no. 14894 (2 Jan. 1934).

28. National Socialism — a contradiction of true *Deutschtum*

. . .

Can one conceive of an ethos or a mentality that is more contrary to the great spirituality and quiet depth of this noble German character than the loud, propagandistic, aspiritual conduct of National Socialism, its mechanical enforcement of conformity in all aspects of life, and its disavowal of German traditions and German culture, in which 'Goethe counts for less than the most trivial poet of the German war of independence'?

. . .

The surge of National Socialism, right down the line, from its deification of race to its mechanical unitarianism, from its rejection of German history and tradition to its obtrusive ethos so full of outrageous hubris, is a tidal wave beating against the German character and German culture, a corruption of German life and traditions such as history has never before witnessed.

That is Austria's great German mission at this hour: to be the refuge of true *Deutschtum* of the German spirit and German tradition, which are outlawed and denied in Germany today.

Austria, once the head of the Holy Roman Empire of the German nation, is now called upon to be the custodian of the spirit of the German nation. In holding back the tidal wave of National Socialism, it is not only doing an inestimable service to *Deutschtum* in its splendid Austrian manifestation, but also to *Deutschtum* as a whole. It is preserving Germany's honour in its own eyes and in the eyes of the world. It is an oasis in which the German genius may freely flourish, and it proves to the world that true *Deutschtum* lives on; for *Deutschtum* and National Socialism cannot be equated — indeed, they are a profound contradiction in terms. It is from Austria that a future Germany, having freed itself from National Socialism, will have to draw its life-blood.

Source: *Österreichs Sendung*. *Dietrich von Hildebrand*, Christlicher Ständestaat, k, Vienna, I/i, 33.12.1903, pp. 3ff.

29. Dollfuss on the struggle against National Socialism

If today our big brother intentionally or unintentionally misunderstands us — we have only ever defended ourselves, we have never been the aggressor! (Vienna, 11 September 1933)

For me the struggle against National Socialism is not first and foremost a struggle against a political party striving to gain power. For me the struggle against National Socialism is a struggle against a false ideology! (Vienna, 29 January 1930)

We intend, at a time when the world stands in horror of a certain kind of *Deutschtum*, to show the world that we are the standard-bearers of traditional, Christian, German civilisation. (Dornbirn, 29 June 1933)

We are convinced that this German people in the Alpine region and on the Danube must today, where *Deutschtum* is shaken through by a serious crisis, remain an island on which old Christian German culture is preserved. (St. Pölten, 9 July 1933)

Those who believe that they can overthrow the government through their acts of terror from within and without are mistaken. We have hardly begun to draw on the means of power that we have at our disposal. But if it becomes necessary to preserve peace in our country, then we will not hesitate to resort to extreme measures. (Hollabrunn, 25 June 1933)

Source: Anton Tautscher (ed.), *So sprach der Kanzler. Dollfuss' Vermächtnis*, Vienna, 1935, pp. 105, 119, 89, 89, 118.

We will only have peace, and relations with Germany will only be normalised, when the National Socialist movement has disappeared from Austria.

Source: *Unser Staatsprogramm — Führerworte*, Bundeskommissariat für Heimatdienst, Vienna, 1935, p. 36.

30. Austria, the 'last warning voice of *Deutschtum*'

Anti-Nazi demonstration at Hitler's birthplace

The entire border town of Braunau was a sea of flags: the red, white and red and green and white flags could be seen everywhere — *Heimatschutz*, Ostmark Battle Corps, *Freiheitsbund* — in a word, all loyal defence forces bore witness that the Fatherland Front, united behind Dollfuss and Starhemberg, is the surest guarantee of an independent Austria and at the same time constitutes the cornerstone of our young state. Many thousands of men and women came from the border areas, and here, in this border town, on Adolf Hitler's name-day, pledged their allegiance to their country.

. . .

Provincial Governor Dr Gleissner, who was greeted with long, thunderous applause, then declared:

'Nothing separates us from our brothers on the other side of the [River] Inn. Our whole way of feeling is German. But historical experience tells us that we must preserve this German people here. We German-Austrians are the last warning voice of *Deutschtum* trying to prevent another iron wall being built around the German people that would keep them down again for a hundred years.'

. . .

Federal Leader Starhemberg [of the *Heimatschutz*], greeted with loud applause, declared:

'It is a sad sign of our times that we are forced to hold a borderland demonstration against the Third Reich here at the border, that . . . after so many centuries of a common past, after so many centuries of duty to the nation in Austria, the German River Inn should form a frontier between, as it were, two varieties of *Deutschtum*, between an independent, autonomous Austria and a *Deutschtum* which, under its national flag, has become equal to Bolshevism.

'What dominates the German Reich today, if not in name then certainly in deed, is nothing other than the Bolshevism of the Germanic race, the kind of Bolshevism that can exist within the context of *Deutschtum*. . . .

'That is why our fight against this terrorism under a national flag is not just a fight on behalf of objectives specific to this government alone; our fight against National Socialism is a struggle for Germandom itself, in the interests of the entire German people. . . .

'By no means do we feel we are in a weak position; on the contrary, we are determined to fight with the same weapons as are being used against us. . . .

'Self-defence is the only way!' (Long, tumultuous cheering.) 'There are times when reports to the authorities are of no help, when the fight cannot even be fought with the weapons of the Army or with machine-guns, there are times when drastic measures are called for. These times have come, and we are determined to make abundant use of the right which accrues to every people, namely the right to defend oneself and to resort to emergency action if need be. There's no time to be lost when danger is imminent. We should rather hit back in a most direct manner!. . . .

'We do not believe it is necessary to avenge things of the past. I would like to make it quite clear that I feel we should make our peace with all the combatants who opposed us in the February uprising, provided they are prepared to stand down from their inane attempts to spread their Marxist ideas. *Austria can only be rebuilt when those workers who have until now been organised along Marxist lines are to be found in the ranks of the population loyal to the fatherland. . . .*'

After the speeches by the Federal Leader Starhemberg and Provincial Governor Dr Gleissner, both of whom spoke out sharply against the National Socialist acts of terror, thousands of hands were raised in the solemn oath: *Austria for the Austrians!*

Source: *Der Heimatschützer*, no. 25, 23 June 1934, pp. 3ff. Emphasis added.

31. *Anschluss*, yes; Hitler and the Habsburgs, no

From a policy declaration by the Austro-Marxists, May 1933

. . . . When in October 1918 . . . German-Austria, deprived of the basis of its economic existence and threatened by the gravest dangers, found itself isolated, Social Democracy declared *Anschluss* with the German Reich to be the aim of the German-Austrian people.

. . .

We have been striving for *Anschluss* with the German [Weimar] Republic — but we reject *Anschluss* with a fascist prison.

. . .

Anschluss with a free and peaceful Germany of the future remains our goal; any endeavours to bring about *Anschluss* of Austria with the fascist and nationalist Germany of today will be opposed by us as a danger to the freedom of the Austrian people and to peace in Europe.

. . .

We want German-Austria to be a sanctuary of German freedom, German democracy, of the unencumbered development of German literature and

German civilisation, but above all of the German workers' movement and German socialism, too, until such a time when the whole of Greater Germany is free again.

We shall oppose any restoration of Habsburg rule just as we shall steadfastly resist subjugation to Hitler's tyranny.

Source: Arbeiterzeitung (Vienna), 13 May 1933. Emphasis added.

32. Austria's self-defence and the European peace

From a press conference with Prince Starhemberg, 10 August 1934

It goes without saying that the knowledge that National Socialism in Austria does not in any way represent a nationwide movement is of great comfort to us and a boost to our confidence. Beyond this, we are able to witness the steady growth of an unmistakably Austrian patriotic awareness, a desire on the part of Austria to assert itself. Chancellor Dollfuss' tragic death has brought about a remarkable reaction. Wide circles among the loyal population are being driven by the fervent determination to defend Austria to their last dying breath against any kind of *Gleichschaltung* and against National Socialism in any form. The proud acceptance of what is seen to be a European mission is fast gaining ground. Let it not be interpreted as Austrian presumption or arrogance when we say that we believe *the preservation of an independent Austria is a fundamental guarantee of the preservation of world peace*.

Source: Ernst Rüdiger Starhemberg, *Die Reden* (ed.), Österreichischer Pressedienst, Vienna, 1935, p. 25. Emphasis added.

Part IV

RESISTANCE ON THE FOREIGN POLICY FRONT

33. Basic foreign policy declarations by Chancellor Dollfuss, 1932–1934

(a) The Geneva Protocol guarantees the safety of Austria and Austria's sovereignty in the face of efforts to enmesh it, against its will, in political and economic entanglements. (Vienna, 28 July 1932)

(b). . . . I have every confidence that we are a country with a viable future, and it is in this deep conviction that I have undertaken to conduct Austria's affairs of state. But the path to liberation is a hard and stony one. We are of the firm conviction that our people have a future. (3 Sept. 1932)

(c) Austrian politics essentially consists of foreign policy. This is to be explained by Austria's central position in Europe and the fact that it borders on six states whose political and economic development have as much bearing on Austria as developments in Austria have on its neighbouring states. (Vienna 7 April 1933)

(d) Our foreign policy can have but one goal: to ensure our independence on all sides and to see to it that we alone determine the future destiny of our country. (Salzburg, 6 May 1933)

(e) Our honour, our freedom, Austria's independence, are unnegotiable facts; they are, and must continue to be, absolute conditions. (Grossmugl, 29 October 1933)

(f) We believe that, by maintaining our independence and striving for economic recovery, we are serving a cause far beyond our borders — that of union and peace in Europe. (Vienna, 7 December 1933)

(g) We are not an object of politics, we are a subject! Those days when we were deeply anxious of what might happen if the freedom of this country were indeed violated are well and truly over. (Klosterneuburg, 25 March 1934)

Source: (a) Anton Tautscher (ed.), So sprach der Kanzler. Dollfuss Vermächtnis, Vienna, 1935, p. 91; (b) Speech at a lunch given by the Anglo-American Press Association in honour of the Chancellor. From Edmund Weber, Dollfuss an Österreich, Vienna, 1935, p. 49; (c) Tautscher, op. cit., p. 83; (d)–(g) ibid., p. 90.

34. Mussolini on Austria's role in the new Europe

From a conversation with Starhemberg, July 1930

'An "Anschluss" with Germany must never be permitted, nor a union either. . . . I have told you already Austria must survive and as an Austrian, not a German land. Out of the Heimwehr you must create a militant Austrian movement. You must also have the courage to take up the struggle against a wrong conception of nationalism. Politically, Austria is necessary to the maintenance of Europe. The day that Austria falls and is swallowed up by Germany will mark the beginning of European chaos. Austria must also retain her culture, for she is the bastion of Mediterranean civilisation. Germany is led by the Prussians, and Prussia stands for order and military efficiency. It also stands for war and brutality. Prussia means barbarism. That is why you must fight for an 'Austrian' Austria. Perhaps the day will come when you and other Danubian countries will be able to create a new Danubian organisation.'

. . .

'What is your attitude to the Jewish question?'

'The Heimatschutz rejects anti-semitism, and its ranks contain many patriotic Austrian Jews.' Mussolini expressed approval. Finally he said 'You must defend Austria against the Communist danger, but also against any attempt at an ''Anschluss'' with Germany or at bringing her under Prussian domination in any form. You are young and known as a fighter, an ''activist'', and you must rally the youth of Austria and rouse them in their country's cause. I shall always be at your disposal in the fight for Austria. Come to me if you need help.'

Source: Ernst Rüdiger Starhemberg, *Between Hitler and Mussolini*, pp. 24ff.

35. Attempts to prevent a Rome-Berlin axis lined up against Austria

Report by Dollfuss as recorded in the minutes of the Christian Socialist Party Executive Meeting of 20 April 1933

. . .

Allegation that, with Italy's collusion, attempts are being made in Austria to form a so-called concentrated national grouping headed by Jakoncig. I hope he didn't know anything of this. Nazi, Styrian *Heimwehr*.

. . .

When I heard with Italy's collusion, and since there is danger when two powerful states negotiate that the third, less powerful state would be crushed, I resolved to go to Rome.

. . .

Suvich [Fulvio Suvich, Under-Secretary of State at the Italian Foreign Office], Foreign Minister and thoroughly conversant with the situation in Austria, studied at Graz in peacetime, paid me a visit because I had asked him to, so that I could talk to him beforehand. He is well informed about the state of affairs in

Austria, also about personalities. I was surprised at his first-hand knowledge.

. . .

The results of the talks with Mussolini and the other gentlemen: Italy is positively interested in maintaining Austria's independence and its present policy line. Mussolini is very much in favour of the Christian Socialist Party. If I were to declare that the *Heimwehr* was not loyal, he would — as far as he was personally involved — abandon all other friendships and, with absolute confidence, support any action by the Christian Socialist Party and its policy of preserving the state. This outcome, I think, has ensured the exclusion of all other influences. Austria is entirely free to decide its domestic and foreign policy towards the National Socialists. Not only that, it can count on support. We have not signed anything, no treaty. But these ascertainments are valuable. The fact that Mussolini sees in me the chancellor of an independent state also played a role.

Vatican: As with Mussolini, so also with Pacelli [later Pope Pius XII], I did not hesitate to talk about our situation, beginning with the Nazis. He expressed his basic agreement. Recent observations that Rome is coming to terms with the situation in Germany and, as a matter of principle, is applying this attitude to Austria. This would also be negative from an ideological standpoint. In our country the National Socialists are the spiritual successors of the 'Separation from Rome' movement. The Church must therefore show no tolerance, but support the Christian Socialist Party. If the Church is tolerant, young people, unimpeded by any moral restraints imposed by the Church, will join up with the Nazis. That is why Rome is interested in the survival of the Christian Socialist Party. I repeatedly expressed this to Pacelli, and I have the impression that this is the way the Vatican feels too.

. . .

Source: Protokoll der Vorstandssitzung des Christlichsozialen Parteiklubs vom 20. April 1933, in Walter Goldinger (ed.), *Protokolle des Klubvorstandes der Christlichsozialen Partei 1932–34*, Vienna, 1980, pp. 227ff. and 230ff.

36. Berlin's assessment of Dollfuss' first visit to Rome

The Ambassador in Italy to the Foreign Ministry

Rome, 20 April 1933

POLITICAL REPORT

Subject: Visit of the Austrian Chancellor to Rome; Italy's policy toward Austria.

. . .

The Chancellor evidently felt impelled to outline to the Italian Government the guiding principles of Austria's domestic-policy, especially with regard to its attitude toward Reich German National Socialism and its effects on Austria, and to obtain in Rome some sort of backing against the anticipated progressive strengthening of the National Socialist movement in Austria, with its implication for the Anschluss question.

. . .

Result of the visit

The close relationship between the two countries by and large has assuredly been further strengthened by the Chancellor's visit during which, we may be certain, other subjects were discussed in addition to the aforementioned topic, such as the significance which the four-power pact has for Austria, the Austrian loan, and economic questions concerning Austria and Italy. It is most certain that the Chancellor departed with the impression that Italy regards preservation of an independent Austria as one of the cardinal points of her European policy.

. . .

It is of course also conceivable that under the impact of a sweeping National Socialist victory on the German pattern in Austria, which might take place some time hence, Italy would recognize the accomplished fact and adjust her policy accordingly. Herr Dollfuss, for his part, however, appears to be very confident about the future in this respect. He explained to me that the situations in Austria and Germany were not at all alike. The Austrians, to be sure, had the Reich-German experience before their eyes, but this did not mean that developments would now follow an identical course; on the contrary, what had been witnessed served more in the nature of a warning. This applied particularly to the setting up of the office of Reichsstatthalter in Bavaria, which had given exceptional impetus to the Christian Socials in Austria. If that is true, it is incomprehensible why Herr Dollfuss is then so set against new elections.

HASSELL

Source: ADAP 1918–1945, Series C, vol. I, no. 173 (20 April 1933).

37. Austria and the European powers

Note by Mr Sargent

Foreign Office, 29 June 1933

M. Rost, the financial adviser to the Austrian Government appointed by the Financial Committee of the League . . . came to see me this afternoon.

. . .

M. Rost proceeded to discuss some political aspects of the present Austrian situation, and in doing so I think he was speaking at the instigation of Dr Dollfuss.

. . .

In the matter of foreign support Dr Dollfuss realises that Great Britain, although sympathetic, is far off, and that France is unreliable and too flagrantly anti-German. In these circumstances he feels compelled to rely almost entirely on the Italian Government, and he is by no means convinced that Signor Mussolini would continue to give him support if he once came to terms with the Austrian Socialists. Dr Dollfuss is very angry with General Gömbös for having paid his visit to Hitler, which he considers to have been a stab in the back to himself. In fact, what he suspects is that Gömbös has come to some arrangement with Hitler whereby he has acquiesced in the absorption of Austria into Germany in return for the retrocession of the Burgenland to Hungary. Dr Dollfuss has definitely asked the Hungarian Government whether any such arrangement was made. No answer has yet been received.

. . .

He still feared that an incursion of Nazi bands into Austrian territory might in the near future bring about a sudden and dangerous international crisis. M. Rost said that he had been asked by Dr Dollfuss to warn us of this possibility, in the hope that we could consider in time what action we would be prepared to take in defence of Austrian independence if it were thus suddenly attacked.

Source: *DBFP, 1919–39*, 2nd Series, vol. V, 1933, no. 233 (4 July 1933).

38. Dollfuss protests in Berlin

In an instruction to the Austrian Ambassador in Berlin, Tauschitz, dated 18 July 1933, the Chancellor wrote:

. . .

Seen objectively, the struggle against the National Socialist Party in Austria is — from the point of view of the natural rights of nations and from Austria's position under international law — nothing more than an absolutely justified reaction to incessant terrorism and, under international law, illegal interference on the part of the present German government in the internal affairs of Austria. If the measures against National Socialism which the Federal Government finally saw itself forced to take to maintain security and order in the country are regarded by the National Socialist forces in the Reich, and thus also by the Government of the Reich, as being directed against Germany, then this is a conscious or unconscious misinterpretation or distortion of the situation. . . .

. . .

No matter how much the Federal Government regrets the conflict, which is clearly most detrimental to both parties involved, and is prepared all the sooner to re-establish friendly relations with the German Reich, it will nevertheless be obliged under all circumstances to insist that the sovereign rights of the independent Austrian Republic be respected unconditionally by the German Reich and its agencies.

. . .

Source: *Beiträge zur Julirevolte*, pp. 45 ff.

39. Germany complains about Dollfuss

Sir W. Selby (Vienna) to Sir R. Vansittart

Vienna, 21 July 1933

The German Minister, Dr Rieth, called upon me at the Legation this morning to return the courtesy visit I had paid him on my arrival.

. . .

Dr Rieth complained bitterly of the attitude of Chancellor Dollfuss and the present Government of Austria towards the Nazi movement in Austria itself. He said that the resistance which was being offered to the Nazi movement was solely due to the fear of the other parties — Christian Socialists, Heimwehr, Landbund, & c. — that if once they made any concession to the Nazis their political future would be placed in jeopardy. It was for that reason, and that reason alone, that Chancellor Dollfuss had rejected every offer of the Austrian Nazi leaders to co-operate with him. They had asked for two seats in the cabinet, a moderate demand considering the backing they had in the Austrian electorate. Chancellor Dollfuss had refused to make this concession, just as he had rejected every other approach from the Nazis.

Source: ADAP 1919–1939, 2nd Series, vol. V, 1933, no. 264 (21 July 1933).

40. On the Dollfuss-Mussolini talks at Riccione, 19–20 August 1933

Official Memorandum on the contents of the discussion

1. *Foreign policy*. Mussolini expressed his concern about developments in Germany, especially about the growing dominance of Prussianism. 'Should there, contrary to Mr Mussolini's expectations, be an invasion from Bavaria, Italy would intervene militarily.' It became quite clear, however, that Mussolini prefers to maintain his policy of 'friendly conversations with Berlin' as long as possible.

2. *Questions of economic policy*. In the course of the discussion it became evident that neither Italy nor France has so far worked out any precise plan for

the reconstruction of the Danubian area . . . Mr Mussolini has no objections to an intensification of economic relations with the states of the Little Entente. On the contrary, he aims to achieve a fruitful relationship with these states, which will include the economic sphere.

3. *Domestic policy.* Mussolini attempted to put pressure on the Chancellor to secure greater *Heimwehr* participation [in the Government]. The Chancellor, however, successfully side-stepped the attempts. Mr Mussolini recommended that the Chancellor prepare a constitutional reform for a corporate state by the end of September and, furthermore, make a major political speech under the motto 'Austria's external independence and Austria's renewal from within' as soon as possible. The Chancellor approves of this idea and has penned in 11 September as a possible date for this speech. In addition Mr Mussolini urgently recommended the unification of the various patriotic organizations under the exclusive leadership of the Federal Chancellor.

Source: *Mussolini-Dollfuss: Geheimer Briefwechsel*, Vienna, 1949, pp. 34ff.

41. Confidential German report on the Dollfuss–Mussolini talks of August 1933

The Chargé d'Affaires in Italy to the Foreign Ministry

Rome, 21 August 1933 — 4.05 p.m.

Today's conversation with the Deputy Director of the Political Department about the significance of Mussolini's meeting with Dollfuss at Riccione gives the following picture:

. . .

Dollfuss outlined to Mussolini Austria's internal and international situation and requested Italy's continued support.

. . .

In outlining Austria's domestic situation, Dollfuss acknowledged that German propaganda had let up somewhat, but at the same time expressed grave concern for the preservation of Austria's independence. Austria wished to remain independent in all circumstances and desired peace and cooperation with all neighbors, especially Italy, Hungary and, as soon as possible, also Germany.

3. Mussolini told Dollfuss that Italy was opposed to Anschluss in whatever form, but at the same time urgently desired an early easing of tension in the German-Austrian relationship.

Source: *ADAP 1918–1945*, Series C, vol. I, no. 408 (21 Aug. 1933).

42. Dollfuss informs Britain of the Riccione meeting

Sir W. Selby (Vienna) to Sir J. Simon

Vienna, 29 August 1933

Speaking of his visit to Riccione with results [of] which he expressed himself as well satisfied, Dr Dollfuss told me that Signor Mussolini had enquired whether he could assist in any way in bringing about *détente* in Austro-German relations. Dr Dollfuss had replied that he could only negotiate with Germany on basis of complete independence of Austria and on condition of Germany refraining from intervention in internal affairs of Austria. Dr Dollfuss could not admit of German intervention as regards representation of Austrian Nazis in Austrian Government.

Signor Mussolini had expressed appreciation of this reasonable point of view and Dr Dollfuss did not doubt had informed German Government of Austrian point of view.

Source: ADAP 1919–1939, 2nd Series, vol. V, 1933, no. 374 (29 Aug. 1933).

43. Austria's conditions for a normalisation of relations with Germany

Sir W. Selby (Vienna) to Sir J. Simon

Vienna, 13 September 1933

. . .

He [Dollfuss] said that he had had soundings from Germany through 'unofficial' intermediaries, but had refused to have anything to do with them, and had made it clear to the German representative here that he could only undertake to deal with direct and official approaches from the German Government. He had had enough of unofficial go-betweens who claimed more or less influence as the case might be with the influences [*sic*] directing the policy of Germany at the present moment.

His position remained the same, he would not contemplate entering negotiations with the German Government except on the basis of
1. The independence of Austria.
2. No dictation by Germany as to the manner in which Austria should order her own affairs.

At present the authorities in control in Germany could not bring themselves to believe that Austria as a whole was not passionately anxious to link her destinies to German Hitlerism, and until they were convinced that there were elements, and strong elements, in Austria bitterly opposed to such subordination to Hitlerite Germany, he saw little chance of an accommodation of the quarrel. Any help he could receive from the Powers by intervention in Berlin to help to remove this prevailing and inaccurate impression would, Dr Dollfuss thought, assist towards bringing Germany to reason. *Chancellor Dollfuss again affirmed his intention to fight the issue with Germany to the last*, but he did not conceal the seriousness of the struggle in which he was engaged. The Hitlerite Government were pouring out money on propaganda in every country on a scale unprecedented even for Germany.

. . .

Dr Dollfuss affirmed that he regarded the situation in Europe as very critical. So far as he was concerned he was determined to do all in his power to prevent Austria from becoming the occasion of another Franco-German war.

Source: *ADAP 1919–1939*, 2nd Series, vol. V, 1933, no. 390 (13 Sept. 1933). Emphasis added.

44. Mussolini's threatening gesture to Hitler

Sir R. Graham (Rome) to Sir R. Vansittart

Rome, 28 September 1933

I talked to Signor Mussolini yesterday regarding Austro-German situation.

. . .

Herr Hitler had offered him a private assurance to respect independence of Austria but Signor Mussolini had replied that Herr Hitler should take an opportunity of expressing this publicly. So far Herr Hitler had not done so.

. . .

He [Mussolini] had made his own attitude perfectly clear to Germany by moving Italian army headquarters at Verona to Bolzano and Florence army headquarters to Verona. This was only a gesture but Germans understood it.

. . .

Signor Mussolini did not believe that we were necessarily fighting a 'losing battle' in supporting Herr Dollfuss.

Source: *ADAP 1919–1939*, 2nd Series, vol. V, 1933, no. 417 (28 Sept. 1933).

45. Dollfuss warns against German expansionism

Sir W. Selby (Vienna) to Sir J. Simon

Vienna, 5 December 1933

. . .

The Chancellor emphasised the enormous accession of strength throughout Central Europe which would accrue to Germany were Germany to succeed consistently with the aims of Herr Hitler in extending her authority to Pressburg. The Chancellor went on to express a certain apprehension as regards the attitude of the Powers towards the Austrian problem, and said he could not avoid voicing his fear lest Austria should be made the pawn in the negotiations which were now proceeding between the Western Powers and Germany, in other words, lest Austria should be sacrificed by one or other of the Powers as the price of reaching an accommodation with Germany of their own difficulties. He said he felt less anxiety in this respect as regards His Majesty's Government than as regards France.

. . .

The Chancellor went on to say that he was disappointed at the progress of the negotiations for the economic relief of Austria. While the Powers had been profuse in protestations of friendship for Austria and support for the cause for which he was fighting, concrete evidence of this friendship and support had not been forthcoming. . . .

. . .

His own difficulties as regards the Nazi movement in Austria increased in the measure that he was unable to show that the support for the cause for which he was fighting, which had been so vociferously proclaimed, was being interpreted in the form of concrete and effective assistance.

Referring to the negotiations now proceeding with his neighbour, Czechoslovakia, the Chancellor said they were making no progress. All that the Czechoslovak Government did was to present to him long lists of their own demands. He was at a complete loss to understand the outlook of the Czechoslovak Government, when so much was involved for them in the maintenance of Austrian independence. 'Had', asked the Chancellor, 'France lost all her influence in Prague?'

Source: *ADAP 1919–1939*, 2nd Series, vol. VI, 1933–4, no. 100 (5 Dec. 1933).

46. Austria Supports the Pan-European movement

From the Memoirs of Count Coudenhove-Kalergi

On our trip back from America we resolved to convene the first European Congress in Vienna in the autumn of 1926 . . .

. . .

Six statesmen took on the honorary presidency of the first European congress; Eduard Beneš, Joseph Caillaux, Paul Loebe, Francesco Nitti, Nicola Politis and Ignaz Seipel. The First European Congress sat from October 3 to 6; over 2,000 delegates took part, representing twenty-four nations. The plenary meetings took place in the huge marble hall of the Vienna concert hall.

. . .

Dollfuss took on the honorary presidency of the Austrian Pan-Europe Committee. He placed one of the most beautiful offices in the world at the disposal of our organisation: the Chancellor's official lodgings in the Hofburg. In Imperial times these rooms had been used to house foreign monarchs. Dollfuss hated pomp and show, and preferred to live in his small private apartment rather than in these imperial halls.

We soon agreed on a plan of action. The Austrian government would support our movement in every way, while we were to do everything we could to promote a united European front, guaranteeing Austria's independence . . .

. . .

Dollfuss, Barthou and Hodža were the three new statesmen who made possible the renewal and reorganisation of our movement after Hitler's seizure of power. It is thanks to them that the Pan-European Promotion Association survived the resignation of its German supporters.

Source: Richard Nikolaus Coudenhove-Kalergi, *Der Kampf um Europa*, Zürich, 1949, pp. 123–7 and 190–6.

47. Italy — the sole guardian of Austria's sovereignty

Sir W. Selby (Vienna) to Sir J. Simon

Vienna, 20 January 1934

Signor Suvich received me at his hotel this morning.

. . .

So far as Italy was concerned, Italy had up till recently felt that the burden of defending the independence of Austria had been thrown on to her shoulders. It had seemed to Italy that France had seen no more in the issues raised by Austria than one calculated to separate Italy from Germany.

. . .

What had at one moment surprised the Italian Government was the attitude of M. Beneš who, I understood Suvich to say, had affirmed that if Anschluss were effected Czechoslovakia would make her terms with Germany. Suvich asked how Czechoslovakian independence could be maintained if Germay (? thwarted) her (? at) Vienna.

Suvich said that Mussolini regarded the maintenance of Austrian independence as vital for Italy and intended to go to the uttermost limit of his capacity to defend it.

Source: *ADAP 1919–1939*, 2nd Series, vol. VI, 1933–4, no. 194 (20 Jan. 1934).

48. Reaction of the Three Powers to Austria's complaints

Communiqué of the British, French and Italian governments on the preservation of Austria's independence (Joint Declaration of 17 February 1934)

The Austrian government had turned to its counterparts in France, England and Italy in order to ascertain their reaction to the files it had compiled to demonstrate Germany's intervention in the internal affairs of Austria. The discussions between these three governments led to a unanimous declaration of the need to maintain the independence and integrity of Austria in accordance with the prevailing agreements.

Source: Michael Freund (ed.), *Weltgeschichte der Gegenwart in Dokumenten 1934/35*. Part I: Internationale Politik. Essen, 1944, pp. 252ff.

49. Czechoslovakia's ambiguous stance

Sir F. Addison (Prague) to Sir J. Simon

Prague, 3 March 1934

. . .

At one moment Dr Beneš [the Czechoslovak Foreign Minister] tells me that he has nothing to fear from Germany whatever should happen, but, later, he will declare that he cannot 'allow' the 'Anschluss', for it would be fatal to Czechoslovakia.

. . .

At the same moment that Dr Krofta was telling the Foreign Affairs Committee of the Chamber of Deputies that the rumours that the Czechoslovak Government intended to send troops to Austria was [*sic*] 'so fantastic that they required no denial', Dr Beneš was apparently informing the Quai d'Orsay . . . that 'an incursion of Italian troops into Austria would be followed by the immediate entry of Czechoslovak troops'.

Source: *ADAP 1919–1939*, 2nd Series, vol. VI, 1933–4, no. 328 (3 March 1934).

50. Prague remains unperturbed by the prospect of *Anschluss*

From a Speech by Eduard Beneš, Czech Foreign Minister, 21 March 1934

. . .

During the war, at the time when we had gained the Western Powers' acceptance of our plan for a division of Austria-Hungary, we quite objectively recommended a unification of Austria with the German Reich. We assumed that this would perhaps also be the most acceptable solution for the Allied nations and would preempt the undesirable solution, as far as we are concerned, of [the creation of] a so-called 'Little Austria'.

. . .

As early as 1917, however, we abandoned this view ourselves, when we realised that Italy and France, and Britain too, were adamantly opposed to it. At the time, Russia was also firmly against a unification of Austria and Germany. . . .

. . .

Should anyone today be puzzled by our wartime stand, then I would like to point out that we were aware then, as we are now, of all the unfavourable consequences that *Anschluss* would bring with it. And if anyone today should be surprised that we had no fears on behalf of our own population with regard to such a development, my answer now would be, as it was then: though at present we still feel that it would be safer and more auspicious for peace in Europe if there were no *Anschluss, we would not fear such an eventuality* today if the major powers in western Europe should be unwilling to prevent it. For, from the very earliest days of our independence as a state and a nation, that is, from the middle of the tenth century onwards, we have been surrounded by this surging German sea and have always known how to cope with it.

. . .

Loyalty towards our friends, international obligations to maintain peace, and our own interests make it impossible for us to accept *Anschluss* as a solution to the Austrian problem.

Source: *Weltgeschichte in Dokumenten*, vol. I, pp. 256, 259, 260. Emphasis added.

51. Yugoslavia comes to terms with the possibility of *Anschluss*

Sir N. Henderson (Belgrade) to Sir J. Simon

Belgrade, 5 March 1934

. . .

The King and the Minister for Foreign Affairs are at heart convinced that, sooner or later, the 'Anschluss' in some form is inevitable, that nothing Yugoslavia can do will prevent it, and that consequently it is better to discount its consequences. Now that Italy has taken the field in Austria, Germany is regarded as decidedly the 'lesser' of two evils, and, indeed, almost ceases to be an evil.

Source: *DBFP 1919–1939*, 2nd Series, vol. VI, 1933–4, no. 331 (5 March 1934).

52. Dollfuss regrets lack of support from the Western Powers

Sir W. Selby (Vienna) to Sir J. Simon

Vienna, 5 March 1934

. . .

I see no other leader in Austria able or willing to continue the fight against Germany, and am therefore of the opinion that, distasteful and even short-sighted as many of the Government's acts may appear to public opinion in Great Britain, it is to the advantage of the latter to give him all possible and practical economic support.

. . .

Yet in his present bewildered and somewhat embittered mood, I learn that the Chancellor feels privately that he can, to his regret, count on practical help and support only from Rome. Surrounded by false or biased counsellors, with his back to the wall, and convinced of the justice of his fight 'for the peace and religious faith of Europe against Nazi political and anti-religious doctrines', he is therefore forced to do as Italy bids until help can reach him from other quarters.

Source: *ADAP 1919–1939*, 2nd Series, vol. VI, 1933–4, no. 332 (5 March 1934).

53. The consultation pact between Austria, Italy and Hungary

From the official version of the Rome Protocols between Vienna, Rome and Budapest, 17 March 1934

(a) *Protocol No. 1*

The Head of the Government of His Majesty the King of Italy, the Federal Chancellor of the Austrian Republic, and the President of the Royal Council of Hungary, animated by a desire to co-operate in the maintenance of peace and in the economic restoration of Europe, on the basis of respect for the independence and rights of every state; persuaded that collaboration between the three Governments in this sense can establish real premises for wider co-operation with other States; undertake, for the achievement of the above-mentioned objects, to concert together, on all problems which particularly interest them and also on those of a general character, with the aim of developing in the spirit of the existing Italo-Austrian, Italo-Hungarian, and Austro-Hungarian Treaties of Friendship based upon the recognition of the existence of their numerous common interests, a mutually agreed policy which shall be directed towards effective collaboration between European states and particularly between Italy, Austria, and Hungary.

To this end, the three Governments will proceed to common consultation each time that at least one of them may consider this course opportune.

L.S. BENITO MUSSOLINI
L.S. ENGELBERT DOLLFUSS
L.S. JULIUS DE GÖMBÖS

Source: John W. Wheeler-Bennett (ed.), *Documents on International Affairs 1933*, London, 1934, p. 396.

54. From the unofficial version of the Vienna-Rome-Budapest Pact

. . .

As a result of the negotiations between Mussolini, Dollfuss and Gömbös, the so-called Rome Protocols were signed on 17 March 1934, in Rome, outlining in final form the alliance between the three states. The secret minutes in the German language covering the negotiations, which are being made public here for the first time, clearly show the internal inconsistencies within this alliance:

1. It was ascertained that the three states deem extensive cooperation in the political and economic spheres to be advisable.
2. The relations between Austria and Germany are the central issue among the political questions, it being ascertained that it would be in the interests of peace . . . if, by mutual agreement, the relations between Austria and Germany were to improve. The Austrian Chancellor stresses that he has no objections to such a trend; the pre-requisite for cooperation with Germany is, however, a guarantee that Germany recognises the independence of Austria in both the foreign and the domestic political spheres.

The Hungarian Prime Minister raises the matter of the need for friendship and cooperation between Italy, Germany, Austria and Hungary; he further emphasises that, in connection with the revision of Hungary's boundaries, his country needs Germany's backing north of the Danube and thus a dependable support in that area. These remarks were also acknowledged and approved by the Italian head of government.

Source: Lajos Kerekes, *Abenddämmerung einer Demokratie. Mussolini, Gömbös und die Heimwehr*, Vienna/Frankfurt/Zürich, 1966, pp. 187ff.

55. A German assessment of the Rome Protocols

The Ambassador in Italy to the Foreign Ministry

Rome, 17 March 1934
Received 19 March II It. 432

POLITICAL REPORT

Subject: Meeting of Mussolini, Dollfuss, and Gömbös in Rome.

. . .

Political result

From the political point of view, Italy is able to register a victory.

. . .

The tripartite relationship of Rome, Vienna, and Budapest has been consolidated again through the Rome conversations and this will have its effect also in the international sphere. Austria has thereby received a new and conspicuous pledge of her independence.

Source: *DGFP, 1918–1945*, Series C, vol. II, no. 332 (17 March 1934).

56. The SS evaluation of the Rome Protocols

. . .

In March 1934, Mussolini, Dollfuss and Gömbös signed the 'Protocols' in the Palazzo Venezia. In this document, the signatories expressly guaranteed the mutual independence of their respective states.

The then French Foreign Minister, Louis Barthou, saw in the position that Italy adopted towards the Austrian question an opportunity to influence Italy's general attitude toward the German Reich. The Austrian Federal Chancellor, Dollfuss, attempted to exploit every possibility that this political situation offered Austria. In doing so, he took no consideration of German interests as a whole. Austria's continual representations to the Italian government, ruthlessly attacking the German government, rendered the danger of Germany becoming isolated increasingly likely. Around this same time, Hitler travelled to Venice for his first meeting with Mussolini, *Dollfuss left no stone unturned in his attempts to prevent the German Reich and Italy from reaching an understanding.* He had material collated that was intended to incriminate the Austrian National Socialists and the German Reich, and had passed them on to Italy's Under-Secretary of State, Suvich, before Hitler's arrival. The effects of Austria's presentations against the German Reich could be seen in the increasingly critical tone which the Italian press adopted towards the German Reich. May 1934 saw the start of a campaign in the Italian press which was obviously initiated at the behest of the Italian government and was directed against the attitude of the German Reich towards Austria. This action reached its climax in an article by Gayda printed in all Italian newspapers and entitled 'For Austria, stop the terrorist attacks'. Gayda wrote that the acts of terror planned and carried out by agitators from the German Reich threatened to make relations between Italy and Germany increasingly difficult. Because of such activities, it was to be feared that Germany would be cut off by an ever growing wall of separation made up of distrust and hostility that would be of no benefit either for its future destiny or for the peace and harmony of Europe.

. . .

Dr Rintelen pointed to the dangers which this political situation posed for Germany during Weydenhammer's visit. He drew particular attention to the forthcoming talks that Dollfuss would be having with Mussolini in Riccione and with Barthou in Paris, and explained that military concessions towards Austria on France's part, as well as a loan from Paris, were to be expected. He also informed Weydenhammer that he could not extend his holiday plans beyond the end of July and that he did not expect to return to his post in Rome.

Source: Die Erhebung der österreichischen Nationalsozialisten im Juli 1934. Akten der Historischen Kommission des Reichsführers SS, Vienna/Frankfurt/Zürich, 1965, reprinted 1984, pp. 74ff. Emphasis added.

57. Habicht threatens Dollfuss with 'the end'

. . .

The Rome Pact brings to an end, for the time being, a struggle which has now lasted some fifteen years and which had its beginnings in St Germain and Versailles. In the final analysis its central issue was always the question of which role would fall to German-Austria in the struggle for the future of the German nation:

. . .

All in all, Austria has drifted farther and farther away from the Reich in these years — first towards isolation, then increasingly into the arms of foreign powers — but between what has happened so far and what has just taken place in Rome there is an enormous difference.

. . .

However, in Rome — in 1934 — a final break was made with this policy [i.e. an essentially pro-German attitude before 1933]. *Faced with the choice of siding with Germany or with Italy*, who, after France's withdrawal, were left the only remaining antagonists in the Danube area, *Dollfuss, Starhemberg and Fey have opted unreflectingly for Italy*.

. . .

The goal of our struggle is a German Austria under German leadership, and we shall not deviate one inch from this goal, come what may! For us the Rome

Pact — more so than that of Lausanne — is just an episode, but for the Austrians who signed it, it means the end.

Source: *Österreichischer [NSDAP] Pressedienst* (Munich), no. 51, 24 March 1934. Emphasis added.

58. Karl Renner on the Western Powers' policy on Austria and Italy

. . .

The attitude adopted at that time by the West, and by France in particular, now became decisive for the entire future development of Austria's foreign policy and of the political situation in the Danube area. Even before this, Italy, as Austria's closest neighbour, had been given the chairmanship of all League of Nations commissions dealing with loans to Austria, and had invariably made use of this position in the interests of its special policy [towards Austria]. In view of the present predicament, it was considered judicious once again to push Italy forward, committing the protection of Austria to its care, or, as Mussolini later put it, *to make Italy the gendarme of Europe in Austria against Germany*, in the hope that the two central European dictators, Mussolini and Hitler, would become embroiled in bitter, perhaps irreconcilable, antagonism.

Source: Karl Renner, *Nachgelassene Werke*, vol. II: *Österreich von der ersten zur zweiten Republik*, Vienna, 1953, pp. 130ff. Emphasis added.

59. France supports the Dollfuss government

The Minister in Austria (Messersmith) to the Secretary of State

Vienna, 21 June 1934

. . .

Barthou, French Minister for Foreign Affairs, passed through Vienna en route to Bucharest on June 19th. After conference of Dollfuss with Barthou Austrian Government in official communiqué approved by French Legation stated that French Government in cooperation with Italian and British would 'continue to guarantee independence of Austria'. Later in an authorised press interview Barthou stated 'France's whole power stands behind independence of Austria; independence as it is represented in the person of the Chancellor. With regard to National Socialist outrages from which your country suffers so much' Barthou added 'I wish to say the following: we are quite on the side of Dollfuss government. The freedom and peace of Austria must be guaranteed under all circumstances. We will protect this freedom by all means.'

French Legation here stated foregoing was substance of Barthou's statements to Dollfuss and added that Barthou had assured Dollfuss of French Government's confidence in his chancellorship.

Source: *Foreign Relations of the United States, Diplomatic Papers*, vol. II, 1934, p. 28.

Part V

THE 'LIGHTNING COUP' AND CHANCELLOR'S MURDER

60. Hitler demands Dollfuss' death

From a conversation with Rauschning, May 1933

In May 1933 new elections had taken place in Danzig. For the National Socialists the results had been better than they were in the Reich.

. . .

Hitler had just initiated his struggle against Austria's independence with the introduction of the thousand-mark visa fee [on travel to Austria]. He said he had imposed this restriction against the will of the Foreign Office. It was evident with what satisfaction he took on the fight, which he incidentally felt would be over very soon. Every word he uttered was, as it were, aglow with hatred. Hatred and scorn . . .

. . .

'This Dollfuss, these paid scribblers and would-be somebodies, these silly little shrimps who make themselves out to be statesmen and don't realise how they are being manipulated by the French and the English — I'll call them to account. I know', he continued after a pause, 'that we can't just come out with *Anschluss* straight away.'

. . .

Hitler intimated what he intended to do and how everything had been prepared for a revolt in Austria. It became clear that he desired a revolt of this kind and that he positively welcomed the resistance that the Dollfuss government was putting up. From the vehemence of his words one could only conclude that he was thirsting for sanguinary action, conspiracy, retribution in some form.

. . .

A hot, morbid, singeing odour emanated from this conversation. It wasn't so much a conversation as a passionate self-interpretation, which was what every conversation with Hitler eventually turned into.

. . .

'I'll make short shrift of this Dollfuss,' yelled Hitler. 'This man dares to contradict me. Just picture it! They will come to me on bended knees yet. But I shan't flinch from having them executed as traitors.'

. . .

Hatred and a desire for personal revenge echoed in these words, retribution for privation experienced in his youth, for disappointed hopes, for a life of poverty and humiliation. For a while an awkward silence filled the room.

Source: Hermann Rauschning, *Gespräche mit Hitler*, Vienna, 1973, pp. 83–6.

61. Alternative strategies in the battle for Austria

From a confidential report of the German Military Attaché, 5 June 1934

Copy II M 805   Vienna, 5 June 1934
German Embassy   Secret!
The Military Attaché
Secret Doc. no. 246
Report no. 11/34 (Austria)

. . .

Considerations as to what could be done to speed matters up and achieve a solution that is favourable for both the Reich and German Austria. Three possibilities have emerged:

(*a*) A continuation of the existing positional warfare by persisting with, or stepping up, economic pressure and acts of terror in order to grind down the enemy so that he will be forced to the bargaining table;

(*b*) Overthrow of the enemy government by violent assault;

(*c*) Removal of the ruling regime by non-violent means and by agreement with Italy.

With regard to (*a*)

The war can probably be continued in this way without fears that our own resources will be exhausted before those of our opponents. However, an end could not be reckoned with in the foreseeable future. *Our [Austrian] opponents have by no means exhausted their defensive resources and continue to find support abroad, perhaps increasingly so.*

. . .

With regard to (*b*)

Violent assault is always attended by risks, and should only be attempted if there is no other possibility. Today the armed forces are under firm government control and will probably be so for some time to come.

. . .

With regard to (*c*)

An agreement with Italy, assuming that this can be achieved on acceptable terms — and bearing in mind that the political independence of Austria will be a conditio sine qua non for Italy — would deprive the present regime of its main source of support.

signed MUFF

Source: Foreign Ministry Archives, Bonn. Emphasis added.

62. Hitler knew of the imminent revolt

From the Memoirs of General Wilhelm Adam

When Adam also declined to take part in the 'German Games' in Nuremberg, Hitler ordered the General to appear before him at 9 a.m. on 25 July. . . . Clearly preoccupied with other matters, Hitler suddenly said to Adam: 'Today the Austrian Federal Army is going to strike against its own government.' I immediately interrupted: 'It's absolutely impossible that the Federal Army would do that.' Hitler shouted: 'That's not for you to decide; it is going to strike . . . The Austrian government will be thrown out today. Rintelen will be Reich Chancellor (*sic!*). He'll order all Austrian emigrés and members of the Legion to return to their home country.' The Legionaries were armed Nazis who had fled in large numbers to Bavaria, where they had become a public nuisance . . . . We have disarmed them and gathered them together in depots. 'These Legionaries', Hitler continued, 'will return to their home-country unarmed. They will receive weapons once they have crossed the border. Complete arrangements for these weapons to be transported to locations details of which you will receive later.' . . . At three o'clock in the afternoon the telephone in my room rang. To my surprise I heard: 'Hitler speaking. Things in Vienna are running smoothly. We have occupied the Ministry. Dollfuss is wounded. No precise details are as yet known. I'll call you back shortly.' He did not call again.

Source: Anton Hoch and Hermann Weiss, *Die Erinnerungen des Generalobersten Wilhelm Adam. Miscellanea* (Festschrift for H. Krausnick), Stuttgart, 1980, pp. 47ff.

63. The rebels' planned 'decapitation strike'

From a National Socialist account

The misguided strategy of the Marxists' revolt in February had shown us that it was impossible to conquer Vienna and the seat of the government from the periphery. It was clear to the leaders of the uprising that an attempt must be made to capture the entire government at one fell swoop and thereby gain control of the state's nerve centre. Thus the plan was devised for the revolt which, on July 25, was to take a totally militarized state machinery by surprise and hold it in check for several hours . . .

. . .

. . . The control of military operations was in the hands of Fridolin Glass, former leader and federal chairman of the German League of Veterans. He was in charge of SS-Standarte 89, an excellently drilled troop that was completely reliable and had a sound record of discipline . . .

. . .

The plan was as follows: A squad wearing uniforms of the federal army or of security guards was to be taken in several trucks from the gymnasium of the German Gymnastics Club in Siebensterngasse to the Federal Chancellery at Ballhausplatz, where they would occupy the Ministry, arrest the members of the government and, with the help of Dr Rintelen, force a reorganisation of the cabinet. At the same time, another squad would take over the broadcasting system and, by announcing the new government, bring the entire state machinery to a halt and put it out of action. A third group, under the leadership of Max Grillmayer and the Ott brothers, would apprehend the Federal President, Miklas, in Velden on the Wörthersee and prevent him from interfering in the events that were taking place.

Source: Wladimir von Hartlieb, *Parole: Das Reich*, Vienna/Leipzig, 1939, pp. 222ff.

64. The last-minute warning

. . . . Fey was called out of the conference to receive the news of the planned assault. He at once passed the message on to Dollfuss, who then interrupted the ministerial council with the words: 'I have just received an important message. I must have it verified. It is perhaps not advisable for us all to be sitting here together.' Only when asked by Dr Tauschitz, the Secretary of State for Foreign Affairs, where they should go, did Dollfuss instruct the cabinet members to return to their respective offices. Only the Secretary of State for Security Affairs Karwinsky, the Secretary of State for the Armed Forces Major-General Zehner, and Minister Fey were asked to remain behind. He accompanied them to his office, where he asked Fey to repeat the message. This was between 12 noon and 12.10. Fey reported that he had had a police detective sent to Siebensterngasse to observe what was going on. Dollfuss then ordered State Secretary Zehner to proceed to the Ministry of Defence immediately and put the Federal Army on alert.

Source: Die Erhebung der österreichischen Nationalsozialisten im Juli 1934. Bericht der Historischen Kommission des Reichsführers SS, Vienna/Frankfurt/Zürich, 1965, reprint 1984, p. 85 (henceforth *Historische SS-Kommission*).

65. The Chancellor's assassination

Testimony of Witness Hedvicek

I was the Chancellor's doorkeeper. I had just come on duty ten minutes earlier to replace my colleague.

. . .

Suddenly I heard the sound of heavy vehicles entering the premises and thought to myself that reinforcements had arrived . . .

. . .

I saw the men quickly jump down and then in through the window of the guardroom. The rest spread out on the steps. I met the Chancellor as he was on his way to his office in the hall of pillars. I said 'Quick!' and took him by the hand with the intention of taking him through his office into the adjoining corner lounge, then through to a winding staircase in a connecting room, and from there to the archives. From there a door opens into Minoritenplatz, and I intended to get the Chancellor out of the building this way. On the way the Chancellor asked me if I had a revolver. I told him I hadn't. We hurried through the large corner lounge, and as we were about to unlock the door to the next room — the key was in the door — between eight and twelve men in military uniform burst in, each with a pistol in his hand. They all shouted 'Hands up'. The Chancellor raised his hand to protect his face, and then two shots were fired. The Chancellor reeled around and fell to the floor.

Source: Historische SS-Kommission, pp. 171ff.

66. Dollfuss' presentiments of death

I have no false ambitions. I have no desire to do anything other than to help my home country and my fellow Austrians as well as I can, even to the point of self-sacrifice if need be. (St. Pölten, 9 July 1933)

I should tell you quite openly: physical threats hold no great fears for me. (Mauer, 17 June 1934)

I am convinced that for us a new era is approaching. But the battle is not an easy one. We must all fight body and soul for the sake of our home country, just as we did at the front not so long ago. (Vienna, 29 January 1934)

As long as I have the feeling that God expects me to direct all my energies towards improving conditions in our country and restoring peace to it, I will be prepared to do so to the very end. (Klosterneuburg, 25 March 1934)

Source: Anton Tautscher (ed.), So sprach der Kanzler. Dollfuss' Vermächtnis, Vienna, 1935, pp. 144 and 146ff.

67. Dollfuss's death and last words

From the testimony of a witness

Police Inspector Johann Greifeneder, questioned on 31 July 1934, made the following testimony:

. . . I held the head of the wounded Chancellor, and lifted it slightly as Messinger applied a temporary dressing. . . .

. . .

Then the Chancellor regained consciousness. His first question was: 'How are the other Ministers?' — to which I replied: 'As far as I know they are well.' The Chancellor then told us: 'A major, a captain and several soldiers came in and shot at me.'

. . .

Meanwhile the Chancellor asked to be taken to a hospital or for a doctor to be called. The Chancellor also asked for a priest. We tried in vain to arrange this, then I tried to comfort the Chancellor by telling him that his injury was only a flesh wound and that he did not need a doctor. However, the Chancellor did seem to be aware of the seriousness of his wound, because he asked us to lift up one of his arms and legs, which we then did, whereupon he said: 'I don't feel anything. I must be paralysed.' The Chancellor then added: 'Children, you're so good to me. Why aren't the others like that, too? All I wanted was peace. We were the victims of aggression who had to defend ourselves. God forgive the others.' Federal Minister Fey then arrived under escort. . . .

. . .

The Chancellor then asked Fey to ask Mussolini, the Prime Minister of Italy, to take care of his wife and children. Fey promised to do so. Then the Chancellor said that Federal Minister Dr Schuschnigg was to be given the task of forming the new government, or, should Schuschnigg also have been killed, then Skubl, the Assistant Chief of Police, was to take on the task of forming a government.

. . .

The Chancellor then complained that a doctor had still not been sent for, and that he was afraid he would suffocate on the phlegm. In reality it was not phlegm that was making him feel as if he was going to suffocate, but rising blood which we repeatedly wiped from his mouth. The Chancellor then began to breathe more and more stertorously, and gradually he lost consciousness.

The Chancellor's last words were: 'Say farewell from me to my wife and children,' then his breathing became even more stertorous, his body went into convulsions, and he breathed his last.

Source: Historische SS-Kommission, pp. 248ff.

Part VI
THE ARMED REVOLT IN THE PROVINCES

68. Strategy and tactics of the National Socialist revolt

The 'Kollerschlag Document'

1. There is a possibility that the Dollfuss government will one day be forced to step down . . . either a new government will be appointed or a struggle for power will ensue.

2. In either event, there will be a vacuum of sorts for a certain time — an hour at least — in which the authorities are no longer subordinate to the old government but not yet receiving instructions from the new government, and are thus paralysed in their decision-making and their power to act.

3. This period of inertia must be exploited. On news of Dollfuss' resignation, the entire SA will immediately and without further instructions undertake 'unarmed propaganda marches' — officially billed as demonstrations for the new elections, in reality for the purposes of immediately occupying public offices and buildings in the provincial capitals and local administrative centres and of seizing power. The SA brigade leaders responsible for each province will immediately announce that they and the *Gauleiters* [regional NSDAP chiefs] have assumed power as Directors of Public Safety and Provincial Governors respectively, and, in keeping with this, issue strict orders to the authorities in their capacity as new leaders. The motto will be: 'A free and autonomous Austria, equally independent from the *Reich* and from Italy, but reestablishment of genuinely constitutional and legal conditions.'

. . .

4. If the new federal chancellor, an hour after Dollfuss' resignation and not yet in firm control of matters, receives news from all the provinces that the SA has seized power, he will not find it easy to mobilise the law enforcement agencies against us. As far as these are concerned, they will not act against us independently but will await orders.

5. There can be only two consequences:
   (*a*) The new government will recognize the National Socialist movement and buckle under, or
   (*b*) there will be more or less organised, active resistance against us; in short, a struggle for power will develop. In this event, it will not be sufficient for the SA to conduct 'propaganda marches' and occupy government buildings by peaceful means: all available means will have to be employed to secure control . . .

. . .

If we succeed in seizing power in the provinces in this way, Vienna will not be able to hold out on its own but will have to follow.

196

6. It is essential that the movement appears to come spontaneously from the people; it must be staged as a purely domestic affair and must under no circumstances appear as if it were directed from the outside in any way . . .

   . . .

7. The execution in detail shall be as follows:

   (*a*) On receiving news of the government's overthrow, each local SA leader will, on his own initiative and without further instructions, give orders for the 'unarmed propaganda march' in uniform, or at the very least with arm bands. Weapons are to be carried secretly or to be readily available.

   (*b*) This march will lead to an abrupt occupation of public buildings, on which the swastika flag is to be hoisted.

   (*c*) The new provincial governors and directors of public safety to be announced by the appropriate district leaders in accordance with paragraph 3.

   (*d*) Amnesty for all political misdemeanours to be proclaimed, and all expatriates and political émigrés to be recalled.

   (*e*) In implementing this decree, all prisoners are to be released immediately, including the reds. Special instructions concerning the return of the Legion will apply; they will be directed to Vienna with all possible speed.

   (*f*) Government and defence force leaders hostile to us are to be arrested immediately and rendered harmless if they show any resistance. Neutrality towards the reds, as long as they don't do us any harm.

   (*g*) In the event of resistance or a struggle for power, communications and transport systems to be destroyed completely.

   (*h*) Armed confrontation with the police or gendarmerie is preferably to be avoided for as long as possible. Where it proves necessary, however, it is to be carried out with the utmost vigour and maximum force. Clashes with the Federal Army are to be avoided if at all possible.

   (*i*) Following the takeover of power, this power is to be consolidated everywhere, and the SA to be armed and organised as a reliable instrument of power for the new government. The Socialist Defence League and similar units are to be disarmed and disbanded. The law enforcement agencies, in so far as they are subordinate and appear reliable, are to be reinstated in office and provided with swastika armbands.

8. We should be prepared to alter our conduct towards the law enforcement agencies immediately in the event of the police or gendarmerie carrying out their official duties; this is to be openly resisted with force by SA personnel. This resistance must be organised in such a way that the forces of the executive, which generally appear in small numbers, will find themselves pitted against superior numbers determined to fight to the last. The individual representative

of the authorities must know that he will be risking his life if he opposes us. These tactics are to consist of small-scale actions with the objective of grinding down the opposing forces, and should under no circumstances lead to premature open rebellion or to attack. Wherever the law enforcement agencies appear in closed ranks and in large formations, they are to be avoided so that they will strike their blows at thin air.

9. Should a death sentence by court-martial be passed on one of us in the near future, there will be an attempt to free the prisoner either by cunning or by force. Those involved are to disappear immediately afterwards. In no event should a general uprising, which would rally all the forces of the executive together, be sparked off by this, as there would be little prospect of success.

10. If, on the resignation of Dollfuss, Fey should on his own initiative take over the dictatorship, proceedings shall follow the same pattern.

Source: Beiträge zur Julirevolte, pp. 54f.

69. The uprising in Styria

From a National Socialist account

Storm over Styria (July 1934)

. . .

The execution of the National Socialist revolt in Styria in July 1934 had to take into account the geographical nature of this province. The revolt had to be launched from all corners of the province, then merge, and finally gain ground beyond its narrow confines to meet up with the revolt in the other regions.

Thus the brown columns marched into battle for the Reich from four areas: Upper Styria, West Styria, Lower Styria and East Styria. And the heart of the province — its capital — was to flare up with the desire for battle and victory of this quintessentially German people.

It is pointless to ask why, at that time, victory for National Socialism in the Ostmark [Austria] and here in Styria could not yet be achieved. Were the province and its people not yet ripe for such a joyful victory? Were the German people as a whole not ready to become united in brotherhood? — At all events *the arch-enemy of the Germans was still too powerful and these conscious Germans still much too weak.*

. . .

And then on 25 July 1934, the signal to launch the attack flared up in Vienna. The SS-*Standarte* 89 went on the march and struck out.

On 22 July the final, decisive conferences among the National Socialist leaders had already taken place in Styria, and the highest state of readiness been put into operation. Something of immense significance was about to happen.

In Upper Styria the SA-*Standarte* J 9 stood ready for action with four assault units. Unit no. 1 was located in Schladming, no. 2 in Stainach-Irdning and Bad Aussee, no. 3 in Liezen, and no. 4 in Eisenerz.

In addition to this rifle battalion of some 1,500 men, there were about 300 men of the SA Reserves available for the forthcoming action, a further 50 or so men of the Mechanised SA, and finally 200 SS men. Beyond this, about 800 men from various sections of the population had volunteered their support in the fighting. However, only about 1,000 rifles, a number of machine guns and submachine guns were available to these selfless troops.

. . .

The first assault unit occupied Schladming and Gröbming with its District Commissioner's headquarters, as well as the surrounding villages, and advanced towards Mandling in order to seal the province off on the Salzburg side.

No. 2 Assault Unit occupied Stainach-Irdning and advanced into the Salz-kammergut as far as the outskirts of Bad Aussee.

No. 3 Assault Unit accomplished its mission to occupy Liezen, the Pyhrn Pass, the Selz Valley, Admont, Rottenmann, Trieben and Gaishorn. At 5 p.m. on 25 July 1934, the District Commissioner's Headquarters and Gendarmerie District Command Headquarters at Liezen were occupied, and control of public life had passed into the hands of the National Socialists. Now followed the swift advance to take the strategically important Pyhrn Pass, which was reported as accomplished in the early part of that night . . .

. . .

Units of the Federal Army which had been ordered to the military training area in the Dachstein region succeeded in pushing forward unobserved over the Brunnenstein and the Hintersteiner Alm, and descending on the left flank of the SA after passing through the narrow Hinterstein pass, unaware of the favourable strategic position they had thereby gained. The Federal Army appeared to be of the opinion that the SA had already retreated; this would explain why the soldiers made their way through the Hinterstein pass entirely without stealth or cover. They were met with rifle and machine gun fire from the SA, and within a short time the Federal Army unit was dispersed.

At the same time, the Upper Austrian Home Defence Corps, advancing south-eastwards across the Pyhrn Moor, parallel to the road, pushed forward towards the right flank of the SA. From the Brand ridge the SA placed them under heavy fire and was able to repel the advance. However, when the wooded heights northeast of the lime-kiln came alive with advancing soldiers and *Heimwehr* personnel, when heavy enemy rifle and machine gun fire forced the SA to take cover, and a mortar platoon of the Federal Army went into action, the situation took a serious turn for the National Socialists defending the pass.

. . .

Several days before 25 July 1934, numerous conferences among the leaders had already been taking place in southern Styria, the area of the SA Mountain Infantry *Standarte* 47. Deployment plans were being drawn up and the initial measures for an imminent power takeover in the country by the NSDAP being discussed.

. . .

Then on 25 July 1934, when Vienna Radio announced that the Dollfuss government had resigned, this signal to strike out was greeted with great jubilation.

At the same time, in Radkersburg, the SA appeared on the streets, armed and in uniform. With loud voices they proclaimed that the NSDAP was in power. The town was festooned with swastikas, public administration buildings, the post office and the railway station were occupied . . .

. . .

Meanwhile, the rebel leaders were issued with an ultimatum from the provincial security authorities to lay down their arms. As a result of skilful negotiating, this ultimatum was repeatedly prolonged. At 8.30 p.m., however, negotiations broke down completely. The disarming of the gendarmerie, which was a necessary consequence, was carried out without a struggle. As a result, another 100 rifles, some machine guns and several hand grenades were seized. After this action it was decided to proceed to Mureck with the majority of the SA units — about 150 men — in order to join the SA located there in an attack on the Strass garrison. At about 2 a.m. on 26 July, the Radkersburg National Socialists arrived in Mureck to find around 800 freedom fighters from the entire district assembled there.

. . .

One battle — the July uprising — had been lost, but not the war. And war was waged against the tyrants, war and fighting continued until a liberated Austria found its way back to the Reich.

Source: Otto Reich von Rohrwig, *Der Freiheitskampf der Ostmarkdeutschen von St. Germain bis Adolf Hitler*, Graz/Vienna/Leipzig, 1942, pp. 205–40. Emphasis added.

70. The federal army's battle in Styria

From a confidential report of the Ministry of Defence

Federal Province of Styria

. . .

During the afternoon hours of 25 July, uprisings by National Socialist supporters took place in most of the towns and villages in Styria, with the exception of the provincial capital, Graz. These mainly took the form of attacks on gendarmerie stations, the occupation of post and telegraph offices and of government and district administrative buildings, as well as the taking of hostages, the arrest of persons loyal to the fatherland, and acts of violence against the local volunteer defence units.

The fight for the occupation of Leoben
. . .

At 15.30 hours on 25 July, the Austrian Home Defence Corps district of Leoben was mobilised on the orders of its local group leader, Dr Josef Kolmayr. To protect the town, vigorous patrolling commenced and the most important administrative buildings were occupied.
. . .

In the course of the night of 25/26 July, the rebels approached the outskirts of the town from almost all sides, so that the local security authorities, in cooperation with the *Schutzkorps* and the *Heimwehr* were forced to restrict their defence to individual key points in the town (the gendarmerie command headquarters, town hall, savings bank and labour office).

No. 1 Mechanised Rifle Battalion advanced into Leoben at 0915 hours . . .; for reasons of safety, the tanker vehicle remained behind in the gendarmerie barracks at Bruck a.d.M. At that time the town appeared to be completely quiet. During the debussing of the battalion next to the mining college and the parking of the transport vehicles in the yard, the insurgents suddenly opened fire. Undetected, they had moved snipers into numerous houses throughout the town; heavy rifle fire issued from the windows and roofs of neighbouring houses.
. . .

In heavy fighting and under constant fire from an unseen enemy, the advance units had reached the Waasen Bridge at about 10.50 hours. Serious fighting developed around the bridge and the streets immediately adjacent to it (Kärntnerstrasse, Donawitzerstrasse and Vordernbergerstrasse). The battle was the more difficult due to the bridge being under the control of the rebels, who were covering it with infantry and machine gun fire from the slopes to the west. The auxiliary forces, moreover, were subjected at the rear and flanks to repeated fire coming from rooftops and barricaded windows. It was here that the battalion sustained its heaviest losses.
. . .

The battalion commander ordered the mortar platoon, with a rifle squad to provide fire protection cover, to a position 'Am Glacis', the main direction of fire to be towards the limekilns and the parish hall in Donawitz. A heavy machine gun of the Reserves fired with success upon advancing rebels on the slopes north of the main railway station (Bärenkogel-Münzenberg), the aim being to contain the enemy which had gathered there. Thanks to this protective fire, the battalion's attack won ground along Donawitzerstrasse and Kärtnerstrasse to beyond the railway line, then further through Vordernbergerstrasse up to the Vordernberger brook. Approximately 2,000 men with 12–15 heavy machine-guns and several submachine-guns had been in action within this battle sector.
. . .

In the Leoben area of operations, the number of captured rebels brought in

during the next few days amounted to about 1,100; as for weapons and ammunition, six heavy machine guns, 300 infantry rifles and about 7,500 live rounds were confiscated. . . .
Review of the fighting in Styria

. . .

The guiding principle that ensured the successful suppression of the revolt was that of the most practical concentration and utilisation of the available forces, which were by no means large in number. It was a case of overpowering a well-equipped enemy, highly trained in the use of weapons and to an extent in field skills, an enemy undeniably possessing determination and courage. The rebels had supplied themselves with sufficient motor vehicles, with whose help they were able to concentrate their forces at important locations in the province and thus, in some sectors, confront the security forces with superior numbers.

The brigade command rightly felt that the main task was to take swift action backed by the simultaneous deployment of sufficiently large and powerful units. Motor vehicles were allocated to those units chosen for auxiliary services, and their commanders entrusted with mopping-up operations which involved the 'neutralising' of long valley stretches and extensive areas of the province. And so that their initiative should in no way be restrained, they were given complete freedom in the utilisation of the resources placed at the disposal of the troops. This form of employment proved most successful; as early as the afternoon of 28 July, public calm and order could be regarded as having been fully restored throughout Styria.

. . .

The revolt claimed many victims on both sides. The mobilised forces of the executive suffered total casualties of 41 dead and 87 wounded, while the rebels sustained 42 dead and 59 wounded. Five non-participating civilians were killed and 18 injured. The number of rebels who fled to Yugoslavia probably amounted to several hundred.

In the course of investigations to trace participants in the rebel movement, more than 3,000 arrests were made.

Twenty heavy and five light machine-guns, about 1,000 rifles and 36,000 live rounds, as well as considerable amounts of other weapons and equipment, were confiscated.

Source: Bundesministerium für Landesverteidigung, *Die Julirevolte 1934. Das Eingreifen des Österreichischen Bundesheeres zu ihrer Niederwerfung*, Vienna, 1936, pp. 87, 113ff., 118 and 127ff.

71. Announcement by the federal government

To the armed forces of Austria, the Gendarmerie, to the Police and all formations of the volunteer Schutzkorps

The criminal attempt to overthrow the lawful public order in Austria by force of arms has failed; the struggle is over.

. . .

Your action and your sacrifices of blood on this occasion not only restored peace in our country but also preserved the peace in Europe. If the rebellion had succeeded, there would have followed not a new order but a terrible chaos and the very great danger of war. *Your sacrifices have saved the world sacrifices a thousand times over.* For this we also thank you!

. . .

Source: Bundesministerium für Landesverteidigung, *Die Julirevolte 1934. Das Eingreifen des Österreichischen Bundesheeres zu ihrer Niederwerfung*, Vienna, 1936, p. 190. Emphasis added.

72. Appeal by Prince Starhemberg to the *Heimatschutz*

Comrades in the Austrian Heimatschutz!

With deepest respect and emotion I bow before the fresh graves of 51 Austrian Home Defence Corps fighters. In never ending gratitude and loyalty I bow before these silent heroes of our units, men whose blood bears witness to their patriotism, and who became martyrs to our cause. In us, in the Austrian *Heimatschutz*, they will live on . . .

. . . Carry on showing the world that the moral fortitude which was inherent in old Austria and which made it great and powerful is still alive, that this idea of Austria, though today it embodies a state which is struggling for survival, has its supporters and champions who will have it recognised by the world.

It was for this idea that the Federal Chancellor, Dr Dollfuss, gave his life . . .

Austria will never die. Austria will become great and powerful, because this is our resolve.

Source: *Der Heimatschützer*, Vienna, 11 Aug. 1934.

Part VII

THE NAZIS ADMIT AND ANALYSE THEIR DEFEAT

73. The Austrian population and the army remain loyal

The [German] Legation in Austria to the Foreign Ministry

MUFF

SECRET   Vienna, 26 July 1934

No. Geh./278

Report no. 16/34 (Austria)

Concerning the events of 25 July 1934.

1. I had known for a long time that the National Socialists were considering the idea of, and had also made certain preparations for, a raid by an SA-formation disguised in Federal army and police uniforms on the Government during a Cabinet meeting.

Such an undertaking had prospects of lasting success only if it was accompanied by a popular rising or by intervention by the army on the side of the prospective new Government. The abortive attempt at a *Putsch* was to all appearances based on this last idea.

Time and again I have pointed out in my reports that I consider any *active* participation by the army to be out of the question. The course which the *Putsch* took has shown I was right. Although close contact is said to have been established between the leaders of the *Putsch* and various high-ranking officers, the army nevertheless remained firmly in the hands of the State Secretary for National Defence, who had escaped capture by the conspirators.

. . .

3. My report No. 11/Austria of 5 June 1934, compares the situation in Austria with trench warfare. The NSDAP's attempt to extricate themselves from this by force has failed, since it was based on false assumptions. The moral setback suffered by the aggressor is considerable, the initiative has passed to the other side.

. . .

4. In the above-mentioned report I said that the international consequences of a violent attack were immeasurable. This is the situation we are faced with today.

Source: DGFP, 1918–1945, Series C, vol. III, no. 125 (26 July 1934).

74. The 'masses' were lacking

The Head of the Volksbund für das Deutschtum im Ausland to the Foreign Ministry
Vienna-Raab, 31 July 1934

As I was able to ascertain, it was thought — also by the provincial representatives invited to the conversations last week — that an uprising would only have a chance of success in about two months' time.

. . .

The most serious and irresponsible mistakes were made right at the beginning: The first was to make the Government resign under pressure whilst the Vice Chancellor was in Italy, thus showing that the situation was completely misjudged. The Duce would naturally make use of him so as by this means to reinstate the 'legal Government' against the usurpers, and St[arhemberg] would of course be the man to accept such help.

. . .

The second mistake which was made in the local preparations was the lack of arrangements for conveying messages from the Office of the Federal Chancellor — this had apparently been overlooked — to cancel the action should the members of the Government leave the building prematurely. For it was even more senseless to undertake the action when, barely a quarter of an hour later, it was already possible to assemble a 'legal' government under Schuschnigg, thus defeating any possibility of forcing the hand of the Army and the Police by means of a proclamation. But to all appearances the 'up and coming men' simply waited to be fetched in in triumph after everything had been done by the smaller fry who were the ones who had to risk their necks.

. . .

It was only during the night that rioting began in earnest in different parts of Styria (Leoben, Judenburg, Western Styria, and frontier regions in Lower Styria) and heavy shooting began with serious losses on both sides. But everywhere the disastrous effects of the failure in Vienna, which had in fact completely destroyed the chances of success, immediately became evident.

At no point did the Army and the Police refuse to obey, and this sealed the fate of the military uprising, because it had always been realized that it would never be possible to succeed *against* the Army and the Police.

. . .

It is characteristic of the attitude of the Army and the Police — we, of course, were never believed when we predicted it! — that, for instance, Major Smolej who fell in the assault on Völkermarkt is a member of the Party and that Kappitz, who for a long time has not even been allowed to have a command, captured Feldkirchen. However, the man in the ranks can do nothing but obey — he is, after all, much too much of a soldier. How did such miscalculations come to be made!

. . .

The 'masses' are lacking. We are unable to prove that they exist and, at the moment when the matter was becoming really dangerous Italy intervened and her Consul at Klagenfurt enquired twice on Friday of the *Land* Government and of Barger whether he should not give the order to march. 'The most modern weapons for war had been made available!'

. . .

At home all the horrors of persecution will now be unleashed against our people, with the approval of 'the whole of Europe', which wishes to cover up the general offensive against the Reich.

. . .

The Schuschnigg era is precisely what we have been wanting to avoid at all costs.

Source: ADAP 1918–1945, Series C, vol. III, no. 143 (2 Aug. 1934).

75. 'A clear defeat' for the Third *Reich* and the NSDAP

The [German] Military Attaché in Austria to the Reichswehr Ministry

No. Geh. 307   Vienna, 30 August 1934

Report No. 21/34 — Austria

1. The abortive *Putsch* of 25 July has *closed a chapter in the 'German' struggle for Austria*. After the assumption of power by the National Socialists in the Reich, the National Socialist Party in Austria became the only authoritative exponent of the German idea in that country. In pursuit of the principle of totalitarianism it had grasped the leadership in the struggle; all the other national forces in the country were at most tolerated as hangers-on.

. . .

The Party's struggle for Austria, while provoking ever sharper counter-measures on the part of the Government, led from constitutional to unconstitutional methods, from propaganda to terrorism, and ended, inevitably, in an attempt at a forcible *Putsch* and in incitement to open revolt.

As everyone possessing any insight had predicted, *the outcome of this policy was a complete débâcle, and, at the same time, a defeat for the Reich*, embroiled as it was in party politics. A political situation abroad fraught with extreme danger was suddenly revealed to the startled world.

. . .

The meeting between Mussolini and Dollfuss which had been about to take place in Riccione might have given some indication of what, if anything, was to have been expected in future from cooperation with Italy.

However, the Party did not want to wait, since it could not but expect an unsatisfactory outcome for itself from such negotiations. Moreover, it was no longer in a position to wait, since the momentum of its action could no longer be reconciled with the slower political developments. Thus the Party, i.e. its present leaders — the Landesleitung in Munich — bears full and sole responsibility for the present situation. It has furnished proof of its political ineptitude.

2. *Austria's relationship with the Reich*, is, however, a fateful question for Germany.

. . .

Austria's significance in relation to greater Germany is in the first place defensive, situated as she is on the periphery of the Reich proper, and forming a south-eastern borderland. She thus blocks the way to any Italian advance across the mountain frontier, and forms a bastion against Silesia, forcing Czechoslovakia into Germany's sphere of influence. From the offensive point of view, however, Austria is the spring-board for the south-eastern area of Europe.

. . .

3. *The struggle for a 'German' Austria* must therefore continue but at a different level and by different means from those employed hitherto.

Source: *ADAP 1918–1945*, Series C, vol. III, no. 186 (30 Aug. 1934). Emphasis added.

Part VIII

HITLER RETREATS IN PANIC — A POSTHUMOUS VICTORY FOR DOLLFUSS

76. The *Reich* dissociates itself from the events in Austria

Report in the Völkischer Beobachter

Reich Government orders arrest of insurgents crossing the border

Berlin, 26 July

At three o'clock on Thursday morning, after we had gone to press, we received the following official bulletin:

Reports on Vienna Radio and from official Austrian news agencies indicate that agreements have been made between the Austrian insurgents and Austrian government agencies to ensure the safe conduct of the insurgents to Germany. These agreements have no relevance and no legal validity for the government of the German Reich.

The government of the German *Reich* has therefore given orders for the insurgents to be arrested should they attempt to cross the German border.

. . .

At the request of the Austrian governmental agencies and the Austrian insurgents, the German Ambassador in Vienna, Dr Rieth, expressed his willingness to approve a settlement between the two with regard to the safe conduct and removal of the insurgents to Germany, but he did so without first clearing the position with the government of the German *Reich*. As a result of this he was immediately recalled from his post.

Source: Völkischer Beobachter, Berlin edition, 26 July 1934.

77. Nazi insurgents to be sent to concentration camps

Note by the State Secretary

Berlin, 26 July 1934

. . .

At 10 p.m. the Reich Chancellor rang me up from Bayreuth and asked (apparently knowing about my telephone conversation) what news I had from Rieth in Vienna. He said at once that Rieth should have had nothing to do with the transport of the rebels to the German frontier, nor with playing the part of a mediator at all.

. . .

At 11 p.m. the Reich Chancellor rang up again and asked whether the agreement with the conspirators was still valid, as Federal Minister Schuschnigg had said in his broadcast that the condition was that there should be no further deaths. But, according to the same broadcast, Federal Chancellor Dollfuss was dead. I told the Reich Chancellor I had understood from Herr Rieth that what was meant was: no further deaths. Rieth had told me more than once that he had been urged to take note of the agreement for the reason that 'further bloodshed was to be avoided'. The Reich Chancellor replied that he would have the expelled conspirators taken into protective custody and transferred to a concentration camp. I, for my part, raised the question of a telegram of condolence from the Reich President to Federal President Miklas. The Reich Chancellor agreed.

Source: ADAP 1918–1945, Series C, vol. III, no. 115 (26 July 1934).

78. The end of fighting units at Austria's border

Memorandum by the State Secretary

Berlin, 1 August 1934

General von Reichenau rang me up at mid-day today.

. . .

He had just had an hour and a half's discussion with the Reich Chancellor [Hitler] about the Austrian situation, and the Reich Chancellor had flatly declared that he intended to wind up the National Socialist Party in Austria and to disband the Austrian Legion, merely retaining a charitable organization for the care of Austrian refugees under the unimpeachable cover of the Red Cross.

Source: ADAP 1918–1945, Series C, vol. III, no. 141 (1 Aug. 1934).

79. Austrian regional NSDAP leadership disbanded

Memorandum by an Official of Department II

Berlin, 7 August 1934
e.o. II Oe. 2047

. . .

The Führer has ordered that the Landesleitung Austria be dissolved at once. The reasons for this dissolution are ones of foreign policy. Appropriate provision will be made for the members of the former Landesleitung Austria.

Source: ADAP 1918–1945, Series C, vol. III, no. 149 (7 Aug. 1934).

80. Right of veto for Franz von Papen

The Führer and Chancellor to Ministers Hess and Goebbels, Herr von Papen and the Office of the Secret State Police

Berlin, 8 August 1934

In order to ensure the uniform policy which I wish to see pursued in future, I hereby order that neither Party authorities nor anyone else may discuss, either on the wireless or in the press, questions concerning German-Austrian policy, unless agreement has previously been reached between the Reich Propaganda Minister and the present Minister in Vienna, Herr von Papen. In particular I forbid Party authorities to discuss such questions on the wireless on their own initiative.

Source: ADAP 1918–1945, Series C, vol. III, no. 151 (8 Aug. 1934).

81. Austria will not be a colony of the Third *Reich*

Minister Papen to State Secretary Bülow

. . .

Vienna, 17 August 1934

Political Report

The presentation of my credentials yesterday went off in the usual manner . . . The meeting with the Federal Chancellor and the Federal President went off with the appropriate courtesies, but I had the feeling that I was visiting a churchyard instead of meeting German-Austrian statesmen at a ceremony of welcome. . . .

. . .

The Reich Chancellor was not only determined, for the sake of a *détente* in Europe, to respect Austria's formal independence, but he also recognized Austria's right to settle her own internal affairs independently.

. . .

The Federal Chancellor first thanked me for the frankness of my statements and then gave the basic points of the policy which he intended to pursue. He emphasized that he, a Tyrolese by birth, had always felt special sympathy for Austria's German rôle and for his country's *volksdeutsch* tasks. *Nevertheless he was firmly resolved not to allow Austria to become a colony or province of the German Reich.* The advantage of the newly formed Cabinet was that it now only included 'Austrians' in this sense. He noted with gratitude my assurances that the Reich Government wished to safeguard Austria's integrity at home and abroad. It remained to be seen whether this promise would be kept.

Source: ADAP 1918–1945, Series C, vol. III, no. 167 (19 Aug. 1934). Emphasis added.

82. Posthumous victory for Dollfuss

Berlin, 19 August 1934

GUIDING PRINCIPLES FOR GERMAN POLICY *VIS-À-VIS* AUSTRIA IN THE IMMEDIATE FUTURE

(These guiding principles were approved by the Reich Chancellor on 13 August 1934.)

In accordance with the Reich Chancellor's letter to Herr von Papen of 26 July 1934, relations between the German and Austrian States are to be 'guided once more on to a normal and friendly course'. The pre-requisites for this are, on the part of

1. *The Reich*: to avoid any appearance of meddling in Austria's internal affairs;

2. *Austria*: to put a stop to the fight from Austrian soil against the National Socialist régime in Germany and to restore peace with those sections of the Austrian people whose sympathies are with Greater Germany.

From this emerge the following guiding principles for the

1. *Policy of the Reich*

(*a*) to deal with the Austrian question is the exclusive concern of those persons whose function it is to conduct foreign policy;

(*b*) any participation in Austrian affairs by Party offices in the Reich is to be stopped;

(*c*) no Austrian fighting organization of any kind will be tolerated in the Reich if it attempts from there to intervene in the development of Austria (Landesleitung, Legion, Kampfring, etc.);

2. *Policy of the Party*

(*a*) complete separation, as regards organization, of the Party in the Reich and the Austrian Party;

(*b*) exclusion of all persons compromised by having been leaders of the fight so far from the leadership of the Austrian Party. Nor must such persons be 'rewarded' for their 'services' by being appointed to important posts in the Reich, for they have committed serious political crimes and murders; the position of the Party members in Austria, if nothing else, demands that they be so excluded.

Points for implementing policy within the above framework:

(*a*) Above all, easing of the atmosphere without false considerations of prestige. This entails the stopping of all aggressive press and wireless propaganda. The best thing would be for Austria to be mentioned as little as possible in the Reich for some time; this will deprive the counter-propagandists of material. The Führer has ordered that in future political statements about German-Austrian policy in the press and on the wireless may only be made after having previously been agreed upon between the Reich Propaganda Minister, the Foreign Minister and Herr von Papen.

(*b*) Attempts to bring about normal relations must be made without undue haste, as otherwise we will only cause the forces at present in opposition to one another (Christian Socialists — Heimwehr) to unite.

Source: *ADAP 1918–1945*, Series C, vol. III, no. 167 (19 Aug. 1934).

83. Reorganisation of the *Kampfring* of Austrians in the Reich

The Führer and Chancellor to the Führer's Deputy

Berlin 19 August, 1934
Rk. 7394

In pursuance of the policy which I have adopted with regard to German-Austrian relations, I request you to order, with immediate effect, that the Kampfring of the Austrians in the Reich to be so reorganized as to exclude in future any political activities on the part of the Kampfring involving interference in Austria's internal affairs. The Kampfring is to be converted into a Relief Society [*Hilfsbund*], concerned only with the cultural, social and economic care of its members. In order to make this change apparent also to the world at large, the direction of the Kampfring should be placed in other, suitable, hands.

ADOLF HITLER

Source: *ADAP 1918–1945*, Series C, vol. III, no. 165 (19 Aug. 1934).

84. Hitler regrets and orders a new course

The Führer's Deputy, Hess, to Herr Frauenfeld

Munich, 21 August 1934

Dear Party Comrade Frauenfeld:
I have received your letter of August 17 about Austria.

I must once more state quite plainly that, by order of the Führer, the Reich German Party must have nothing at all to do with the National Socialists in Austria. It is likewise strictly forbidden for Austrian leaders in Germany to exert any kind of influence on the NSDAP here. The Führer's order is not merely a formality but is definitely an order which must be obeyed unconditionally. Failure to obey this order will entail severe punishment, which, in cases where the interests of the German Reich are threatened, may even include imprisonment.

It is simply and solely a matter for the National Socialists residing in [to decide] where and in what form they should build up anew a purely Austrian NSDAP.

. . .

You and all other Austrians will believe me when I say that the Führer and his collaborators find it very hard to adopt this harsh attitude, but Germany's vital interests, and therefore indirectly also the interests of the German-speaking peoples and not least of the Austrian NSDAP itself, are at stake. As you know, after November 1923 the Führer took decisions which led to an entirely new and absolutely lawful policy being pursued by the NSDAP in Germany, decisions to which he adhered and which were later to prove justified and to achieve success. Let me assure you that, despite everything, the decisions now taken by the Führer in respect of National Socialism in Austria will one day, and that in a perfectly legal manner, enable all your wishes and ours regarding Austria to be fulfilled.

Source: ADAP 1918–1945, Series C, vol. III, no. 173 (21 Aug. 1934).

85. Warning to the German press against interference in Austria's affairs

Senior Counsellor Renthe-Fink to Counsellor of Embassy Erbach

Berlin, 28 September 1934

STRICTLY CONFIDENTIAL

. . .

The competent Head of Department at the Ministry of Propaganda has issued to the German press, at a Press Conference held on 17 September the following strictly confidential directive on the treatment of Austrian affairs, which is based on the attitude taken up on principle by the German Government and in particular by the Führer and Chancellor.

1. Austria's relations with Germany must be considered as part of the general European situation and not merely in the light of specifically Austrian problems, that is to say, the press should not give as much prominence to discussion of every-day events inside Austria as it does to discussion of the big political problems of the Danube area.

2. In this connexion stress must, of course, be laid on the German Reich's fundamental interest in developments in the Danube area and on her right to have a say in the affairs of this region. It must be strongly emphasized that Germany cannot allow herself to be excluded from the Danube area and is prepared to collaborate in any solution acceptable to her in this respect.

3. All discussions which might be interpreted as one-sided interference by Germany in Austria's domestic affairs should be avoided; that is to say, the German press should refrain from giving the Austrian Government any advice

on how to overcome their domestic difficulties. News on conditions inside Austria may be published as hitherto, but comment should take the foregoing points into account.

Source: *ADAP 1918–1945*, Series C, vol. III, no. 222 (28 Aug. 1934).

Part IX
REACTIONS OF FOREIGN POWERS

86. Italy's preventive measures

Rome's Governmental Communiqué of 26 July 1934

Immediately after the news of the assassination of Chancellor Dollfuss, i.e. at 4 p.m. on July 25, orders were issued for movements of land and air forces to the Brenner Pass and Carinthia in view of possible complications. These forces are large enough to deal with any eventuality. It may be assumed, however, that at the moment the situation in Austria appears to be returning to normal, it will not be necessary to go beyond measures of a preventive nature.

Source: Michael Freund (ed.), *Weltgeschichte der Gegenwart in Dokumenten, 1934/35*, Part I: 'Internationale Politik', Essen, 1944, p. 267.

87. Mussolini sees Hitler as Dollfuss' murderer

From Starhemberg's Memoirs

. . .

I began by thanking the Duce once more for the help he had given us, and also expressing the thanks of the new Chancellor, Schuschnigg. The Duce replied: 'What I have done was dictated by my friendship for Austria, my friendship for Dollfuss and for you. But it was also done in the vital interests of Italy. And,' he continued, 'it was done for Europe. It would mean the end of European civilisation if this country of murderers and paederasts were to overrun Europe.'

. . .

'There is no doubt that the National Socialist Government was the instigator of this revolution and that Hitler had Dollfuss murdered.' Visibly stirred, but without raising his voice, he exclaimed three times: 'Hitler is the murderer of Dollfuss, Hitler is the guilty man, he is responsible for this.' He continued to speak of Hitler, very contemptuously, calling him 'a horrible sexual degenerate, a dangerous fool'. His strictures on Nazism were severe. It was a 'revolution of the old Germanic tribes of the primeval forest against the Latin civilisation of Rome'. He grew almost violent as he said that National Socialism and Fascism could not be put on the same plane.

. . .

'Perhaps the Great Powers will recognise the German danger. It may be possible to organise a great coalition against Germany. I cannot always be the only one to march to the Brenner,' he said, laughing almost scornfully. 'Others must show some interest in Austria and the Danube Basin.'

Source: Ernst Rüdiger Starhemberg, *Between Hitler and Mussolini*, pp. 169ff.

88. Condolences from the French Prime Minister

Telegram of 26 July 1934

It was with the deepest regret that the government of France received the news of the abominable assassination which cost Chancellor Dollfuss his life. In the name of the French government I wish to express our deepest sympathy to you. *The Chancellor fell as a victim of his loyalty to his Austrian fatherland, whose independence he defended until the very end.* Firmly devoted to protecting this independence, the whole of France shares in Austria's mourning.

Source: Michael Freund (ed.), *Weltgeschichte der Gegenwart in Dokumenten, 1934/5*. Part I: 'Internationale Politik', Essen, 1944, p. 266. Emphasis added.

89. Mussolini's judgement of Dollfuss

Telegram

His Excellency, the Royal Italian Prime Minister Mussolini to Vice-Chancellor Prince Starhemberg

26 July 1934

Federal Chancellor Dollfuss's tragic end causes me great grief stop Allied to him by the bonds of personal friendship and common political views, I have always admired his constancy, his deep modesty, his great personal courage stop The independence of Austria, for which he died, is a cause which Italy had defended and which will now be defended with all the more determination stop In a time of unprecedented difficulties Federal Chancellor Dollfuss served the people he himself had risen from, with absolute selflessness and with no regard to danger stop His memory will be honoured not only in Austria but throughout the civilised world, whose moral condemnation of this act has already struck home at those directly, and those indirectly, responsible stop Please accept this expression of my condolences, which is at the same time intended as a reflection of the outrage and sympathy felt by the Italian people.

MUSSOLINI

Source: *Neues Politisches Archiv* (Staatsarchiv), Vienna, Fasc. 459, no. 908.

90. A *Reichswehr* report on Italy's military reaction

Memorandum by an official of the State Secretary's Secretariat

SECRET   Berlin, 27 July 1934

Secretary of Legation Adolf von Bülow informs us from the Reichswehr Ministry that, according to recent reports reaching them, large numbers of troops are encamped on the mountain slopes on both sides of Vipiteno. Their strength is estimated at roughly one division. Units of the 11th Infantry Division have been recognized. It has been established that there is another division in the Sarentino north of Bolzano. On the evening of [July] 26 the formations of the 11th Infantry Division were issued with live ammunition. In general it has been established that since yesterday the units stationed in the Bolzano area have been moved further north towards the frontier.

The Reichswehr Ministry are of the opinion that these measures are in preparation for possible further incidents.

[THEODOR] KORDT

Source: ADAP 1918–1945, Series C, vol. III, no. 128 (27 July 1934).

91. War on Austria's behalf?

An Italian view

Sir,

I have the honour to report that when I saw the [Italian] Under-Secretary of State for Foreign Affairs this morning . . .

As regards the immediate future, he thought there was nothing to be done but to watch developments closely. *Suggestions had been made that perhaps England, France and Italy might go beyond their February declaration and declare that interference with the independence of Austria would be regarded as a casus belli.* He did not, however, believe that His Majesty's Government would lend themselves to any such declaration in view of the marked disinclination of British public opinion to assume further continental liabilities.

. . .

In conclusion, Signor Suvich said that the most encouraging feature of recent developments was that they at least disposed of the Nazi contention that they enjoyed the backing of practically the whole of Austrian opinion.

Source: ADAP 1919–1939, 2nd Series, vol. VI, 1933–4, no. 539 (27 July 1934). Emphasis added.

92. Berlin protests against Italian threats and insults

Telegram

The Ambassador in Italy to the Foreign Ministry

No. 173 of 28 July					Rome, 29 July 1934 — 12.15 a.m.
Today I had my first conversation with Suvich since the events in Vienna, and I began by complaining vigorously about the attitude of the Italian press; I said that I more than anyone could sympathize with Italy's views and could understand the sharp tone taken by the Italian press in view of the terrible occurrences in Vienna. Nevertheless the Italian press was almost without exception lacking in any restraint or objectivity, it was adopting an incredible tone, was printing impudent cartoons, was insulting the Führer and the Reich Ministers in office, and did not even shrink from open disloyalty. Suvich replied that he could in any case not accept my last phrase.

. . .

I then pointed out to Suvich that open threats of violence had been uttered in quite a number of newspapers and asked him what the meaning of these threats was in conjunction with the military measures which had been announced. Suvich replied that, as had been clearly stated in the communiqué, the military measures were of a purely precautionary nature. No action was intended as long as no foreign troops marched into Austria either from Germany or from Yugoslavia, and as long as the Austrian Government remained in control, which was now clearly the case.

Source: ADAP 1918–1945, Series C, vol. III, no. 132 (29 July 1934).

93. The costs and effects of Austria's defeat of Hitler

Commentary from 'The Observer', London, 29 July 1934

The important, perhaps historic, sequel to Wednesday's outrage is the increasing concentration of a whole world's thought, not upon Vienna, but upon Berlin.

. . .

	The panic-stricken measures subsequently taken by HERR HITLER to sidetrack the world's indignation had the inevitably opposite effect of directing and strengthening it. . . .

. . .

The panic in Berlin is the good that comes out of the evil. DR DOLLFUSS, who heroically defended a weak Austria against a powerful and unscrupulous intrigue, is himself the price that had to be paid for Austria's survival. The price is bitter, and is universally resented. But thereby he has unforgettably served both his country and Europe.

Dr Dollfuss did more than any man in Europe to save Europe, including Germany, from the Nazi terror of Berlin. That is his true monument . . .

94. Dollfuss and German culture

Commentary from 'The Times', London, 30 July 1934

. . .by his death he [Dollfuss] testified that there is indeed a Germanic civilisation worth saving.

95. The three-power declaration of 27 September 1934 regarding Austria's independence

After having proceeded to a fresh examination of the Austrian situation, the representatives of France, the United Kingdom, and Italy have agreed in the name of their Governments to recognize that the Declaration of February 17, 1934, regarding the necessity of maintaining the independence and integrity of Austria in accordance with the Treaties in force, retains its full effect and will continue to inspire their common policy.

Source: John W. Wheeler-Bennett and Stephen Heald (eds), *Documents on International Affairs 1934*, London, 1935, p. 298.

96. Italy and the independence of Austria

Extract from a Speech by Signor Mussolini, 6 October 1934

We have defended and will defend the independence of the Austrian Republic, an independence which has been consecrated by the blood of a Chancellor, who may have been small in stature but whose spirit and soul were great.

Those who assert that Italy has any aggressive aims, or that she wishes to establish some kind of protectorate over that Republic, are either ignorant of the facts or are consciously lying.

Source: As Document 85, above.

97. The Stresa agreement, 14 April 1935

Joint Resolution of the Stresa Conference

. . .

3. The Representatives of the three Governments examined afresh the Austrian situation.

They confirmed the Anglo-Franco-Italian declarations of 17 February and 27 September 1934, in which the three Governments recognized that the necessity of maintaining the independence and integrity of Austria would continue to inspire their common policy.

Referring to the Franco-Italian protocol of 7 January 1935, and to the Anglo-French declarations of 3 February 1935, in which the decision was reaffirmed to consult together as to the measures to be taken in the case of threats to the integrity and independence of Austria, they agreed to recommend that representatives of all the Governments enumerated in the protocol of Rome should meet at a very early date, with a view to concluding the Central European agreement.

. . .

The three Powers, the object of whose policy is the collective maintenance of peace within the framework of the League of Nations, find themselves in complete agreement in opposing, by all practicable means, any unilateral repudiation of treaties which may endanger the peace of Europe, and will act in close and cordial collaboration for this purpose.

Source: Wheeler-Bennett and Heald (eds), op. cit., pp. 80ff.

98. On Austria's key position in Europe

From the speech of the British Foreign Secretary, Sir Samuel Hoare, in the House of Commons on 11 July 1935

'We have again and again set forth our well considered opinion that Austria strategically and economically occupies a key position in Europe and that a change in her status would shake the foundations of European peace. We shall therefore, also in the future, manifest our heartfelt and sympathetic interest in the brave efforts which her government and her people are making in order to maintain and to strengthen their independent existence. This is one of the reasons why the British Government would be pleased without delay to see the conclusion of a Danube pact and of non-aggression and non-interference for Central Europe.'

Source: Red-White-Red Book. Justice for Austria, Vienna, 1947, pp. 59ff.

Part X

99. Austria's defeat of Hitler as an argument of the Second Republic

From the Red-White-Red Book of the first post-war coalition government of the Austrian People's Party and Socialist Party which was to form the basis of Austria earning the right to be treated as a Liberated Country

PREFACE

This book forms the first part of a publication destined to show the fate and attitude of Austria during the twelve years existence of the 'Third Reich' and to establish the reasons for her claim to the status and the treatment of a 'liberated state' in the interpretation of the Moscow declaration [of 1943]. . . .

Particular importance must be given to the period before Hitler came to power to the Second World War. The judgment of this period and in particular of the 'Anschluss' which comes within it, in the public opinion of the world, is today still in many instances under the impression of former National Socialist propaganda, which knew well to create the illusion not only with regard to their then adherents in Austria, but also with regard to its adversaries in distant countries, of an Austria, the majority of whose inhabitants were striving towards the 'Third Reich', and to represent the occupation, which was a feat of violence, as a peaceful reunion desired by both parties. In that period the Austrian people wrote the first chapter of the resistance movement with their blood and paid the first instalment of her 'passage', a point all the more important, as Austria at that moment stood alone in the struggle.

. . .

When in the early hours of 12 March 1938, the German army on every point of the Austro-German frontier marched into Austria and the squadrons of the German Air Force thundered over the helpless country, only a very few people realised that Hitler had thus started his war against the peace and liberty of the world. In faithful compliance with its European peace function, Austria had, during five years, withstood the over-powerful pressure of National Socialist aggression. Her fall — inevitable under the conditions which then reigned — was the bursting of the dike through which the elements of the brown deluge were to pour over the whole of Europe.

Their first victim, left in the lurch, by the whole world, was Austria.

It is not often that history allows the meaning and significance of a country, the mission and tragedy of her people to appear so evident as in this case. Rarely — perhaps never a European state and every single one of its inhabitants had been put to the test in a harder and more ruthless way than it happened here; for during years Austria, economically weak, suffering still from the unsolved problems of a hardly overcome world war, had stood *alone* and *immediately* opposite an adversary, whom in the ensuing years a whole world, armed to the teeth, could only at the cost of immense sacrifice and by the putting forward of all her strength, overcome after a struggle of nearly six years.

May the nations and statesmen whose historical task it is to-day to re-establish peace and to secure it, remember this fact and dispense to Austria and her people that justice, which has always been the best foundation of peace.

. . .

These are in brief outline the practical and psychological elements on which an unbiassed and just judgment of the fate and attitude of Austria should be based. One may formulate the situation of Austria from the point of view of the right of nations and political economy, from the date of the occupation until this day. One way or the other, the following facts remain:

1. Austria was the *first* free state — and during five years the *only* state which offered practical resistance to Hitler's policy of aggression.

. . .

There follows a summary of the strategy employed by the NSDAP and the Third Reich against Austria.

The meaning and aim of this procedure consisted:

1. To intimidate the Austrian population which in its majority rejected National Socialism.

. . .

2. The economic situation in Austria — difficult in itself — was to be increased in order to cause social and political unrest.

3. The outside world was to believe that revolutionary conditions prevailed in Austria so that confidence in Austria should be shaken.

4. The claim of the National Socialist Party programme for the incorporation of Austria was to be camouflaged before the general public of the world as an irrepressible and passionate desire on the part of Austria.

As in spite of all difficulties, in spite of the unequal proportion of forces between the aggressor and the attacked, and in spite of the absence of adequate diplomatic and economic foreign support, the Austrian Government, its executive and the vast majority of the Austrian people did not flag in their resistance against the National Socialist attempts at violation. National Socialism further augmented its terrorism, until it finally in the *July Putsch of 1934 proceeded to the first comprehensive attack* against the *existing European order*. That this 'Putsch' had been organized and directed from the Reich is sufficiently known to the world and confirmed by documentary proof.

. . .

The July 'Putsch' broke down within a few days. The political summary of the procedure of National Socialist aggression is the following:. . .

> The Austrian patriots killed in the defence of this National Socialist attempt are the first martyrs of the free world in the struggle against Hitler. The rapid breakdown of the 'Putsch' is the proof, that not only the Austrian Government, but also the Austrian people, declined to be ruled by Hitler.

. . .

> To charge the so-called 'Anschluss' and its inevitable consequences to the Austrian account, however, is and remains a concealment of actual facts. *The occupation of Austria was not an Austrian but a European affair. He who would assert the contrary, consciously or sub-consciously adopts the slogans of Hitler's and Goebbels' propaganda!*

. . .

> And when in our days Barbarism again broke forth, harder and more dominating than ever, Vienna and little Austria desperately clung to their European convictions. Five years long Austria withstood with all her might, and only when she was abandoned in the decisive hour, this Imperial city, this capital of our old Austrian culture was degraded to a provincial town of that Germany to which it never belonged.

> *Austria's* cry for Justice is therefore established on the following fundamental facts:

> *Austria* is a 'liberated' country in the sense of the repeated declaration of the Allies.

> *Austria*, as long as she existed as a state, offered active resistance to German aggression and the Austrian people have also after the occupation continued this resistance actively and passively and have thus, within the outlines of possible action, contributed to her liberation.

Source: Red-White-Red Book, op.cit., pp. 3, 5, 7, 25ff., 205ff.

100. The first 'Austria Day' in the United States

Speeches of American public figures, 25 July 1942

On 25 July 1934 Dr Dollfuss was murdered on direct, personal orders from Hitler. For every true Austrian this day is a day of deep grief.

And yet, this black day has given us courage and hope. American statesmen have chosen this very day to speak up publicly on our behalf.

On 25 July Senator Claude Pepper and Congressman Herman P. Eberharter gave deeply moving speeches before us Austrians. *No fewer than 13 governors declared 25 July to be 'Austria Day' in their state*: in California, Colorado, Iowa,

Kentucky, Louisiana, Maryland, Massachusetts, Nebraska, New Jersey, New Mexico, North Carolina, South Dakota and Tennessee.

Subsequently, on 27 July, Secretary of State Cordell Hull declared that the United States government has never adopted the standpoint that Austria was legally incorporated into the German Reich.

. . .

Senator C. Pepper's Speech
Eight years ago today, Hitler suffered his first defeat. Brave Austria, small in numbers though great in spirit, gained another of its many memorable victories. It was on this day in July 1934 that Hitler's evil plans to conquer the world first became plain for all the world to see. But more than that, it became evident to the outraged world just what criminal methods this common scoundrel was prepared to use in order to loot the entire world.

. . .

But this attempt [to overthrow the Austrian government] failed, in spite of the ruthlessness of the attack, despite the barbaric way in which it was executed, and despite its meticulous planning. But its defeat was not to be put down to a lack of determination on the part of the aggressors — it was attributable to the iron resistance that the intruders met with and were unable to overcome, whether in the government or in the army or among the public.

Although the fighting continued for several days, Hitler's band of Nazis was forced to withdraw and Hitler, who, in his bottomless depravity, was not ashamed to rob the country in which he first saw the light of day, experienced his first humiliating defeat.

. . .

The world, after many tragic experiences, now knows that this noble man Dollfuss and the brave Austrians who for a time were able to bring Hitler's expansionist drive to a halt not only saved Austria but also temporarily secured the freedom of the rest of the world.

. . .

It should be stressed, though, that this small, intrepid man Dollfuss did not abandon his country, but rather sacrificed his own life for it. And so it will be emblazoned on the pages of history that wise old Austria made the first blood sacrifice in the attempt to halt this beast's march through the world.

. . .

However, it is regrettable that those Austrians who love their home-country and freedom have not received greater recognition from among the ranks of those who are equally determined to crush Hitler's tyranny and the perfidy of the Axis powers anywhere in the world. . . .

Source: Donau-Echo (magazine for Austrian émigrés), Toronto, Canada, 15 Aug. 1942. Emphasis added.

SELECT BIBLIOGRAPHY

PRIMARY SOURCES

Auerbach, Helmuth, *Eine nationalsozialistische Stimme zum Wiener Putsch vom 25. Juli 1934*, in VfZG 12 (1964), pp. 201–8.

Beiträge zur Vorgeschichte und Geschichte der Julirevolte, ed. Bundeskommissariat für Heimatdienst, based on official sources, Vienna, 1934.

Berchtold, Klaus, *Österreichische Parteiprogramme 1868–1966*, Vienna, 1967.

Das Braunbuch. Hakenkreuz gegen Österreich, ed. Bundeskanzleramt, Vienna, 1933.

Documents on British Foreign Policy, 1919–1939, 2nd series, vols V (1933) and VI (1933–4), London, 1956 and 1957. (Quoted as DBFP.)

Documents on International Affairs, 1933 and 1934, ed. John Wheeler-Bennett and Stephen A. Heald, London, 1934 and 1935.

Die Erhebung der österreichischen Nationalsozialisten im Juli 1934. Bericht der Historischen Kommission des Reichsführers SS, Vienna/Frankfurt/Zürich, 1965, new edn 1984.

Die Julirevolte 1934. Das Eingreifen des österreichischen Bundesheeres zu ihrer Niederwerfung, ed. Bundesminister für Landesverteidigung, Vienna, 1936.

Documents on German Foreign Policy 1918–1945, Series C, vols I, II, III, London: Her Majesty's Stationery Office, 1957, 1959. (Quoted as DGFP.)

Mussolini-Dollfuss. Geheimer Briefwechsel, Vienna, 1949. (Quoted as *Geheimer Briefwechsel*.)

Papers Relating to the Foreign Relations of the United States (Diplomatic Papers) 1933 and 1934, Washington, DC, 1950 and 1951.

Protokolle des Klubvorstandes der Christlichsozialen Partei, 1932 bis 1934. ed. Walter Goldinger, Vienna, 1980. (Quoted as *CS Protokolle*.)

Protokolle des Ministerrates der Ersten Republik, 1918–1938, ed. R. Neck and A. Wandruszka, Kabinett Dr Engelbert Dollfuss, vols 1–5 (20.5.1932–17.2.1934), Vienna, 1980–4.

Red-White-Red Book. Justice for Austria. Descriptions, Documents and Proofs to the Antecedents and History of the Occupation of Austria (from official sources), Part I, Vienna, 1947.

Reichold, Ludwig, *Kampf um Österreich. Die Vaterländische Front und ihr Widerstand gegen den Anschluss 1933–1938*, Vienna, 1984. A documentation.

Unser Staatsprogram — Führerworte. Bundeskommissariat für Heimatdienst, Vienna, 1935.

Starhemberg, Ernst Rüdiger, *Die Reden*, Vienna, 1935.

Suvich, Fulvio, *Memorie, 1932–1936*, Milan, 1984.

Tautscher, Anton, *So sprach der Kanzler. Dollfuss' Vermächtnis*, Vienna, 1935. (Quoted as *Dollfuss' Vermächtnis*.)

Weber, Edmund, *Dollfuss an Österreich*, Vienna, 1935.

Weltgeschichte der Gegenwart in Dokumenten, 5 vols, ed. Michael Freund, Essen, 1944.

SECONDARY SOURCES

Ackerl, Isabella, 'Das Kampfbündnis der NSDAP mit der Grossdeutschen Volkspartei vom 15. März 1933' in *Justizpalast*, pp. 121–8.

Andics, Hellmut, *Der Staat, den keiner wollte. Österreich 1918–1938*, Vienna, 1962.

Bauer, Otto, *Die Österreichische Revolution*, Vienna, 1923.

——, *Der Aufstand der Österreichischen Arbeiter*, Brünn, 1934, new edn Vienna, 1947.

Benedikt, Heinrich (ed.), *Geschichte der Republik Österreich*, Munich, 1954.

Bielka, Erich, 'Theodor von Hornbostel (1889–1973)' in *Neue Österreichische Bibliographie*, vol. XXI.

Binder, Dieter A., *Dollfuss und Hitler — Über die Aussenpolitik des autoritären Ständestaates in den Jahren 1933/1934*, Graz, 1979.

——'Der grundlegende Wandel in der Österreichischen Aussenpolitik 1933 — Ein Beitrag zum quasi-neutralen Staatus der Ersten Republik' in *Geschichte und Gegenwart*, vol. 2, no. 3, Sept. 1983, pp. 226–43.

Bluhm, William F., *Building an Austrian Nation. The Political Integration of a Western State*, New Haven/London, 1973.

Bock, Fritz, *Das Schicksalsjahr 1934*, Vienna, 1983.

Bracher, Karl Dietrich/Sauer, Wolfgang/Schulz, Gerhard, *Die nationalsozialistische Machtergreifung*, Cologne/Opladen, 1962.

Busshoff, Heinrich, *Das Dollfuss-Regime in Österreich in geistesgeschichtlicher Perspektive*, Berlin, 1968.

Carsten, Francis L., *Fascist Movement in Austria: From Schönerer to Hitler*, London/Beverly Hills, 1977.

Diamant, Alfred, *Austrian Catholics and the First Republic, 1918–1934*, Princeton, 1960.

Desput, Josef F. (ed.), *Österreich 1934–1984. Erfahrungen, Erkenntnisse, Besinnung*, Graz/ Vienna/ Cologne, 1984.

Ebneth, Rudolf, *Die österreichische Wochenzeitschrift 'Der christliche Ständestaat', 1933–1938*, Mainz, 1976.

Edmonson, C. Earl, *The Heimwehr and Austrian Politics 1918–1936*, Athens, Ohio, 1978.

Eichstädt, Ulrich, *Von Dollfuss zu Hitler*, Wiesbaden, 1955.

Etschmann, Wolfgang, *Die Kämpfe um Österreich im Juli 1934*, Vienna, 1984.

Falschlehner, Gerhard, 'Das Österreichbild in den Politischen Zeitschriften des Ständestaates', unpubl. Ph. D. diss., University of Vienna, 1981.

Fischer, Ernst, *Ende einer Illusion*, Vienna/Munich, 1973.

Funder, Friedrich, *Als Österreich den Sturm bestand*, Vienna/Munich, 1957.

Furlani, Silvio/*Wandruszka*, Adam, *Österreich und Italien. Ein bilaterales Geschichtsbuch*, Vienna/Munich, 1973.

Goldner, Franz, *Dollfuss im Spiegel der US-Akten*, St Pölten, 1979.

Gregory, John Duncan, *Dollfuss and his Times*, London, 1935.

Hartlieb, Wladimir von, *Parole: Das Reich*, Vienna/Leipzig, 1939.

Hillgruber, Andreas, 'Das Anschlussproblem (1918–1945) aus deutscher Sicht' in: Kann, Robert A./Prinz, Friedrich E. (eds), *Deutschland und Österreich*, Vienna/Munich, 1980, pp. 161–8.

Holtmann, Everhard, *Zwischen Unterdrückung und Befriedung. Sozialistische Arbeiterbewegung und autoritäres Regime in Österreich, 1933–1938*, Munich, 1978.

Hoor, Ernst, *Österreich 1918–1938. Staat ohne Nation. Republik ohne Republikaner*, Vienna/Munich, 1966.

Hornbostel, Theodor, 'Fremde Einflüsse auf die Politik der I. Republik Österreichs' in *Österreich in Geschichte und Literatur 2*, 1958, pp. 129–38.

Huemer, Peter, *Sektionschef Robert Hecht und die Zerstörung der Demokratie in Österreich*, Vienna, 1975.

Jacobsen, Hans-Adolf, *Nationalsozialistische Aussenpolitik, 1933–1938*, Frankfurt a.M./Berlin, 1968.

Jagschitz, Gerhard, *Die Jugend des Bundeskanzlers Dr Engelbert Dollfuss*, Vienna, 1967.

——, 'Der österreichische Ständestaat 1934–1938' in Weinzierl, Erika/Skalnik, Kurt, *Österreich 1918–1938. Geschichte der Ersten Republik.*, Graz/Vienna/Cologne, 1938, pp. 497–516.

——, *Der Putsch. Die Nationalsozialisten 1934 in Österreich.*, Graz/Vienna/Cologne, 1976.

Das Jahr 1934. 25 Juli. Protokoll des Symposiums in Wien, 8. Oktober 1974, Jedlicka, Ludwig/Neck, Rudolf (eds), Munich, 1975.

Jedlicka, Ludwig, 'Das autoritäre System in Österreich' in *Aus Politik und Zeitgeschichte. Beilage zur Wochenzeitung 'Das Parlament'*, B 30 of 25.7.1970, pp. 3–15.

——, *Vom alten zum neuen Österreich. Fallstudien zur Zeitgeschichte 1900–1975*, St Pölten, 1975.

——, 'Das Jahr 1934' in *Österreich 1918–1938*, pp. 73–93.

——/Neck, Rudolf (eds), *Vom Justizpalast zum Heldenplatz. Studien und Dokumentationen. 1927–1938*, Vienna, 1975.

Kann, Robert A./Prinz, Friedrich E. (eds), *Deutschland und Österreich. Ein bilaterales Geschichtsbuch*, Vienna/Munich, 1980.

Kerekes, Lajos, *Abenddämmerung einer Demokratie. Mussolini, Gömbös und die Heimwehr*, Vienna/Zürich 1966

Kindermann, Gottfried-Karl (ed.), *Grundelemente der Weltpolitik*, 2nd edn, Munich, 1981 (3rd enlarged edn, Munich, 1986).

——, 'Zur neuen "Selbstfindung Österreichs" ' in *Zeitschrift für Politik*, vol. 32, no. 3, Sept. 1985, pp. 279–95.

Kleindel, Walter, *Österreich. Daten zur Geschichte und Kultur*, Vienna/ Heidelberg, 1978.

Klingenstein, Grete, *Die Anleihe von Lausanne. Ein Beitrag zur Geschichte der Ersten Republik in den Jahren 1931–1934*, Vienna/Graz, 1965.

Koerner, Ralf Richard, *So haben sie es damals gemacht ... Die Propagandavorbereitungen zum Österreich-Anschluss durch das Hitler-Regime 1933 bis 1938*, Vienna, 1958.

Leser, Norbert, 'Österreichs Demokratie am 19. Juni 1931. Das Koalitionsangebot Ignaz Seipels an Otto Bauer' in *Christliche Demokratie*, vol. 2, no. 1, Feb. 1984, pp. 52–62.

——, *Zwischen Reformismus und Bolschewismus — Der Austromarxismus als Theorie und Praxis*, Vienna/Frankfurt/Zürich, 1968.

Mikoletzky, Hans Leo, *Österreichische Zeitgeschichte*, Vienna, 1969.

Meisels, Lucian Otto, *Die politischen Beziehungen zwischen den Vereinigten Staaten von Amerika und Österreich, 1933–1938*, Vienna, 1960.

Neck, Rudolf (ed.), *Österreich im Jahre 1918*, Munich, 1968.

Nick, Rainer/Pelinka, Anton, *Bürgerkrieg — Sozialpartnerschaft. Das politische System Österreichs, I. und II. Republik. Ein Vergleich*. Vienna/ Munich, 1983.

Österreich muss sein! Der Österreichisch-deutsche Konflikt. 2nd enlarged edn Vienna, 1934 (Documentation).

Otruba, Paul, 'Hitlers Tausend Mark Sperre und Österreichs Fremdenverkehr 1933' in Neck, R./Wandruszka, A. (eds), *Beiträge zur Zeitgeschichte. Festschrift Ludwig Jedlicka zum 60. Geburtstag*, St Pölten, 1976.

Pauley, Bruce F., *Hahnenschwanz und Hakenkreuz. Steirischer Heimatschutz und österreichischer Nationalsozialismus 1918–1934*, Vienna/Munich/Zürich, 1972.

Rath, R. John, 'The First Austrian Republic — Totalitarian, Fascist, Authoritarian or What?' in Neck, R./Wandruszka A. (eds), *Beiträge zur Zeitgeschichte, Festschrift Ludwig Jedlicka zum 60. Geburtstag*, St Pölten, 1976, pp. 163–88.

——'Authoritarian Austria' in Sugar, Peter F. (ed.), *Native Fascism in the Successor States, 1918–1945*, Santa Barbara, California, 1971, pp. 24–43.

Rauschning, Hermann, *Gespräche mit Hitler*, Vienna, 1973.

Reich von Rohrwig, Otto, *Der Freiheitskampf der Ostmarkdeutschen. Von St. Germain bis Adolf Hitler*, Graz/Vienna/Leipzig, 1942.

Renner, Karl, *Nachgelassene Werke*. Vol. II: *Österreich von der Ersten zur Zweiten Republik*, Vienna, 1953.

Ross, Dieter, *Hitler und Dollfuss*, Hamburg, 1966.

Schausberger, Norbert, *Griff nach Österreich. Die Kontinuität der sogenannten Anschlussproblematik*, Vienna, 1974.

Schieder, Theodor, *Hermann Rauschnings 'Gespräche mit Hitler' als Geschichtsquelle*, Opladen, 1972.

Schuschnigg, Kurt, *Dreimal Österreich*, Vienna, 1937.

——, *Ein Requiem in Rot-Weiss-Rot*, Vienna, 1978.

——, *Im Kampf gegen Hitler. Die Überwindung der Anschlussidee*, Vienna/Munich/Zürich, 1969.

Shepherd, Gordon Brook, *The Austrian Odyssey*, London/New York, 1969.

——,*Dollfuss*, London/New York, 1961.

Sporrer, Maria/Steiner, Herbert (eds), *Fritz Bock. Zeitzeuge*, Vienna/ Munich/-Zürich, 1984.

Starhemberg, Ernst Rüdiger, *Between Hitler and Mussolini*, London/New York, 1942.

Streitle, Peter, 'Zur Rolle Kurt von Schuschniggs im österreichischen Abwehrkampf von der Ermordung Bundeskanzler Dollfuss (25.7.1934) bis zum Juliabkommen 1936', unpubl. Ph. D. diss., University of Munich, 1986.

Veiter, Theodor, 'Das 34er Jahr' in *Bürgerkrieg in Österreich*, Vienna/ Munich, 1984.

Verosta, Stephan, 'Die österreichische Aussenpolitik 1918–1938 im europäischen Staatensystem 1914–1955 . . .' in Weinzierl E./Skalnik K., *Österreich 1918–1938. Geschichte der Ersten Republik*, Graz/Vienna/Cologne, 1983, pp. 107–46.

——, Foreword to Schuschnigg, *Ein Requiem in Rot-Weiss-Rot*, Vienna, 1978.

Wagner, Georg (ed.), *Österreich — Von der Staatsidee zum Nationalbewusstsein*, Vienna, 1982.

Wandruszka, Adam, 'Die Krisen des Parlamentarismus 1897 und 1933 — Gedanken zum Demokratieverständnis in Österreich' in Neck R./Wandruszka, A. (eds), *Beiträge zur Zeitgeschichte. Festschrift Ludwig Jedlicka zum 60. Geburtstag*, St Pölten, 1976, pp. 61–80.

Weinzierl, Erika/Skalnik, Kurt, *Österreich 1918–1938 — Geschichte der Ersten Republik*, 2 vols, Graz/Vienna/Cologne, 1983.

Wiltschegg, Walter, *Die Heimwehr. Eine unwiderstehliche Volksbewegung?*, Munich, 1985.

INDEX OF PERSONAL NAMES